HAY, HELL, KIDS AND CATTLE

by

Dillard H. Gates

SKETCHES BY

NONA ASH

Published by:

Dillard H. Gates
6123 Idaho St.
Vancouver, Washington
98661

Copyright © 1997 by Dillard H. Gates
Library of Congress Catalogue Card Number 98-92838
ISBN: 1-57502 790-9

All rights reserved. No portion of this book may be copied or reproduced without the written consent of the author.

To obtain additional copies of the book contact:
Dillard H. Gates
6123 Idaho St.
Vancouver, Washington 98661
Phone: (360) 695-1289
Fax: (360) 735-0643
E-mail: dhgates@juno.com

First printing May 1998.
Second printing March 1999.

Printed in the USA by

3212 East Highway 30 • Kearney, NE 68847 • 1-800-650-7888

Dedication
This book is dedicated to the memory of my family, especially Mom and Dad, and to the good folks of the Gates Community, Custer County, Nebraska.

Acknowledgments
First and foremost I want to acknowledge my wife, Ann, who has patiently listened to these stories for the last fifty-two years; and surprisingly, after listening urged me to put them down on paper.
I would also like to thank Nona Ash Pool Goodrich for creating the sketches for me. They contribute a visual component that adds life to the stories.

HAY, HELL, KIDS AND CATTLE

by

Dillard H. Gates

INTRODUCTION

Every person sees a different rainbow. No two people, even in a small group, are standing in precisely the same place. Each sees the sun's rays reflected through a different mass of moisture droplets. While each sees a different rainbow, what each sees is similar and can be described in common terms so that the phenomena can be recognized by all as a rainbow. So it is with individuals living within a family, a community, or any group of people regardless of size. If there is more than one observer, there is more than one perspective, more than one version, and more than one interpretation.

This book is an attempt to present one perspective of life on a dryland farm in central Nebraska during the drought and depression of the 1930s, the Roosevelt years. The perspective is that of a boy-child falling about in the middle of a family of sixteen kids. I was the scion of a father who sired six children, lost his first wife to influenza, married the hired girl and continued on to sire an additional ten kids almost without breaking the rhythm.

The perspective may be one of many, but it is mine. It was developed as a result of being surrounded and often overwhelmed by brothers and sisters, younger and older, larger and smaller, playing and working, and trying to get my share. I was disciplined by a demanding, hard working, concerned, and supportive father. I was nurtured by a loving, tender hearted, rough handed, workhorse of a mother who tried her best to get food on the table at meal time, do the laundry, bake the bread, tend the garden, wipe dirty noses, kiss hurts, and clean the house. She frequently went about her tasks with a child on her hip or pulling at her dress and another growing under her apron.

I grew up poor but not knowing it, believing that the drought, the depression, and FDR were related debilitating anomalies all very bad for the United States. But I was taught that I should work, be honest, not go into debt, not accept help from the government, persevere, believe in myself, and the situation would change. Eventually the country would get back to normal again.

Kids were a natural and pervasive part of the environment in which I existed. They were as much a part of my surroundings as are trees to a forest, water to a river, or sand to the desert. They were ubiquitous. Kids are somehow intermingled in most incidents or activities

mentioned in this story. Often they are not specifically named. To reference them in each incident would be like introducing each day with a preface such as "On awakening this morning I was surrounded by air containing oxygen, hydrogen, nitrogen, and carbon dioxide." Some things are a given. In this epistle, kids are.

Dillard H. Gates

I endured early childhood, moved awkwardly through adolescence, survived the death of my father when I was sixteen, witnessed the beginning of World War II and completed high school. Then because we were at war, I joined the military service before I was old enough for the draft. It never occurred to me that the brown beans, salt pork, slab-sided shacks, and my brothers and sisters were not worth fighting for, despite the fact that FDR was the Commander in Chief. Maybe I was fighting for a chance to break away from the dust, the dirt, and the work, and to see how other people lived. Except for the fact that I thought it was my duty, I don't know why I enlisted. Maybe it doesn't make any difference, but I suspect it does.

In any case these are my memories, presented from my perspective. They extend from my earliest recollections, through school, to when I entered military service in 1943. Others may have observed the same incidents as I, but interpreted them differently. If so, I invite them to describe their rainbows as they saw them.

HOW THIS BOOK GOT ITS NAME

The name for this book is not a product of my imagination. It resulted from a bit of colorful prose used to encapsulate a situation, a livelihood, and a way of life. It captures the brevity of speech, sense of humor, and wit that were characteristics of my Dad.

Back in the 30s, my Dad, Howe P. Gates, went to the Mayo Brothers' Clinic in Rochester, Minnesota, to get some repair work done on a faulty internal system. He stayed at a nearby hotel which in part accommodated patients and their families.

The hotel guests were a diversified lot ranging from dryland dirt farmers like my Dad, to working people from small towns of America, to gentile and hoity toity men and women of the big cities. The guests began chatting, talking of themselves and inquiring of others about their families, where they lived, their businesses, and other mundane topics.

A woman in the group stood out from the others. Her countenance, manner of speech, and lofty attitude led Dad to believe she was from New York City. She seemed to be participating primarily to observe the strange speech and curious behavior of the peasants from the prairies and to be entertained for the evening.

Following a period of small talk, the fancy lady directed her attention to Dad and noted her curiosity by asking, "Where are you from?" Dad, who appeared gruff to many, was generally soft-spoken but outspoken and had a well developed, if dry, sense of humor. With sixteen kids, a dryland farm in Nebraska mortgaged to the Federal Land Bank, the drought and depression in full swing, a sense of humor was necessary for survival.

His solemn response to the query was, "Custer County."

"Oh, where is that?" the lady inquired further.

"Nebraska," Dad retorted.

"And what do you do there?" she further queried.

"Farm," was Dad's rejoinder.

She smiled and blinked her eyes to favor Dad with the full benefit of her presence. In a condescending tone of voice she continued the questions, "And what do you raise on your farm?"

Dad shrugged his shoulders, returned her gaze and responded abruptly, "Hay, hell, kids and cattle!"

I am one of the kids included in his terse remark. Along with my brothers and sisters I contributed my bit to help Dad raise the hay and cattle. We didn't see Dad raise much hell, except with us kids. But Dad did not consider it raising hell, it was just a part of the educational process. However, consistent with Dad's remarks to the lady, when he was not around, we kids raised a bit of hell ourselves.

The stories related in this book all seem to be encompassed by the few words spoken by my father to the fancy lady from the city. **"HAY, HELL, KIDS AND CATTLE."**

HOW IT ALL BEGAN

This is a book of my memories, but I have to rely on the memories of others for the story of my entry into the already sizeable Gates family. You may ask, "What difference does it make?" Well, everything has to have a beginning, and this is mine. Maybe the circumstances of my introduction to this world were some indication of, or had an effect upon, my subsequent behavior. When I was growing up, Mom always told me not to be in such a hurry.

Much later and over a long period of time, my wife has told me I am the most impatient person she has ever known.

I am told that January 23, 1925, was a cold and stormy day on the farm at Gates, Nebraska. The farm had been homesteaded by my great grandfather Stillman Gates. It is located about one mile south of the Middle Loup River, seventeen miles north of Broken Bow, sixteen miles west of Sargent, and thirteen miles east of Anselmo. Gates was a crossroads village with a post office, a country store, a garage, a church, and a twelve-grade school. Gates was a farm community of old families whose history went back to homestead days. It was a community of neighbors and friends who helped one another in times of need. It was, I am sure, also a community with its share of intrigue, fusses, squabbles, and back-biting. It was a community of mostly good people, no saints, all sinners, trying to get along and do the best they could or at least survive under difficult circumstances.

For some time Mom had been planning to paper the dining room. Even though she was now heavy with child and the weather was threatening, Mom decided to do the papering. Better get it done before she had another kid to take care of. A neighbor and longtime friend, Gladys Jacobsen, had agreed to help. Farm women helping each other was the ordinary way of getting things done in those days. Doing heavy work while pregnant was also situation normal. If Mom had taken time off from work when pregnant, there would have been little done around our house. Thus Mom twisted the crank on the old, hand-operated telephone hanging on the wall and gave Gladys a call. Gladys hooked up a team and drove the mile and a quarter to our place to help Mom. Gladys, too, was pregnant, but was about three months behind Mom. She brought her two little girls, Pauline and Helen, along to play with some of my older sisters while the women pasted and plastered paper on the wall.

Following Gladys's arrival the telephone had been removed from the wall in preparation for hanging paper. The women busied themselves with their work, interspersed with wiping snotty noses, changing dirty diapers and chasing kids.

With hands on her extended belly Mom slouched to a chair. "Gladys," she exclaimed, "The time has come."

Mom and Gladys were used to on-farm emergencies and did not panic easily. Giving birth was not an emergency, but something had to be done. One of the older girls was sent to the shop where Dad was repairing machinery to summon him to the house. Dad saw the scene of kids and chaos and agreed that Mom was right, the time had come. He picked up the phone which had been removed from the wall and carried it over to where the wires could be reconnected. He held the phone in his arms while Gladys turned the crank and tried without success to call Dr. Spivey. The Doctor was not available.

Dad had lots of experience delivering farm animals and had, I suppose, witnessed or even participated in the birth of some of the older kids. Apparently I was already displaying signs of impatience. In no time at all Dad was holding his ninth (eighth living) child in his hands. He whapped my bottom, handed me to Gladys and proceeded to help Mom with the chores which follow immediately after birth. Incidently, that whap on the bottom was but the first of many I was to receive during the next sixteen years. And I suppose the subsequent whaps were as necessary as the first, though for different reasons.

Other than the fact that I was delivered by Dad my birth was normal. The doctor arrived several hours later but was informed his services were not needed, given a cup of coffee and sent back to town. Unlike the Doctor, the bill for "Services rendered" was subsequently delivered on time. As a matter of principle it was returned unpaid.

Dillard H. Gates

I was my mother's first boy and third child. However, there were five other children in the family when I was born, ages about seven to fifteen. These were the children of Dad and his first wife, Ethel Bartlet Gates, who had died of influenza a year or so before Mom and Dad were married. The circumstances of my arrival apparently had little effect on the ardor of my parents. They went on to have an additional seven children.

I was named "Dillard" not after an itinerant salesman but because Mom liked the name, and "Herbert" for my grandfather, Herbert P. Gates. Years later Mom told me Grandpa Gates was pleased as I was the first of his many grandchildren to be given his name. I do not remember Grandpa Gates. Regrettably, he died when I was just little tyke.

MOM

My first awareness of Mom was as a presence more than a person. Like the first rays of light that signal the beginning of a new day she was there at the dawn of my first consciousness. My earliest memories of Mom are not of her relationship with me but with all the babies.

Above all else, Mom was a mother. Our house was always full of kids, some of which she had borne, all of which she mothered. They ranged in size from babies to teenagers who may have sometimes resisted her mothering instincts, but she mothered them. She clucked and cooed to the newest family member as it rested in her arms, snuggled tightly against her body, receiving nourishment from her ample breasts. She changed the dirty diapers, usually not store-bought but cut from the still usable outer portions of worn-out flannel bed sheets. She bathed the babies in the big dishpan. She carefully fitted a band around the babies middle to cover and protect the protruding navel. She dressed the babies in little hand-me-downs passed on by the toddlers, now watching curiously as the newest entry into the family assumed the stellar role. The babies in our household were dressed only in simple garments but were clothed in love.

Caring for the babies was more a ritual than a chore for Mom, and somehow the next older kid or two was generally included. No child in the family felt less loved with the sudden entry of a new baby into the family for they were loved and their love naturally extended to the one who replaced them. Love flowed from an inexhaustible source from person to person. It was passed back and forth, but, unlike the hand-me-downs it didn't wear out.

The interaction among mother, baby, and children was a continuous, multifaceted bonding process. The kids and the kitchen seemed to be Mom's primary concerns. If she wasn't caring for the kids, she was in the kitchen, cooking, cleaning, or washing for the family. Oftentimes she would mix the two tasks as she placed the baby in the highchair or tied it with a dish towel into a rocking chair so she could watch it as she worked.

Mom herded and shuffled and shooed us kids around and got her work done. She sorted us out each morning and got us off to school. And she always had a hot dinner ready for us when we returned from school during the mid-day recess.

Mom baked bread, up to ten loaves, three times a week. And if we were lucky, she prepared extra dough and made a pan of cinnamon rolls. Mom's cinnamon rolls were unsurpassed in this world. They were sweet and gooey and sticky and even though she made them often, I could never get enough.

Mom's cinnamon rolls remained a favorite with me throughout her life. In later years when I visited her she always had a pan of fresh cinnamon rolls for me. She taught my wife how to make them and Ann has always been proud and content to say that she makes the second best

cinnamon rolls in the world. In the hours before her death at ninety-four, as Mom lapsed in and out of consciousness, I am told she whispered to my sisters attending her, "I wish Dillard was here. I would fix him a big pan of cinnamon rolls."

Mom's role as a disciplinarian was mixed. We all accepted the fact that Dad's word was final; however, we were not always aware of the subtle influence Mom may have had in the development of Dad's final word. We kids worried little if Mom said she was going to spank our bottoms. She did occasionally, but it didn't hurt much. I think the main reason we minded Mom, even to the extent we did, was that we didn't want to hurt her feelings. If somehow one of us offended her to the point that she cried, which we did occasionally, it was devastating to

the offender. But Mom was always quick to forgive following an, "I'm sorry, Mom."

Mom's place in the family was somewhat of an enigma. She was the cook, the cleaner, the baby tender, the consoler, the constant source of care and love to the kids, and the wife of Howe Gates. As a child I had little understanding of what a wife was supposed to be.

Mom and Dad did not always agree, but they did not bicker or argue. On a rare occasion when Dad overtly criticized something Mom had done she might respond, "If you don't like it maybe next time you should do it yourself." However, they must have had relations unknown to me as babies continued to appear on a regular basis.

Dillard H. Gates

DAD

I am not certain of my earliest memories of my Dad. I do remember lying on his lap when I was three or four, with my head on his chest listening to his big watch tick. It was a big, thick, gold watch that he had inherited from his father. He carried it in the breast pocket of his overalls attached by a leather thong. That watch was a great source of entertainment and security for all of us kids as we sequentially occupied that choice spot, Dad's lap. Sometimes the lap was shared by two or more kids as Dad lay back in his big chair resting or reading the *Omaha Bee News*, later the *Omaha World Herald*.

As a little guy I recall the lap was always there, as a place of refuge, a place to rest, or to find solace. I also remember that the lap sometimes served as the "executioner's block" as I was placed across the knees, with pants tight or bottom bare, to receive what is today referred to as behavior modification. And, generally, behavior was modified. As a result some attempt was made, at least in the short run, to pay a bit more attention to the rules that had been broken, or to try to make sure that Dad didn't find out about it next time.

THE BEGINNING OF THE LEARNING CURVE

In the family into which I was born, kids were expected to learn the rules early and well. Of course there was always another chance to learn if somehow one failed to perform adequately the first time, or if performance just sort of tailed off over time. However, some reinforcement to encourage adherence to the rules, sharpen the memory, and enhance the learning process often accompanied the next chance. The nature of the reinforcement was influenced by the severity of the breach of the rules and the age of the kid breaking the rule. It was also a function of the mental attitude and the identity of the reinforcer, be it Mom, Dad, another one of the kids, the hired lady, the hired man, or a neighbor.

The rules, though unwritten, were generally understood by those to whom they applied. All rules did not apply equally to all members of the household. That is, different levels of performance and behavior were accepted from toddlers than teenagers. Each individual sort of had to figure out which rules applied, about how far they could be stretched, and the consequences of exceeding the limits. When Dad wasn't around, someone else would take what was considered by them to be the proper action. However, it was well understood by all in the household that, in the final analysis, if there was a problem and if it reached his level, Dad had the final word. One of the things we all tended to learn early on was to try to settle our problems at the lowest possible level, with the hope that Dad would not have to get involved.

As I look back, I am led to believe that the imprints made on the seat of the pants by the toe of a boot or the business end of a razor strop were indelible, though invisible to the eye and were firmly planted in my

mind. They are a part of what makes me what I am. I was being programmed by the environment in which I lived, and that environment was dominated by my Dad. The environment has changed, but the recall function of that computer between my ears still functions and the act-consequence relationships phenomena remain an integral part of the memory system. Though I may have experienced a few uncomfortable moments during the programming process I am thankful that it happened, when it happened. For without it I may not have had the strength, the fortitude, or the direction to guide me through the ensuing years.

THE DINING ROOM TABLE, AN EDUCATIONAL INSTITUTION

I remember our dining room table. It was big, probably about ten feet long. It had benches, which Dad and Hap had built, along each side for seating. Dad's big chair sat at the head of the table and Mom's chair at the other end. Her end was closer to the kitchen. The entire family and whoever else was around, be it hired men, neighbor kids, or someone who had just dropped by, assembled at that table for meals three times a day. In our home, we took our meals together, breakfast, dinner and supper. There were exceptions, but we were expected to be there for meals, to eat what was put in front of us, and to clean up our plates.

Mealtime at our home may have appeared to be controlled

bedlam but was also a time for learning. Kids would be talking all at once or shouting, trying to get the attention of Mom or Dad to let them know what had happened or to try to get their version of a story told first. When noise reached a certain crescendo or when for some other reason he wanted to bring a bit of order to the chaos, Dad would tell us to quiet down a bit. We responded for a while, but soon the noise level would escalate and the process would be repeated.

To say that seating arrangements around our table were formalized or fixed would be a bit of an exaggeration. However, there was a general arrangement of sorts. Dad sat at the head of the table and the little kids sat on the bench at the side of the table to his left, somewhat in sequence, with the youngest closest to Dad. Actually the first place at the table for the littlest one was on Dad's knee. When the little one was big enough to sit by itself it would then move from Dad's knee to a high chair and then to the first spot on the bench. When that side of the table was full, and again somewhat by ascending age, the older kids progressed onto the bench behind the table. This seating arrangement allowed Dad to have access to the little ones in order to serve them food. Also, they were within reach so that corrections could be made if their behavior was not up to acceptable standards. As the kids got a little older they were better able to serve themselves and had also developed a sense of acceptable behavior, so Dad didn't need such ready access to them.

When there were hired men present, and much of the time there were, they occupied the end of the bench behind the table next to Dad and on his right. When neighbor kids, guests, or drop-ins were present, and that was frequent, they were squeezed in wherever room could be made. If things got tight enough, some of the bigger girls might have to eat in the kitchen. But one thing was clear, there was always room "at the table" and there was always something to eat. If anyone left the table hungry at our house it might have been because they did not like fat pork or mutton or beans or taters and milk gravy, but not because the quantity was limited. There was always ample amounts of quality food on Mom's table. Sometimes the selection was a bit limited.

The dining room table was probably the single most significant and influential educational institution of my life. We learned table manners, or at least acceptable behavior while at the table. We learned to share. We learned that sometimes you had to put up with something you didn't like, but make the best of it. We began to learn that you are responsible for your own actions. If you put something on your own plate you were expected to eat it or to sit at the table until you did. We learned there was a hierarchy of authority influenced by age, size, and gender. We learned many other things as well that would influence us throughout life. And we learned that Dad was the boss.

Dillard H. Gates

PANCAKE POTATOES

I learned about being consistent when I had progressed only a seat or two up the bench on Dad's left. We generally had lots of taters at our house, and the way I liked them best was mashed then smothered in milk gravy. I especially liked for Dad to take a big spoonful of mashed potatoes and plop them down hard on my plate so they would spread out flat like a pancake. Pancake taters was really a favorite with me. One day we had mashed taters for dinner and I asked Dad to please give me some. As usual he took a big spoonful of mashed potatoes, raised the spoon high and plopped them onto my plate forming a big pancake tater just like I had always wanted. However, this time, and for reasons known only to a four year old, I pushed my plate away and announced emphatically, " I don't want pancake taters."

Dad didn't ask why or offer an alternative. But in a single motion he pushed back his chair, snatched me off the bench and stretched me over his knee. He played a quick, hot tune on the seat of my pants and plunked me back on the bench with the plate of pancake taters in front of me.

"Now what do you like?" he asked.

With a burning bottom and tears blurring the vision of my heretofore favorite food, I blubbered, "I like pancake taters."

I still like mashed taters, but lack Dad's knack of plopping them on my plate to form a tater pancake.

SITUATIONAL MANNERS, A HIRED MAN'S DILEMMA

It was not just the kids who were subjected to the educational process at the dining table. Manners, or acceptable behavior, at our table had evolved over the years. It was a kind of behavior that was responsive to the situation and tended to get the job done with some degree of efficiency. However labeled, adaptive behavior or situational manners, it worked reasonably well in our house.

At mealtime the food was placed on the table then the family and whomever else was present was called to " come set up." Since the food was all on the table, the meal was normally started by a person taking some food from the closest serving dish and then passing it along to the next person. Of course there was an informal system to the process. Potatoes and meat were generally passed around before the gravy. Vegetables could be passed anytime, as could the bread.

When a person was ready for seconds he or she would call out, "Please pass the meat," or whatever the item desired. The dish containing that food item would then be picked up by the person nearest to it and passed along toward the person making the request. Oftentimes, the dish was delayed along the route as someone helped themselves to the food before passing it along. On occasion this would cause a problem, as the serving dish might be empty, or nearly so, when it was handed to the person who originally made the request for seconds.

Bread, and there was always lots of it, was sliced and placed on a platter, more or less in the center of the table. Normally, if there was anything that could be called normal at our table, the bread plate was passed around at the beginning of the meal. However, depending upon the situation, that is, who was at the table, who made the request, and the location of the bread platter, a request for another slice of bread resulted in various responses. The bread platter might be passed, or the person closest to the bread platter, especially if it was one of the kids, might pick up a slice and toss it to the person making the request. Either way was acceptable, kinda, depending upon the situation.

One Saturday night during the summer Dad brought home a new hired man. His pay was the going rate; a dollar a day plus board and room. As usual at our place the hired man was to take his meals with the family. I don't remember his first meal with us, but he evidently survived without incident. In retrospect, it may have been a traumatic experience for him.

However, during the course of Sunday dinner, the hired man made the request, "Please pass the bread."

The bread platter was close to my younger brother Jack, who was about five or six years old. Jack promptly grabbed up a slice of bread and lobbed it in the direction of the new hired man. He snagged the slice of bread in mid-air and dropped it on the table beside his plate.

" Pass me the bread properly," he retorted angrily.

Somewhat taken aback, Jack passed the bread platter. As I recall, there were no further comments or incidents during the remainder of the meal. After the meal I tagged along as Dad asked the new hired man to come outside with him.

Once they were out in the yard, Dad stated firmly to the new hired man, "Get your clothes. I'm taking you back to town."

"Why?" asked the new hired man in astonishment.

"It's very plain you're not going to work out here," Dad commented. It was obvious that the new man was a slow learner. He had been unable to adapt to the situation in which he found himself. Jobs were scarce in those days, and I bet before the depression ended he had to learn to accept a lot worse things than a buck a day and a slice of bread tossed his way. Dad loaded the man into the car, took him back to Broken Bow, and returned Sunday evening with a new hired man.

LIVING AND LEARNING

Being born into the middle of a large and expanding family was in itself not notable, but it was an assurance that I was in the middle of a lot of activities that occurred on the Gates farm and environs.

All of the time I lived on the farm every drop of water utilized in our house for drinking, cooking, washing, bathing, and cleaning was carried into the house from the windmill and pump located just to the east of the house. Every drop of waste water was collected in large buckets or cream cans, carried out of the house, and dumped in the back yard. Every stick of wood used for cooking, baking, heating, canning, washing clothes, cleaning, etc. was cut out in the yard and carried into the house. And eventually the residual ashes from the cook stove and the heating stove were carried out and dumped on the ash pile in the back yard.

When one of us kids became big enough to work the pump handle, carry a small bucket of water, or carry in a few sticks of wood we were expected to do so. By the time we were five such activities had become chores that we were expected to perform on a regular basis. To be told that the wood box or the water pail was empty or the water in the reservoir on the cook stove was low was not just an acknowledgment of a fact, but rather a first reminder that you were expected to do something about it. A second reminder, if necessary, was usually a bit more specific. A third reminder, usually necessary only for those at early stages of the learning curve, was accompanied by motivational factors that made the drudgery of such chores pleasant when compared to the alternatives offered. As a result, the wood boxes were seldom empty, there was generally fresh water in the house, and the waste water was dumped, though occasionally after the waste water can had overflowed onto the kitchen floor.

The waste water containers were too large for the smaller kids to handle. One was an old five gallon bucket. When near full it would require two little kids, one of the bigger kids, or an adult to carry it out. The large cream can that sat under the sink and collected waste water from the wash basin held about fifteen gallons. It required a couple of the big kids or adults to carry it into the back yard where it was dumped.

The chores were not always carried out with enthusiasm or a spirit of joy. Rather they were often accomplished with a bit of grumbling and bickering among those who had been assigned the tasks. Despite the complaints, the protestations and lamentations of overwork, the chores got done without permanent damage to the physical or mental well being of any of us. Unbeknownst to us at the time, it was part of the learning process that was a side effect of doing useful and necessary work and contributing to the welfare of the family. It was a part of learning responsibility. It was a part of growing up.

Dillard H. Gates

WASH DAY

Monday was wash day. Long before I started to school, I remember the drudgery of Mom doing the washing on top of everything else that had to be done during a routine day.

After breakfast when the school age kids were off to school and the breakfast dishes done or stacked in the big dish pan, Mom set the big wash boilers on the stove and filled them with water. While the water heated she began to sort clothes into piles for washing. Each pile of colored clothes, white clothes, especially greasy clothes would make a

separate load. When she was done sorting, the kitchen floor was covered with piles of dirty clothes. Mom did the laundry for the kids, which usually included at least one in diapers, the adults of the family and often times a hired man or so. In some cases if clothes were especially dirty, she would put them into a boiler, add homemade lye soap, and boil them for awhile at the beginning of the washing process. If time permitted before the wash water was hot, she would do the breakfast dishes or care for one of the little kids who was always underfoot. When the water in the boilers was hot Mom would transfer it into the washing machine, shave some slices of homemade lye soap into the hot water, and add the clothes.

The washer was a single tub, hand-operated machine. It had a large agitator that churned the clothes when the large handle on top was moved back and forth. That was the washing process. I don't know how long Mom agitated each load, but it seemed like a long time.

When the washing job was done the clothes were lifted from the hot water with a laundry stick (probably an old broom handle) and put through the hand-operated wringer attached to the side of the washing machine. This required a bit of coordination, a strong right arm to turn the wringer handle and a hot water tolerant left hand to direct the clothes from the laundry stick to the rollers. As the handle was turned the clothes passed between the rollers, the water was squeezed out and drained back into the laundry tub. The squeezed clothes fell into a tub of rinse water sitting on a couple of chairs next to the washing machine. The laundry was rinsed by hand and once again put through the wringer. The dirty hot water was drained from the washing machine, and the process was repeated as many times as there were piles of clothes on the floor.

Doing the washing was not only a hard job, it was dangerous. Long before my time, a half-brother, still a toddler, had been fatally scalded by hot water from the washing machine. We kids were often reminded of the tragedy as Mom hurried about trying to get the washing done while trying to keep the kids out of harm's way.

. Following the final rinsing and wringing the wet laundry was put into a basket, carried to the back yard and then hung on the clothesline to dry. Once dry it had to be taken down and brought back into the house and folded, some sprinkled and set aside to be ironed the next day.

Even though it was laundry day, other aspects of the household continued. Dinner had to be prepared for the men and the little ones at home, as well as for those who would be coming home from school during the noon break. By the time school was out at four o'clock in the afternoon, Mom would have the washing done. The kids would do the chores and help Mom as she prepared supper for the family. And yet the day's work was not finished. Supper dishes had to be done and the smaller kids gotten ready for bed. The school kids then gathered around the kerosene lamp sitting on the dining room table to do their homework. Dad sat on his chair at the end of the table reading the paper or a book. Yes, I remember laundry day at the Gates household. Mom eventually got a power washer, but otherwise wash day remained about the same on the farm.

A LESSON IN LIFE, THE SIGNIFICANCE OF A CHALLENGE

Nubbing seed corn was just one of the jobs to be done as spring planting time approached. When I was five or six, Dad and my older brother, Hap, were in the granary nubbing seed corn. I was there, probably trying to help a little, learning to nub corn, but mostly just being with Dad and Hap.

Back in the years before hybrid corn we selected corn for seed from the regular corn crop. That is during those years when we grew enough corn of sufficient quality from which to select seed. The selection process had several steps. First, the largest ears were selected from the corn which had been shucked and stored in the granary. The idea was that corn from the best and biggest ears was genetically superior seed and would result in a more productive corn crop the following year.

The second step was to nub the selected ears of corn. The nubbing process consisted of removing the rounded or odd shaped kernels from each end of the ear of seed corn. It was necessary to remove the odd shaped kernels as they would not properly feed through the planter plates in the seed boxes of the listers Dad used to plant corn. The misshaped kernels were removed by a couple of techniques. One technique was to shell (remove) the kernels from each end of the ear of corn. This was usually accomplished by rubbing the kernels off with the base of the thumb or with a cob. The other technique was to cut off each end of the ear of corn utilizing a corn knife, a large machete-like tool. Once an ear of corn was properly nubbed it was tossed into a pile to be shelled later.

As Dad and Hap sat there nubbing corn, I must have decided I needed a diversion. From the other side of the granary bin I challenged Dad, "I bet you can't hit me with an ear of corn. If you try, Dad, I'll show you how well I can dodge."

Dad did not respond and continued to nub corn as if he had not heard me. I jumped about and repeated the dare. Dad continued to ignore my antics. My attention span was limited, and, after a short period of being ignored, I forgot about the original challenge and went back to just messing around.

As I was squatting down across the bin from Dad, thinking only about little kid things, I was bowled over by an ear of corn that struck me along side of the head. An ear of corn is hard and rough and the top ends of the kernels are sharp.

As I struggled to my feet rubbing the abrasions on the side of my head, I blubbered tearfully, "Why did you do that, Dad?"

At first Dad ignored my plea and continued nubbing corn. I continued rubbing my head with the back of my grubby little hand, now covered with a mixture of blood, tears, and snot. "Why did you do that Dad?" I insisted.

Dad tossed another nubbed ear of corn onto the seed pile and laid down his corn knife. He looked up from his work, beckoned to me and said, "Come here, Dill."

I stumbled across the corn littered bin and into his outstretched arms. He sat me on his knee and retorted, "Dill, I'm sorry I hurt you, I didn't mean to hit you so hard, but I have some advice for you. You are just a kid, but you can't learn any younger. Do not challenge someone unless you are prepared to back up the challenge."

I felt safe and secure on Dad's knee despite the fact that my head hurt. I may have looked at him in a questioning manner as I did not comprehend what he was telling me. "You bragged that I could not hit you with an ear of corn," he continued, "but you did not remain alert to the challenge. Never make a challenge you are not prepared to meet. And if you do challenge someone, keep your eyes open and stay prepared until the challenge is resolved."

This may have been a harsh teaching method for one so young, but it was effective. I remember the challenge, Dad's response to the challenge, and his profound advice. I don't really know how much influence it may have had on me in subsequent years, but I think that somehow the lesson was one that became firmly fixed in my memory bank. It provided at least a modicum of guidance as I grew from that sobbing, bewildered little boy to meet the challenges of life.

THE GATES SCHOOL

Gates School was established in 1882 by Stillman Gates. Classes were first held in a room of his sod house with Harry Gates, his son, serving as the teacher. The students had to provide their own desks, books, slates and writing materials.

In 1883 a sod school house was built one mile west of the present Gates School on land owned by Stillman Gates. The cost of the school house was reported to be $66.00. A frame school house was built in 1893 to replace the soddy. In 1920 the frame school house was moved a mile east to the southeast corner of the Gates intersection. There it was combined with the White Pigeon school house which had been moved from its original location one mile to the east. The two schools were combined to form the Gates Consolidated School, District C-23.

The new school had thirty-seven students in grades one through nine. Belle Gift (Young) taught grades one through six and Sid Vose taught grades seven through nine. At the beginning of the school year 1923-1924 Gates School was expanded to include grades one through twelve with four teachers.

With some modifications, the school house remained pretty much the same for the next twenty-two years. The school yard included outdoor one-hole toilets for the boys and the girls. A wooden screen was constructed in front of the toilets to shield the doors and to provide a bit more privacy for the users. There was also a barn with stalls and mangers for a half dozen or so horses, a tack room and a feed room. There was a garage on the northern end of the yard containing six stalls open to the south and a coal bin. A concrete tornado cellar was located just southwest of the entrance to the primary-room entry hall. Water was provided by a well and hand pump located near the south side of the school house. There was no electricity or central heat in the building. Heat was provided by a coal-burning "pot bellied" stove in each room.

Gates School had an enrollment of seventy students when it burned to the ground March 3, 1937.

The men of the community quickly made modifications to the old Gates church, located about one hundred yards west of the store on land owned by my father, Howe Gates (grandson of Stillman Gates). The old church was partitioned down the center forming two rooms. Primary grades one through four were housed in the west side and intermediate grades five through eight in the east side. An old farmhouse about one and one-half miles east of Gates was also modified to accommodate high school grades nine through twelve.

The cause of the fire was never officially determined; however, secrets are hard to keep. Many years later rumor had it that Oscar Swick, a high school freshman at the time, bragged about setting the fire because he didn't like school and just wanted to see it burn.

A new brick school house was built and ready for use during the fall of 1937. The two-story structure with four classrooms was centrally heated by a coal fired furnace. There was also a small room on the second floor between the two classrooms. The room was constructed as an office; however, it was used as a locker room for boy's sports. The lower two rooms housed grades one through eight, and the upper story housed grades nine through twelve.

The last class to graduate from Gates High School was in 1942. Since then Gates School has continued with grades one through eight with two or three teachers. Sometime during the intervening years a large addition was constructed and serves as a gymnasium, recreation area, and general community meeting place.

Dillard H. Gates

THE SCHOOL BELL

The Gates school house had a large bell housed in a cupola on the roof. The bell rope hung down into the hallway that separated the two high school classrooms. It was attached to a wooden hook on the wall and was supposed to be left alone unless a teacher pulled it or granted permission to a student to ring the bell. Occasionally, the bell rang out of sequence, signaling only that some kid was up to mischief or could not resist the temptation to give the rope a jerk as he passed by.

Depending upon the atmospheric conditions, when the rope was pulled vigorously the bell could be heard not only on the school grounds, but for miles around. The tolling of the bell controlled the activities of the school.

The first bell of the day rang at 8:30 in the morning. That was the half-hour bell and told all within hearing distance that school would begin in thirty minutes, at 9:00 o'clock.

The next bell was the five minute bell, which sounded at 8:55. By that time most of the students had gathered on the school grounds or in their classrooms. Some might still be putting their riding horse in the school barn or be across the road at the Gates store making a quick purchase of a pencil or paper for the days school work. Wherever you were when that bell sounded, you knew you had five minutes to be at your desk.

The 9:00 o'clock bell indicated it was time for kids to be at their desks or risk being scolded or counted tardy. It was time for another day of school to begin.

The bell rang again at 10:30 signaling the beginning of recess. It rang again fifteen minutes later when recess was over.

The 12:00 o'clock bell released the students for a one-hour lunch break. The bell rang again at 12:55, telling the kids they had five minutes to terminate whatever they were doing and return to their seats.

The 1:00 o'clock bell signaled the beginning of afternoon school. The bell rang again at 2:30 and 2:45, signaling the beginning and end of afternoon recess.

At 4:00 o'clock the bell tolled again, indicating the end of the school day. The school house doors burst open and kids from all twelve grades flew from the confines of the classrooms and scattered like a covey of quail.

THE GATES CHURCH

The old Gates church, while not officially a part of Gates school, served for decades as an annex to the school. The wooden structure had been built in 1905 about one hundred yards west of the Gates intersection, on the north side of the road, on land belonging to Stillman Gates.

There was an unwritten agreement between Stillman Gates and the Methodist denomination which constructed the church building that the church could be built on his land at no charge and could remain there without cost as long as the building was used for church or community purposes only. My father purchased the farm on which the church was located in about 1923 and owned it until his death in 1941.

Regular church services were held in the building for twenty-five years or so following its construction. Subsequently, the old church building continued to be used for funerals, intermittent church services, a community meeting place, an auditorium for Gates School, a poling place, a gymnasium, and as a school. As far as I can recall, the last religious service held in the old Gates church was my father's funeral in March 1941.

Dillard H. Gates

THE PRIMARY YEARS

I was greatly influenced by my teachers and that to which I was exposed within the school setting. I also found out that learning is not confined to the classroom and that there is life outside the school. My family, my friends, the neighbors, and the community all had some role in molding the boy, that piece of clay that was me.

READING, RITING, RITHMATIC, RESPECT AND RESPONSIBILITY

School started for me in September 1930. I was an excited five-year old looking forward to entering the first grade. I already knew my teacher Miss Wells, as her family were long time residents of the community and family friends.

Having Miss Wells as a teacher was a memorable experience for me. She had a warm, beautiful smile and big brown eyes that twinkled when she smiled and snapped when she was less than satisfied with the behavior of one of her students. She was gentle and kind and I believe able to get us to perform because of our respect for her. I quickly fell in love with Miss Wells, but had to compete with all the other boys in the primary room for her attention. She was my teacher for four years. I was crushed when she got married when I was in the second or third grade. It was difficult to accept the fact that she was now Mrs. Vanek. She was always Miss Wells to me.

Life goes on and memories are a wonderful thing. Fifty years after I had moved on from the primary to the intermediate grades at Gates School, I accidently ran across Mrs.Vanek at a farm sale in Milburn, Nebraska. She still had the same beautiful smile and twinkling eyes, and I immediately recognized her. She, my wife Ann, and I spent a couple hours together reminiscing about old times at Gates School. In 1996, Ann and I were fortunate enough to visit Mrs. Vanek again, this time in a nursing home in McMinnville, Oregon, just a few months before she died. Though confined to a wheel chair, she still had the same beautiful smile and sparkling eyes. For a couple of hours she showed us pictures of her children and grandchildren. She was justifiably proud of her family, especially the grandchildren. Once again we talked about the Gates community and the Gates School, and then it was time to go. At the time I was both thrilled and saddened. Thrilled to once again see Miss Wells, that wonderful teacher with the beautiful smile, that I had loved since I was a little boy. But saddened to realize that this would probably be the last time I would see her. May you rest in peace Miss Wells, you brought joy to this world.

The primary grades classroom was arranged with several rows of seats facing the front wall. The wall was mostly covered by a large blackboard, an American flag, and large posters displaying the proper form for writing the letters of the alphabet and numbers 0 to 9 using the Palmer method. The teacher's desk was in the left-front corner of the room. From this position she could survey her domain which included, more or less, twenty grubby little kids willing if not eager to do her bidding. A large coal burning stove surrounded by a metal heat jacket occupied the front-right corner of the room. A door connecting the primary and intermediate rooms was located in the east wall. The outdoor exit in the southeast corner of the room lead to an entry hall where coats were hung and, in season, overshoes stored.

The area between the front of the desks and the front wall was occupied by about a dozen little red chairs. At recitation time each class was called to come forward and sit on the chairs. The children in the other three grades were to stay at their desks, go ahead with their work and ignore the reciting class.

OPENING EXERCISES

When the school bell rang at 9:00 o'clock, the kids tumbled into the room and stood by their seats until the teacher said to be seated. Miss Wells took the roll call as tardiness and absences were reported on our monthly report cards. We then got up from our seats and stood stiffly and proudly facing the flag while the teacher lead us in the "Pledge of Allegiance."

Opening exercises included all four grades and usually consisted of simple exercises that could be done sitting or standing beside the desk. Good posture was emphasized. Miss Wells taught us a little ditty to help remind us to sit and stand properly:

Dillard H. Gates

> *Perfect posture, perfect posture*
> *Do not slump, do not slump*
> *We must grow up handsome*
> *We must grow up handsome*
> *Hide that hump, hide that hump*

Miss Wells often read stories from a book or teacher's magazines. Sometimes we would tell riddles, recite little verses, or play simple word games. This was a transition period, from outside play or other activities to the classroom. The idea was to get us to settle down and get ready for the work and study which was to follow.

Once a week an activity known as "Current Events" was the main activity for opening exercises. Each student was expected to bring to school a clipping from a newspaper of a current news item or picture. If no newspaper was available at home, Miss Wells had a small newspaper entitled *Current Events* from which we could select an item to show the class. Like all the kids I participated in the activity, but for a year or so I did not understand its significance. When the teacher said "current events" it sounded like "curnivents" to me. I could not figure out the meaning of that sound, but I knew that when I heard it I was supposed to be ready to say something about the news.

News of the Italian war with Ethiopia was used several times in Current Events and was of real interest to me. I remember how terrible I thought it was for the cruel Italians under the dictator Mussolini to attack the primitive people led by Hallie Sallasie. I was elated to hear that the poor Ethiopian soldiers dug holes and covered them with brush to trap Italian tanks. I thought the Italian soldiers were getting what they deserved when the Ethiopians set their trapped tanks on fire and speared them as they tried to escape. In my mind it was heroic for men defending their country with sticks and spears to defeat the tanks and guns of their enemy. I didn't know where Ethiopia was or what the fight was about, but I thought the Lion King was great and that Mussolini and his army were vile villains.

Later in life when I learned the truth about the Italian war with Ethiopia my feelings were confirmed.

Miss Wells also taught us a little verse that I did not appreciate at the time, but which stuck with me. I finally came to understand its significance and have tried, but often failed, to include its meaning into my relationships with others.

> *Hearts, like doors,*
> *Open with ease*
> *To very, very little keys.*
> *And don't forget*
> *That two of these*
> *Are " thank you"*
> *And "if you please."*

Many years later as a university professor I quoted the ditty in the classroom when I thought it appropriate. I continue to repeat it to my grandchildren and hope its essence will be inculcated into their behavior toward others.

LEARNING TO READ

Reading was an important activity in our home, especially during the long winter evenings. The pages were illuminated only by the dim light of a kerosene lamp, but we read.

My Dad, though he had only attended school through the fourth grade, was a voracious reader. He seemed to have a reverence for books. He subscribed to and read the daily newspaper and various farm magazines. My favorite farm magazine was The Furrow put out by the John Deere Company, as it had jokes and cartoons on the back pages. Dad also bought lots of books at farm sales and local auctions. His acquisitions varied from a twelve volume set of The History of World War I which took up about four feet on the bookshelf, to a series of The One Hundred Best Mystery Stories to The Complete Works of Sherlock Holmes and various other reference books and novels. During long winter nights in the dim, flickering light of the kerosene lamp, he worked his way through most of the books. His first wife (deceased) had been a school teacher, and many of her books remained in the book cupboard.

Even more important than the fact that Dad liked to read was that he encouraged us kids to read. We were taught to respect books and to accept the consequences if we purposefully tore a page or otherwise damaged a book.

I enjoyed being read to. But as far back as I can recall I wanted to read by myself. I wanted to read the books my older sisters brought home from school, but most of all I wanted to read the funny papers, especially

Dillard H. Gates

"The Katsandjammer Kids." The pictures were great, but I didn't like being limited to pictures. I wanted to know the words that were in the little balloons above the heads of those delightful, funny characters. If I could just read maybe I could find out how those two little boys were able to get into so much mischief, fool the big folks and get away with it.

I suppose the first word I learned to read in school was "Spot" as I looked at a picture of a spotted dog on the first page of my reading primer. My reading vocabulary doubled when I learned to read the word "see." Now I could not only recognize Spot, but I could see him as well. In time I progressed from "See Spot" to "See Spot run," and then to "Run Spot run." Like an opening flower, the world of words and reading unfolded before me. Then like pollen scattered from the stamens of opening flowers, the words and soon the ideas found their place and began to fertilize and stimulate my young but curious mind.

I do not recall being a quick learner or a particularly good reader, but I liked to read and struggled hard to improve. Early on I began to realize that if I could read, all of the information contained in the The Book of Knowledge would be available to me.

I do not know the method Miss Wells used to teach us to read or the specific progress made each year. I do know that somehow during the primary years I learned to read: to sound out words, to know the vowels and the consonants, and to break words into syllables. I learned the rudiments of spelling, how to write, penmanship, and how to put words together into sentences.

Miss Wells may have been a teacher at a little country school, but she could "read the handwriting on the wall." She taught us that the ability to read opened doors to the unlimited knowledge of the world. If we could read, then in our minds, we could go any place in the world. We could experience the deeds and thoughts of great men who had gone before us. By the end of the fourth grade under Miss Wells' tutelage I was ready for the expanded adventures which reading could bring.

I can never thank her enough.

A RECITATION WHILE WRITHING

The recitation period stimulated an array of emotions depending on how well I was prepared and what I was expected to do. I was shy and reluctant to stand in front of the class to recite. With a little encouragement and praise from Miss Wells, I was generally able to do what she asked of me; however, I vividly remember one exception. Just prior to our recitation period I held up my hand, with index finger extended. That was the accepted signal to the teacher that I was requesting permission to go outside to the toilet to do number one. If I had been requesting permission to go to the toilet to do number two, I would have extended two fingers. I really had to go and shook one hand vigorously to attract attention while grasping my crotch firmly with the other.

Miss Wells, unaware of the urgency of the situation, continued to ignore my request and called the class forward for our recitation period. The pressure was building and I knew I was in trouble. I continued extending my arm giving the appropriate finger signal as my classmates assembled in the front of the classroom and we all took our places on the little red chairs. I sat there gritting my teeth with my legs tightly crossed still hoping the teacher would heed my call. Instead she called on me to stand in front of the class and read. I was really torn. I could not disobey Miss Wells even though I had an urgent problem that was becoming more critical by the second. I uncrossed my legs, stood, and stepped in front of the class as they sat in their little red chairs. As I held my book before me and began to read, something else started as well. As I stood there in front of my classmates and Miss Wells, I raised my book to hide my face as a hot liquid streamed down my leg and puddled at my feet.

Miss Wells was undaunted as she had undoubtedly encountered similar problems before and asked me to please sit down. I was ashamed and humiliated, but in one respect greatly relieved. In my wet overalls, red-faced and with head hanging low, I slumped in my chair for the remainder of the class period. When called, the other kids stood and recited while carefully avoiding the evidence of my embarrassment as it slowly seeped into the cracks of the rough wooden floor.

This was a traumatic experience for me, but I did not hold it against Miss Wells. I thought she should have acknowledged my request to go to the toilet, but she did not. Maybe I had waited until it was too near recitation time to make the request, or she may have made a mistake. Regardless, she was Miss Wells, my teacher. I loved her and she could really do no wrong.

RITHMATIC

Somehow learning the numbers was not as memorable an experience for me as learning to read and write. I learned the numbers, how to count to ten and even to one hundred. I practiced writing numbers on scratch paper and somewhere along the line realized there was no end to the number of numbers. Maybe that is why Miss Wells discouraged us from counting on our fingers.

We learned how to add and how to take away. We learned that if we were to get the correct answer in addition we had to keep the columns straight. Miss Wells helped us overcome that problem with this little ditty and showed us the truth in the ditty with accompanying examples:

Peter White
Could never add right
The figures 3 and 8
I'll tell you why
He didn't try
To keep them nice and straight

Correct	Incorrect
Nice and straight	Not nice and straight
3	3
+8	+ 8
=11	= 8 3

  Rithmetic became more complex as we progressed to carrying over numbers when adding more than one column and to borrowing numbers in subtraction. Even when I didn't know for sure what I was supposed to do, I soon learned if I just followed instructions and did what Miss Wells told me to do I could get the correct answer. I suppose in many cases I learned the mechanics of the procedures before I understood the concepts. Multiplication was still more difficult. It was another level of mental gymnastics to grasp the concept that the answers to the problems 3 x 2 and 3 + 3 were the same. I finally learned that it was a lot quicker to multiply 8 x 8 than it was to add a column of eight 8's. I imagine that I counted a lot of little piles of corn kernels before I saw the light, but eventually it happened, and I realized once again that Miss Wells was right.

  I also had to learn the multiplication tables through the 12's. Many of the writing tablets back then, in the dark ages before calculators and PC's, had a multiplication table printed inside the cover or on the back. I learned the multiplication tables at first by rote probably. The 5's were easy; the 7's and 9's more difficult. I hoped for an easy number when called upon during recitation periods.

  Miss Wells also drilled us using flash cards which had the arithmetic problem on the front and the answer on the back. Students were drilled and tested until correct responses to questions about the multiplication tables were spontaneous.

Division was yet another hurdle to be conquered. For me, division, especially long division, was even more difficult than multiplication. I don't remember the specific techniques Miss Wells used to teach us division, but I suppose it included a combination of explaining, solving problem sets, flash cards drilling, reciting, testing, more drilling, and explanations tempered with lots of patience.

Each year I managed to grasp enough arithmetic to be advanced to the next grade. I liked arithmetic and found satisfaction in being able to solve problems, but I was just not very good at it. Throughout my school years, math was never my strong suit.

RECESS

There was more to school in the primary grades than studying and reciting. There was recess. The area behind the school house on the northwest corner of the school grounds was the play area for the primary room. Weather permitting and under Miss Wells' watchful eyes we played pump-pump pull away, capture the flag, red rover, ante-over, kittenball, and I suppose many other games the names of which I have forgotten. We were taught to take our turn, not to push and shove, and to get along .

There were times when we thought Miss Wells was not looking or when she was not with us on the playground that we did push and shove, hit and stand fast, or, depending on the relative size and temperament of who was hit, we might hit and run. In the winter when there was snow we built snow forts and had snowball fights or played fox and the goose on a big circle stomped in the snow. If the weather was just too bad, we stayed inside during recess and Miss Wells would read to us or we would play inside games.

Generally, several of the garage stalls were unused. The open garage was a good place to play in the early spring as it gave protection from the north wind and was open to the sun.

In the spring most of the boys and a few of the girls played marbles. We all had sacks of marbles made up of colorful glassies, some crockies and our favorite shooter. Miss Wells would not permit us to play keepies. She knew if we did soon the bigger boys would have all the marbles, the little ones none and there would be tears or fights.

Dillard H. Gates

Miss Wells was not a marble player, but she knew the accepted rules for the game. She often served as the arbitrator when a player was accused by another of some infringement such as snugging, stepping over the lag line, not holding the knuckle on the ground when shooting, or shooting out of turn.

As I recall there was little distinction between boys and girls in most of the games we played. But there were instances when a less boisterous or maybe sneaky little girl would hide behind her status as a girl and run to the teacher, fleeing from repercussions for something she had done or escaping from something she feared was going to happen.

In some cases boys and girls alike liked to hit, but some of the girls could not accept the fact they might get hit back.

"He hit me!"
"Did not!"
"She hit me first!"
"Did not!"

These were accusations and defenses frequently heard on the playground. Even at that age it was obvious that girls sometimes wanted to be treated like girls but at other time treated like boys. The problem was that there was no way to determine their mood until after the fact.

Most conflicts were resolved without major damage, and generally the would-be combatants were soon playing again, often joining together and directing their combined resources toward another perceived opponent. To say the least, personal relationships on the playground were fluid and like all fluids shaped by their immediate environment. Certainly fighting on the school ground was frowned upon, but playground spats were not considered anything to get too excited about, either by the teachers or the parents. A quip and a fist were about equal. Sometimes a shove or a sock on the nose was an acceptable response to name calling or teasing.

Dad tried to teach me not to be a bully or pick a fight, but on the other hand I didn't have to let anyone push me around. I was not expected to back down from a position I thought was right. If that met hitting back, so be it. In fact, if pushed far enough, "hitting back first" was sometimes acceptable, if applied with discretion. Dad further taught me that if I did get into a scrap and came out second in a two man contest, I should not come to him for sympathy or help. Being able to take care of one's self was considered a part of growing up. When I did get into a fight at school

I didn't want Dad to even know about it; however, my sisters could hardly wait to blab about it when we sat down to the supper table.

When games such as kittenball were played that called for two competing sides, Miss Wells normally would designate two kids to choose up sides. First choice was decided by drawing straws or guessing closest to a number between one and ten. There were always kids who were the biggest and best players. Choosing up sides was a way to distribute the talent more or less evenly between the two sides. Of course the best players or favorites of the chooser were chosen first. The small, the weak, the clumsy, and the least popular were left to the last. We learned that life is not always fair but we learned to make the best of it.

It may not have been a direct insult to be last chosen, but on the other hand I am sure it did little to enhance the self esteem of that child.

Even so I am not aware that being last chosen had any lasting negative effects. Often the last chosen was small and in the lower grades. Generally they advanced up the skill ladder as they got older and were then chosen earlier in the selection process. In cases when they were eventually designated to do the choosing, they expressed their rights and selected whom they wanted on their team. It all worked out in the long run.

On warm days, at the end of recess thirsty kids of all grades would cluster around the pump to get a drink prior to returning to the classroom. Someone would work the pump handle. Each kid, boys and girls alike, would bend over the pump spout and divert the water with their hands to get a drink.

A BLUE BELLIED YANKEE

The Gates community, with some exceptions, was inhabited by people who had lived in the area for decades. Many families had come to the area as homesteaders. The ancestors of most of the inhabitants originated in central or eastern Europe or Great Britain.

While learning about geography in the primary grades, Miss Wells would discuss the different countries of the world and point them out on the globe that occupied a prominent spot in the classroom. In an attempt to make the subject more interesting and meaningful, she would show us where our grandmothers and grandfathers may have come from. As a part of preparation for geography class, she requested students to find out their ancestors country of origin. She said we could get the information from our parents.

At recitation time the kids reported on their ethnic backgrounds. Some said they were Irish, some Scotch, some French, some German, some English, etc. As each student reported, the teacher would have them stand and point to the country on the globe.

When it came my turn, the teacher said to me, "Now Dillard, where did your ancestors come from?"

"Dad said to tell you I am a Blue Bellied Yankee," I promptly replied.

"Was that all he told you about your ancestors?" she questioned.

"That's all he would tell me," I insisted.

Miss Wells was a bit taken aback by my response. She was trying to use our ethnicity to help teach us geography. The teaching technique was probably valid; however, in utilizing the technique she had omitted to present the concept that now we were all Americans. The point my Dad was trying to make was that we were no longer German, or Irish or whatever. It didn't make any difference where we came from, we were Yankees. We were Americans.

THE FRECKLED FACED GIRL THAT LIVED ON THE HILL

As long ago as I can remember, I had a girl. I may have been fickle and sometimes changed my mind; however, at any given time there was a little girl that I thought was extra special. Whether or not the feelings were mutual, she was my favorite. Ray and Bell Young lived at the top of the Gates hill about one-half mile south of the school. They had two freckle faced daughters, Viola and Marjorie.

Viola, the elder, was quiet and shy. In contrast, some referred to Marjorie as the ornery little girl who lived on the hill. Viola and I were about the same age, but I started school a year before her. She and my sisters played together, and on occasion I would see her at the Gates store or she would be with her parents when they visited our place. I don't remember us actually playing together before she started to school. Usually she tended to hide behind one of her parents, peek around their leg, wrinkle her nose, squint her eyes, and smile shyly. She didn't have much to say and I was only slightly more assertive than she. Our encounters as preschoolers consisted mostly of grinning sessions. But I thought she was really something and considered her my girl.

She started school when I was in the second grade, so then I got to see her most every day. If I happened to be the one choosing up sides for a game, I would always try to choose Viola. If we had to join hands in a circle to play a game, I tried my best to get to hold her hand. Whenever possible I would work the handle on the school pump so she could get a drink.

My closest contact with Viola was on the last-day-of-school picnic at Victoria State Park. The park was located about six miles west of Gates. It had a small lake, a wonderful spring, big areas to run and play, a merry-go-round, picnic tables, and, most importantly several high swings. It was the swings that attracted me the most.

The swings were the most popular pieces of play equipment at the park. There was often a line of kids waiting for a chance to swing. There were no rules or time limits, so, once occupied, a swing could be controlled as long as the occupant desired. When lucky enough to finally get a swing what I really liked to do was to stand in the swing and make it go as high as possible. Sometimes we would pump double; that is, two kids would stand on the swing seat facing each other and pump in rhythm. We often wondered if we could pump hard enough to make the swing go over the top, but it never did. Swinging was enjoyable. Pumping was fun. Pumping with Viola was ecstasy. We could bend out knees in unison, thrust our feet forward and make the swing go high. In the process of pumping our legs and bodies would sometimes touch. I had lots of sisters and would also swing with them; but somehow swinging with them was just not the same as swinging with Viola. Going up in the swing with Viola was for me like swinging toward heaven.

I didn't tell Viola, or anyone else, how much I liked to swing with her. I kept my feelings to myself and waited for the next picnic at Victoria State Park.

THE SHORT LIFE OF A BABY BROTHER

Mom presented the family with another baby shortly after the beginning of my first school year. A boy, born October 10, 1930 was named Richard Dean. He was a happy, healthy baby who, like all babies,

Hay, Hell, Kids and Cattle

became the center of attraction and pride and joy of the family. As babies will, he grew like a weed. When he was big enough to sit up I remember Mom tying him into a rocking chair with a dish towel. She would scoot the rocking chair close to the wall, and Dean would entertain himself by kicking the wall to make the chair rock.

On July 3, 1931 the family was making plans to celebrate the Fourth of July. Dad went to Sargent to take care of business and to get a shave and a haircut. Mom, assisted by the bigger girls, was busy preparing food for the lunch we would take to the Independence Day picnic. In mid-afternoon she fed baby Dean and laid him on Dad's bed for a nap. As always she placed a pillow on each side of the baby to prevent him from rolling off the bed. Dad's bedroom was just off the dining room, which was the main work room in our house. The door to Dad's bedroom was left ajar so that someone would hear if Dean fussed.

Later on Mom stepped into the bedroom just to check on the baby. He was not on the bed where she had laid him. She rushed to the bedside, but he was not there. Mom called for Hap who had just come into the house. Frantically, together they pulled Dad's bed away from the wall. When they did so, they heard a thud as the baby's head struck the floor behind the bed. Hap leaped across the bed and lifted the limp body of baby Dean from the floor. Somehow he had rolled over the pillows and fallen behind the bed. His head had caught between the wall and the bed and he had strangled.

Hap cradled Dean in his arms, carried him from the bedroom and laid him on the dining room table. He tried to breath life into the baby, but to no avail. I was five. I didn't really understand, but I knew my baby brother was dead.

Friends of the family located my father in the barber chair in Sargent. They waited until the barber was finished before calling him outside and telling him of the tragedy.

Dad burned up the road between Sargent and Gates. As he rushed into the house, I remember his anguished cry, "Where's Dean?"

Dad tenderly picked up the body of his infant son and cuddled it in his arms. Grief stricken, with Dean's body clasped to his chest, he sat in his big chair, rocking. Sometime later a neighbor gently removed Dean's body from Dad's lap, wrapped it in a blanket, and placed it on the bed. Never in my life had I seen Dad shed a tear, but he was crying now. Even at my age I was aware that Dad was suffering greatly. I crawled up onto his lap, the lap that over the years had provided so much solace to me, laid my head upon his chest, and tried to comfort him.

There was no Fourth of July celebration at our house. Every year hence when we celebrated Independence Day we were reminded that during this season in 1931 we laid our baby, our brother and son Dean, to rest in the Gates Cemetery.

Richard Dean was my father's twelfth child and Mom's sixth. Dad had buried a young son, Stetcher, in 1918, who had also died as the result of a tragic accident. Having a houseful of remaining kids did not lessen the grief for Mom and Dad.

THE HAY FIELD REVOLT
THE DAY THE KIDS LEFT HOME

Putting up hay was a big job that involved everyone in the family big enough to work. There were periods of time when there were enough big kids still at home that the hay could be put up with family labor alone.

On a hot Friday in the summer of 1932 the hay crew consisted of Dad, my brother Hap, then twenty years old, and two sisters, Alice, fourteen, and Anna, fifteen. At the time I was seven years old but the memories of that day in the hayfield are as vivid to me as yesterday.

Anna was mowing hay with the steel wheeled 1929 Farmall with a mounted power mower. Alice was raking hay with a two-horse team. Dad was operating the four-horse hay sweep, and Hap was up on the stack. I suppose I was there just watching or maybe taking care of my younger brother or one of my little sisters and carrying the water jug to anyone that called for a drink.

Anna finished mowing a field and headed the tractor toward the haystack. There was enough hay down (mowed) to keep the hay crew busy through Saturday. Dad saw Anna heading in and motioned for her to begin mowing another field. From his vantage point on top of the half built haystack, Hap had observed Anna heading in and Dad directing her to continue mowing.

Hap was a hardworking and respectful son. He was husky, strong, and hot headed. He had somehow managed to control his temper thus far in life, and he and Dad gotten along in a fragile father-son relationship. Hap could do anything with his hands; he could do any job on the farm, and even Dad said he could do more work than any two other men. (He was also my big brother whom I idolized.) He was still living at home, working for Dad without wages and accepting whatever money Dad gave him on Saturday night or whenever he made a request. The arrangement was working, but not without stress. I remember Hap complaining to Mom about the situation and telling her that he wanted to leave home and get started on his own. He could talk to Mom about, it but even at his age he was still fearful to broach the subject with Dad. Hap was also courting Amy Johnson, who lived with her family on a farm in the Round Valley community fifteen or so miles southeast of Gates. Hap had a date with Amy for Saturday night. Unbeknownst to Dad, they also planned to do something on Sunday, maybe a picnic at Victoria Springs State park or a movie in Broken Bow. Whatever they had planned, it did not include putting up hay.

When Hap saw Dad wave Anna to the other field, he immediately realized that if more hay was cut, it could not be stacked by Saturday afternoon. That could only mean Dad was intending to put up hay on Sunday.

The thought of spending Sunday in the hayfield rather than with Amy brought long suppressed emotions to the surface. This was too much. The time had come. Hap's temper flared. Momentarily subjugating his fears and choking back tears, Hap, using language that was just never used when addressing Dad, or even when within his earshot, shouted down from atop of the hay stack.

"Dad, I'm not stacking hay on Sunday for any son of a bitch, I'll leave before I do!"

"Well leave then!" was Dad's instant though intemperate response.

The pent up flood of emotions was released, the dye was cast, the damage done. That was a defining moment in the Gates family and on the farm.

Hap literally tumbled from the haystack, grabbed his shirt, and headed toward the house. Alice had heard the heated exchange and saw Hap take off. She quickly swung the rake team toward the stack and tied it to a wagon standing nearby. Though only fourteen, she called to Dad as she took off on a run following Hap.

"If Hap's leaving, I'm leaving, too!"

As she followed Hap toward the house, she stopped to tell Anna what was happening. Anna immediately shut off the tractor and together they ran to catch up with Hap. I doubt that either of the girls understood the significance of their actions, but at the time neither gave it a moment's thought.

It was about mid-day and Mom was busy in the kitchen preparing dinner for the hay crew. All three of the kids, distressed, frightened but determined, burst into the kitchen where Mom was working and blurted out their story. Before Mom could grasp what was happening or why, they grabbed a few clothes and bolted from the house without even a good-bye.

My big brother and my two oldest sisters still living at home had just left home, resolute and in tears. They were fleeing from a situation that in their minds had become intolerable.

Hap headed up the road to try to catch a ride to Round Valley where Amy lived. The two girls headed for a neighbor's house about a half mile away to seek temporary refuge.

Meanwhile back in the hayfield, haying operations had ceased. I watched my father, badly shaken, unhitch the four horses from the hay sweep. He tied them to the back of the wagon then unhitched the rake team Alice had abandoned. He then hitched the rake team to the wagon, loaded me and any siblings that may have been present into the wagon. With the four horses trailing behind, we headed for the barn. It was a quiet ride.

Dad was subdued and obviously distressed. He was a strong man, physically and mentally, but he had received a crushing blow. He was trying to cope with a severe emotional problem: three of his kids had just left home, but there was still hay on the ground that had to be stacked before it spoiled.

After we had watered the horses, put them in the barn, filled the mangers with hay, and put oats in the feed boxes, we went in to dinner. I don't recall hearing Mom and Dad discuss the recent happening during the meal. In fact, as I recall, they seldom discussed anything. Without a doubt, right or wrong, Dad ruled the roost. Mom was generally passive and only reacted to what Dad said or did. She seldom initiated a discussion.

Dad did ask her where Hap, Anna, and Alice had gone. Mom replied that she didn't know. She only knew that they were all crying and they had left.

Following dinner, Dad and I went back out to the barn. Dad slowly unharnessed the work horses and turned them out to pasture. He then turned to me and said, "Get your clothes changed, Dill, and come to town with me. I must hire a new crew to help finish putting up hay."

For me dressing up meant just pulling on a clean pair of overalls. Dad and I got in the old Ford and headed to Broken Bow. I knew that Hap and the girls had left, but I did not comprehend the full significance

Dillard H. Gates

of the event. Dad, never really talkative, was even more quiet on the way to town. However, I do remember him breaking the silence once when he said to me, "Dill, having three kids leave home at once is pretty difficult to take. I didn't realize I was so hard on them."

As I recall, that was the limit of discussion about Hap, Anna and Alice's sudden break with Dad and their unexpected departure from home.

Dad had contacts in town and soon located Frank Jalenek, a man with whom he was acquainted and who had a good reputation for work. Dad told him to get his bag and he would pick him up later after he had located another man. Unemployment was high in Custer County during the depression of the thirties. Even at a wage of only a dollar a day plus room and board, it was not difficult to find men anxious to work on the farm.

After a bit more looking, Dad heard of a young man by the name of Stutzman who was looking for a job. Dad was acquainted with the Stutzman family and knew where they lived in Broken Bow. We went up to their home and Dad talked to young Stutzman and his mother. Though not experienced, the eighteen or nineteen year old indicated he had done some farm work and would like to give the job a try. His mother was protective, a mite "churchy" and concerned for the spiritual welfare of her son. She agreed to let him take the job with the provision that her son would not be expected to work on the Sabbath. By evening, with two new hired men in tow, we headed north for the twenty mile drive home.

The next morning, Saturday, Dad and the new crew headed out to the field where the hay was down waiting to be stacked. Frank was on the stack, Stutzman was running the rake, and Dad was running the sweep as usual. Since the hay crew was still a bit short-handed, Dad had to stop the sweep after pushing each load onto the stacker head and drive the stacker team to lift and dump the load on top of the growing hay stack. The day went well and without incident; however, since no hay had been stacked the previous afternoon there was still hay down in the field at quitting time.

On Sunday morning Dad remembered the admonishment of Mrs. Stutzman. He decided that he and the other hired man, Frank, would try to put up the remainder of the hay. Young Stutzman, maybe a bit chagrined by his mother's intercession when he was hired, told Dad that he didn't mind working on Sunday and that he would like to help complete the job. The three men went to the hay field and, though still short-handed, proceeded with the task of putting up hay.

Around mid-afternoon a car drove into the farmyard and the woman driver asked where she could find her son. A large man sat in the front seat beside her. One of the girls told her he was down in the hay field and offered to show her the way. In a huff she got back into her car and made tracks for the hay field. She first collared Dad as he was sweeping in a load of hay to push onto the haystacker. She demanded to know where her son was and what he was doing in the hay field on the Sabbath.

Dad was not the excitable kind and was not overly concerned about the mother's state of mind. He realized, however, that he had not adhered to the spirit of the understanding reached when he hired her son two days earlier.

Young Stutzman was raking hay in a field nearby. Dad waved and motioned for him to come over to the stacking area where his mother was waiting. He climbed down from the hay rake and sheepishly approached his mother. Obviously he was a bit more susceptible to and affected by her attitude than was Dad. She quickly and emphatically informed the would-be farm hand that she had found another job for him that fit his talents much better than working in a hot hay field on the Sabbath. Stutzman told his mother that he had volunteered to work on Sunday and protested feebly about being pulled off the job after only one and one-half days. She informed Dad to pay her son the wages owed as she was taking him back to town.

The good lady, however, had realized Dad's need for help in the hay field. Before coming out to retrieve her son she had located a replacement for him and had, in fact, brought him with her. She told Dad about the new hay hand in the car awaiting his fate. Only then did the big man in the front seat get out of the car. That is when we first met Ab Myers.

Ab walked over to the rake, climbed aboard, clicked his tongue, said, "gidup," to the team and started raking hay. The newly constituted hay crew went back to work, and before evening all the down hay was in the stack.

Dad had responded quickly and decisively to the critical problem of the loss of his hay crew. When the hay was put up there was still lots of work to do on the farm. Dad had lost not only a hay, crew but the main source of all farm labor as well. He had also lost three of his children. Dad was a strict disciplinarian, gruff and demanding. He expected a lot from us kids. His praise was forthcoming only when one excelled or exceeded expectations. Praise was not a reward for just doing your job.

Frank Jalenek and Ab Myers were good men and continued to work for Dad the remainder of the summer. Both men worked periodically for Dad over the next several years. Ab, a kind and gentle man, almost became a part of the family despite the fact that he had a family of his own in town.

Despite all this, Dad loved and cherished each one of his kids. But in this case Dad had pushed them too hard for too long. Within moments the pressure had soared from normal to explosive. I believe the revolt in the hay field had an ameliorating influence on Dad's treatment of the rest of the kids. He was gentler with us than he had been with the ones who had left.

Even though the ruptured relationship between Dad, Hap, Anna, and Alice was traumatic, it was not permanent. The girls lived with Aunt Mary, Dad's sister in Broken Bow, and Dad supported them through high school. Hap worked as a hired farm hand in the Round Valley community for a year or two. When he and Amy decided to get married, he sought out Dad. Together they arrived at a working arrangement that provided enough financial security so that Hap and Amy could get married. Dad fixed up a little house for them (the shack) and Hap worked for Dad for a couple years or so. Dad then provided machinery and livestock and helped them rent a farm and get started on their own.

I was only seven but I was the oldest son remaining at home. My role in the family scheme of things began to change, if ever so imperceptibly.

THE INTERMEDIATE YEARS

Leaving Miss Wells and the primary room was sweet sorrow. I loved her as a teacher, her kind and gentle manner and sparkling smile, but I was growing up. I was now nine years old, ready to open another door and move toward new horizons.

The period of my life which encompassed the fifth through the eighth grades was crucial from the standpoint of academics. But there was still a lot of knowledge to be acquired in places other than the school house. Life experiences continued behind the school house, behind the barn, in the farmyard, and in relationships with neighbors, family, and friends. All of these experiences were educational and were amalgamated within the developing biological entity that was slowly and erratically moving toward maturity.

MISS MYERS

Miss Myers was the first of my three intermediate school teachers. Our families had been friends and neighbors since the country was settled. We attended Lillian Christian Church where Miss Myers taught Sunday school and directed the choir. She was kind and gentle, an excellent teacher and a great lady despite the fact that most of the kids in her room considered her to be the "old maid" type.

Miss Myers taught the intermediate grades at Gates school for five years, 1929-30 then 1931-35. She put up with little nonsense and expected us to do our work as instructed. I was fortunate to have her as a teacher for even one year.

Miss Myers was also the music teacher for the entire school. She always carried a pitch harp on a string around her neck. I wondered why she insisted on blowing a note on the harp before we started to sing. I knew that different songs had different tunes, but all the sounds coming from the pitch harp sounded pretty much the same to me.

She taught us the scale- do, ra, me, fa, so, la , te, do- frontwards and backwards. I could make the sounds alright, but they helped little in teaching me to recognize musical notes. Even though I didn't appreciate the technical side of learning music, I always liked to sing. I learned and retained a large repertoire ranging from cowboy songs, to folk music, to hymnals and then-popular ballads. I sang them with the family, I sang them to the cows and the horses and sang while driving the tractor.

I later sang them to my wife, especially as we drove down the highway. And by the way, she is about the only one that still encourages me to sing. (love has wonderful ways). I sang to my children until they pleaded, "Radio-off," and I now sing to my grandchildren, sometimes spontaneously, sometimes at their request. My grandson, Gregory, who is seven years old says, "Oh, Papa, you have a song for everything."

Maybe it is, in part at least, because of Miss Myers that I learned and have still retained many of the church hymns I learned as a boy. I still love to sing "The Old Rugged Cross," "The Church in the Valley," "When my Name is Called Up Yonder," " Coming Down The Valley," "Is My Name Written There," and many others. Singing these old songs I learned as a kid is still fun and stimulating.

I have few memories of being in the fifth grade except that I liked school and Miss Myers and tried do what was expected of me. I do recall one specific thing I was first exposed to in Miss Myers class. I did not appreciate its full significance when she read it to the class then took the time to write it on the blackboard but the verse from Longfellow has served as a guiding light for me, though often dim and seemingly far away. I may not remember the verse exactly, but the essence is there:

> "*Lives of great men all remind us*
> *That we too can make our lives sublime*
> *And departing leave behind us*
> *Golden footprints in the sands of time*"

I respected Miss Myers, later Mrs. Ferguson, and we remained friends for the rest of her life. Over a span of fifty or so years I saw her occasionally when I visited friends and family in Broken Bow, Nebraska. It was always inspiring to spend time with her and to talk not only about old times, but about the future, what she was doing and how my career was developing. She was in her nineties when I last visited her in the Melham Memorial Medical Center Nursing Home a few months before she died. She was still sharp as a tack and interested in life, my family, and what was going on in the world. I will remember her always. I was proud and lucky to have had her for my fifth grade teacher and as a lifetime friend. In all humility, I hope that Miss Myers, as she sits behind that teachers desk in the sky peering over the top of her glasses at her students, now disbursed, may spot this humble former student and feel a bit of satisfaction for having had such a positive influence on him more than sixty years ago.

WANTABE COWBOY:
A NECK IS NOT A STABLE SNUBBING POST

Cattle were very much a part of farm life. There were stock cattle which were raised and sold for beef. These cows and calves were normally kept in the pasture or in the fields grazing crop residues. The stock cattle while not wild were handled only as necessary. Then there were the milk cows.

Generally, calves of the milk cows were kept around the farmyard for a few months, and received extra care until they were mature enough to join the stock cows in the pasture. These calves, called bucket calves, were taught to suck a nipple, drink milk from a bucket, and were provided supplemental grain and hay. Bucket calves were gentle and were treated somewhat like pets. But little calves became big calves and in so doing became stronger and less inclined to respond as we kids expected them to.

One summer during threshing season when I was about ten, some of the neighbor boys around my age were at our house as their mothers were helping Mom cook for the threshing crew. We decided to play cowboy and got out Dad's lariat. We planned to lasso one of the bucket calves kept in the corral adjacent to the barn and see if we could throw and hog-tie it like we had seen cowboys do at the rodeo and our dads do while working cattle.

The lariat belonged to my Dad, so I assumed the role of calf roper. We would-be cowboys opened the gate and headed into the corral. The calf was gentle as it was accustomed to being handled by kids; however, it had grown and now weighed probably one hundred fifty pounds. I was a scrawny little kid and would not have weighed more than seventy pounds dripping wet.

As I approached the calf I made a loop in the lariat as I had seen Dad do many times before. The calf stood still, probably expecting to get fed or have his ears rubbed. Getting the loop over the calf's head was anti-climatic for the budding buckaroo within me. I imagined myself dropping the loop neatly over the head of a critter running at full speed. Actually, I didn't even swing the loop. I walked up to the calf and dropped it over his head. I stepped back to pull the loop tight as my support staff, the potential calf wrestlers, rushed forward.

The gentlest animals may be startled by sudden or unexpected activities. This was no exception. Faced with a swarm of, pint-sized but rowdy would-be calf wrestlers rushing toward him, the startled animal did the natural thing. It took off. The frightened calf headed across the corral through the open gate. I was half dragged and running as fast as I could trying to keep up and maintain my grip on the lariat.

Several cars had been parked in the barnyard either by some of the threshing crew or the women helping Mom with the cooking. The fleeing calf, with me in tow, attempted to run between two of the cars. The rope, with the calf on one end and me on the other, became entangled in the bumper of one of the cars. This brought the run-away steer to an abrupt halt, but it continued to thresh and strain trying to free itself as my end of the rope slackened. I eyed the tangled rope and tried to catch my breath as the mini-wranglers caught up with me.

The calf was pulling so hard that we could not get enough slack to slip the lasso from around his neck. It seemed the only solution was to somehow untangle the rope from the bumper. The calf kept the rope tight while we struggled with the problem of how to get it loose. It appeared a solution was in sight as, finally, we were working the rope loose from the bumper; however, I became concerned that if the rope was suddenly freed the calf would take off with Dad's lariat around its neck. I figured I was in enough trouble with the calf and certainly did not want trouble with my Dad. In a flash of inspiration I came up with a brilliant solution to the problem: so I tied the end of the rope around my neck freeing both hands to work on getting it untangled. Now if the rope came free from the bumper, I would still have control of the calf.

I knotted the loose end of the lariat around my neck and concentrated on disentangling it from the bumper. All of a sudden the problem with which we had been struggling was solved. The rope was no longer tangled with the bumper. The calf was free. But I suddenly realized I was not. The struggle against the rope while we tried to free it from the car apparently did little to exhaust the calf. As the calf headed across the barnyard at full speed, the rope was drawn tight and I was jerked from my feet.

As I was dragged across the barnyard on my belly, I grabbed the rope and tried to relieve the pressure from my neck. If I would have had time to stop and philosophize, I might have given some thought to how the calf felt as it struggled to free itself from the lariat. But at the moment I was not inclined to be philosophical. The calf was headed across the road toward a big sandbur patch. I had not yet reached the conclusion that I might be strangled on the end of the rope. My immediate concern was that I was being dragged face down toward a patch of sandburs growing along the road.

It is alleged that the good Lord looks after little kids. In this instance he must have been looking out for a scrawny little boy who wanted to be a cowboy, who was now being dragged by his neck behind a scared and running calf.

Luckily, it was midday and some of the threshing crew were bringing their bundle racks and teams into the barnyard in preparation for dinner. One of the threshers noted my predicament, jumped from his bundle rack, and caught the calf. As he held onto the lariat and relieved the tension of the rope from my neck, other threshers hurried forward and removed the lariat from around the neck of the calf. Now the calf and I were both free: the calf from those pesky kids and the suffocating rope around its neck and me from the threat of being dragged through the sandbur patch.

MILKING, A DREADED CHORE

We milked only enough cows to provide milk for the family. We did not rely on the cream check as a source of cash to buy groceries. There were enough kids around to milk cows, but for some reason Dad just did not want to bother with milk cows any more than was necessary.

Even so, milking was a chore we all disliked. We each tried to dream up reasons why we should not have to milk and shift the chore to one of our siblings. Dad didn't care much who milked, he just wanted the job done and didn't want to hear any squabbling about it. The exception to the general rule was that if someone was working in the field, that person was not expected to have to milk the cows after field work was finished in the evening.

There were many incidents in the cow barn that contributed to the displeasure of the job. While milking, it was necessary to sit on a milk stool holding the milk bucket firmly between the legs. If the cow moved or kicked, the milker was expected to grab the bucket handle with one hand, the milk stool with the other, and stand up and step back from the cow all in one motion without spilling the milk. If you didn't complete the move correctly and landed on your backside instead of your feet, you were still expected to protect that pail of milk. Believe it or not, I became quite adept at the maneuver, but I had lots of practice.

Sometimes if a cow had a sore teat or was not yet completely broke to milk she would have to be hobbled to force her to stand and not kick while being milked. I remember one instance when a cow continued to give us kids trouble when we tried to milk her. She would often kick us over and in some cases cause us to spill the milk. Dad decided to check out the situation to see if it was our imagination or if the cow was really a kicker.

As Dad watched, I sat on the stool, grasped the cow's teats, and started to milk. The cow promptly raised her right leg and kicked me over backwards. Dad agreed that this cow had a problem. He took the milk pail from me, picked up the milk stool, sat down at the cow, grabbed a teat in each hand, and started to milk. The ole cow immediately tried to give him the same treatment she had given me only moments before. Dad parried the kick and tried to continue milking. The cow kicked again. Dad stood up and handed the milk pail to me. He walked over to the side of the milk shed and picked up a piece of 2x4 about four feet long. He stepped to the left side of the kicky cow, raised the 2x4, and struck her a solid blow on the shin of the left hind leg. The cow let out a bellow and raised the wounded leg from the ground. Dad dropped the club, walked back to me, reached for the milk pail, picked up the milk stool, sat down at the cow, and continued to milk. The cow stood with the left leg held in the air as Dad milked. She was unable to kick again with her right leg as she stood on three legs unable to put weight on the wounded left leg.

The old cow limped around and favored her left hind leg for a few days; however, her kicking days were over. From then on, we kids could milk her with no trouble. I guess a cow can learn fast, but, as with a kid, you first have to get it's attention.

For the most part the milk cows were confined to the barn or the adjacent corral at night. Sometimes these places tended to get covered with cow manure or mud or a mixture of the two. The cows lay down where they could, and sometimes it was in a messy place. It is not in the nature of a cow to delineate between where she deposits her pies and where she lays down. As a result, often at milking time the cow's udder and tail were covered with manure and mud.

In the summer when the flies were bad, the discomforts of milking were magnified. The old cow would swing her tail continuously to chase away the flies. In so doing, she would frequently swat me alongside the head or in the face with a long bushy tail saturated with mud and manure. I was not squeamish, but, I did not enjoy a cow pie facial plaster. Sometimes I would try to hold the end of the cow's tail between my left knee and her right rear leg. That worked sometimes but more often than not the cow managed to extract her tail from the meager trap and with the same motion plant it squarely across my face. At the least, this incited me to direct all the profanity in my vocabulary at the cow while spitting and trying to wipe the cow crap from my face. Additionally, in some instances it resulted in the ole cow getting whacked with the milk stool, sometimes to the degree that it was difficult to get her to stand still while the milking was finished.

On some occasions when I had to do the milking I would shanghai one of my always present little sisters to hold the tail of the cow being milked. This worked reasonably well as long as the tail-holding little sister remained alert or until the cow made an extra effort to swat flies. When the messy tail came loose from the grasp of my little sister, the result was the same: a wet, manure covered tail in the face. In addition to cussing and hitting the cow, I sometimes subjected my poor little sisters to similar treatment.

One time, ole Roany, our favorite milk cow, would not stand still because she had chapped teats. I hit her across the top of the neck with a milk stool, and she fell to the ground like a pole-axed steer. I was sure I had killed her. I leaned against the wall and started to cry but ole Roany raised her head then slowly struggled to her feet. Both Roany and I were trembling as I completed milking. The cow trembled as a result of the blow to the neck and I trembled from fright thinking of what Dad might have done if that cow had not gotten to her feet.

CUT AND PULL, CLIP AND PULL
THE RHYTHM OF THE HAND CLIPPERS

Conventional wisdom would have us believe that torture has not been a generally accepted practice in our society for a long time, but those who put their faith in that tenet never had to sit still while Dad cut or otherwise removed hair which had grown beyond the acceptable length. Getting a haircut from Dad, and there was no other choice, was more than just a haircut; it was a test of endurance, will, tolerance to pain and one's ability to accept the inevitable.

Dad could do a great job of roaching the horses' manes and trimming their tails, and shearing sheep with the old hand sheepshears. It was only logical for him to take the next step and apply his skills to the recurring long hair problems of the family. Occasionally we would have a hired man who claimed tonsorial skills, and he would be given a chance to prove himself, but for the most part Dad was the barber, cum hair stylist from the time he held me on his knee and removed my baby curls until his death when I was sixteen.

It was time to get a haircut when Dad said it was time. In the case of we boys, that occurred when the hair on the back of the neck reached our collar or when hair in front hung down to our eyes. The girls generally had somewhat more latitude in the way they wore their hair as they approached high school. However, for the first ten or twelve years their hair styles, too, were a reflection of a session with Dad and his scissors and clippers.

Most assuredly Dad did not peruse fashion magazines or even the Montgomery Ward catalogue to evaluate current hair styles. He probably gave little if any consideration to the hair styles of our peers. The first criterion for an acceptable haircut on Dad's list was "short." The length of hair remaining when Dad finished the job determined how long it would be before he would have to cut it again. For me, it was a measure of how long it would be before I had to endure another torture. This fact alone created stress. I certainly didn't want to look like a peeled onion, but neither did I relish the idea of another bout with my barber. If there was a second criterion on Dad's list I don't know what it was. The desires of the kid beneath the clippers were given little consideration and likely would not have made the list, had there been one.

Dad's barbering equipment consisted of a comb, barber scissors, a pair of hand clippers, and a can of kerosene. Dad would periodically sharpen the cutters of the hand clippers, but whether that improved their hair cutting characteristics could have been a matter for debate, had debate been allowed. A flour-sack dish-towel was placed around the neck of the victim and secured by a big safety pin. The barber chair depended somewhat on the size of the one getting the haircut. A kid might be set on the dining room table, on a box placed upon a chair, on a tall stool, anywhere just so the head to be shorn was within easy reach of Dad and his clippers.

Dad's hair-cutting technique was simple. He placed his left hand on top of my head and grasped the clippers in his right. He dipped the clippers into the can of kerosene, then squeezed the handles together a few times to make certain they were lubricated. Starting at the temple on one side, squeezing and releasing the handles, he moved the clippers upward, cutting and pulling hair, until he reached the hair level he deemed appropriate. He proceeded to make clipper-wide swaths around my head, over an ear, across the back of my neck, and continued until he completed the circuit on the other side.

Each upward thrust of the clippers was little less than agony. The often dull clippers cut some and pulled some as Dad pushed them through my hair. It was a matter of endurance to sit still without flinching or hollering while Dad wielded the clippers. If I told him the clippers were pulling, he would dip the cutting head into the can of kerosene again. Sometimes this helped, sometimes not. If I flinched or jerked too much as a result of the hair pulling, I was rewarded with a cuff on the side of the head and an admonishment to be quiet and sit still. Sometimes with tears in my eyes I wondered which was worse, to grit my teeth and endure the misery of the hair being pulled, or to jerk and yelp and accept the whack which was likely to follow.

Following a trip around my head with the clippers, Dad used the barber scissors to cut the remaining hair to a length suitable to him. He would then attempt to feather the top hair and taper the edges so that it blended, to some degree, with the clipped hair on the sides of my head and my neck. When the job was finished my face was plastered with hair and tears. I had hair down my neck and I smelled like kerosene. But whether I liked the hair cut or not, I was generally relieved that the ordeal was over.

Frequently the first look in the mirror following a barbering session was startling, but the final results varied. There were times when I looked like I was wearing a fuzzy skull cap. Other times I looked like a bowl had been set over my head and the hair cut off below it. Occasionally the results were such that for a few days I was embarrassed when I went to school. I sometimes turned up my shirt collar in an effort to hide the evidence of Dad's handiwork, but I suppose I was successful only in calling more attention to it. A redeeming feature of the entire undertaking was that most of the other kids were in a similar situation. Most had homemade haircuts, and though we did not always suffer in silence, we suffered together.

BUTCHERING, PUTTING MEAT ON THE TABLE

We were poor, but we were never hungry, and meat was a staple of our daily diet. We raised our own animals for slaughter. Dad was the butcher and primary meat cutter, and Mom was mostly responsible for canning or otherwise preserving the meat. Dad slaughtered and butchered pigs, cattle, sheep, and an occasional goat. This was in addition to the dozens of chickens raised for fryers, roasters, or boilers. We didn't really think about chickens as animals to be butchered. When Mom wanted a chicken for a meal, she told one of the kids to go catch one and kill it for her.

HOGS

Aside from chicken, pork was the primary meat in our household. Dad raised lots of hogs, so they were readily available for slaughter. Compared to cattle, pigs were of a size that could be easily handled in the butchering process. In addition, pork was easier to preserve by canning, cooking, salting, or pickling than was beef. Pork was not necessarily the meat of choice in the household, though it was well liked. Its availability was a matter both of economics and convenience.

Butchering was a job common to our family, but it still required planning and preparation. The scalding vat had to be moved into place under the big limb of the huge box elder tree which grew in the middle of our farmyard. Dad and Henry Klaninski, a blacksmith in Sargent, had built a scalding vat that would accommodate a hog of any size. The hog carcass, after it was scalded, could be easily lifted from the vat and rolled onto the scraping platform. This had replaced the more laborious and dangerous method of scalding the hog in a fifty-five gallon barrel of hot water.

In preparation for butchering knives, and scrapers had to be sharpened, and Mom had to assemble the big cooking pans and crocks required to process and store the meat. If a part of the meat was to be salted, she had to make certain there was an adequate amount of smoked salt available.

Dillard H. Gates

An extra hand was usually required to help Dad with the butchering operation. Scalding the carcass, even with the new vat, required more than one man. And until I was around fifteen years old, I was just not strong enough to do the job.

To begin the butchering job, the scalding vat was filled to the appropriate level with water. A can of lye was added to the water to help cut the grease and grime on the pig's skin, soften the hair, and make it easier to properly clean the carcass. Wood was placed under the vat, splashed with kerosene, and ignited.

Water temperature was critical to a good scald. The water was at the correct temperature when Dad could draw his finger through it for two counts without getting burned. If the water was too hot, the hog hair set and would not pull loose during the scraping operation. When that happened, hair removal was more of a shaving than scraping operation. If the water was not hot enough, the hair was not loosened and could not be scraped from the skin.

As the water was heating, the butcher hog was brought to the killing area adjacent to the scraping platform. The hog was controlled by a rope secured around the ankle of a front leg. A hog couldn't move very well if a front leg was pulled back and off the ground. It was time to kill the hog as the water warmed. There needed to be adequate time for the carcass to bleed fully before being hoisted into the scalding vat.

It was a relatively easy job for Dad, or sometimes his helper, to throw the butcher hog to the ground. The hog was then rolled onto its back and held in position with all four feet sticking up in the air. Even a big hog weighing in excess of three hundred pounds could be easily held on its back by a man standing against the animal and grasping a front leg below the knee. The knee was then bent at the joint and tightly held. The man's leg was pressed firmly against the side of the hog as it was pulled against him. The hog could squeal, squirm, and kick, but as long as the leg was held in place and it was balanced on its back, it could not get away. I learned as a thirteen or fourteen year old kid that by using this technique I could hold a hog that weighed several times more than me. Like some other lessons on the farm, the toe of the boot or the back of the hand had provided the primary incentives for learning.

The hog was killed by having its throat cut. We called it stabbing, and Dad usually did the job. However, I remember a few occasions when my big brother, Hap, or another helper being taught the proper technique was allowed to practice. The person that was to stab the hog stood at its head as it was held in place on its back. He placed one hand on the snout of the pig and pushed downward, completely exposing the throat. With the stabbing knife in the other hand, he cut a slit lengthwise through the fat in the neck of the pig. He then grasped the knife firmly and thrust it downward through the slit aiming the point of the knife in the direction of the base of the pigs's tail. A successful thrust slashed or severed the jugular and the blood spurted from the opened throat. Sometimes the one holding the hog was splattered with blood as the animal kicked and squirmed in the throes of death. The hog was held in place briefly, then as its struggles ceased it was laid over on one side to bleed out.

There were always kids around and butchering time was no exception. Unlike some of the breeding activities in the barnyard, it was alright even for the youngest of the kids to witness the entire process. Normally when the hog was being thrown and held on its back prior to being killed, it squealed as only a pig can squeal. I had never heard the word "trauma," but, despite our natural curiosity, witnessing the killing and butchering of an animal must have been a traumatic experience for a little kid.

I recall an occasion when I was around five and Dad was in the process of killing a hog. I was frightened by the loud squeal and headed for the house in a dead run. I had gone only a few yards when I was passed by my equally terrified sister, Sissy, who was a year older than me. After she had passed me and was extending the distance between us, Chris Peterson, a neighbor who was helping Dad called out, "Hey, Sissy, where are you going in such a hurry?"

"I'm just trying to catch Dill," she responded as she looked back over her shoulder while increasing the distance between us.

When the killing sounds had quieted, we both sauntered back to the butchering area. We watched the men scald the hog and tried as best we could to help with the scraping process. We were little, but we were learning. It was but a few years before I was holding the hog as it struggled and squealed as it was prepared for slaughter

The carcass was then hoisted to the scraping platform using a block and tackle secured to the box elder tree limb. The hook of the block and tackle was fastened to the clevis of a singletree which separated the back legs of the carcass. Hooks on each end of the singletree were placed through tendons exposed just above the foot of each leg. Turning ropes were then placed around the carcass and it was rolled sideways into the scalding vat. Once in the vat the carcass was rolled back and forth and turned over to assure that the entire body surface was immersed in the hot water. As the scalding process continued Dad, would periodically reach down and grasp some hog hair between his fingers to test if it was loosening properly. When the hair was right, the carcass was rolled from the scalding vat back onto the scraping platform.

Once on the platform, the carcass was attacked by Dad and some of the kids, all with scraping knives. The kids usually scraped hair from the easy areas, like the sides of the body, while Dad worked on the more difficult areas, like the feet and head. When one side of the hog was scraped to Dad's satisfaction, the carcass was rolled over and the process repeated. When the job was properly done, all hair had been completely removed and the skin scraped clean.

When the scraping process was completed, the carcass was again attached to the block and tackle, hoisted up, and hung from the limb of the tree. The scraping platform was slid out of the way and the butchering of the carcass began. Using a sharp knife, Dad cut open the carcass from the tail to the breast bone. The urethra and anus were tied off to prevent fecal material and urine from leaking onto the carcass and damaging the meat. The guts (entrails) were then removed, caught in a big galvanized wash tub, and set aside. The head was removed, and, with a meat hook inserted through the lower jaw, hung on a peg in the tree. The body cavity was cleaned and the carcass left hanging to cool.

Dad then removed the liver and heart from the entrails and stripped the fat from the intestines and other organs where it had accumulated. The liver provided the basis for supper that evening. The fat was saved until other fat was removed from the carcass, then it was placed in a large kettle, cooked, and rendered for lard.

The carcass was covered with a clean bed sheet and left hanging overnight. The following morning Dad would utilize a saw and knife to split the carcass lengthwise from the tail to the neck along one side of the back-bone. He would then hoist one-half of the carcass onto his shoulder, carry it into the house, and place it on the dining room table that had been cleared to receive it.

Dad was the main meat-cutter. He would quarter the carcass, trim off the layers of fat, then cut it into the appropriate cuts for salting, cooking, pickling, or other methods of preservation. He, Mom, and any of the kids that were big enough and not in school would then begin the process of cutting the slabs and pieces of fat into chunks to be cooked and rendered for lard. Meat scraps and less desirable pieces were put through the hand powered meat grinder and later made into sausage.

There were several methods of preserving the meat. The methods used depended in part upon the time of the year and the weather, the size of the animal that had been slaughtered, the number of people Mom expected to have to feed during the upcoming weeks, and the general preferences of Mom and Dad.

The hams, shoulders, loins, sides, and bellies were normally rubbed with smoke salt. This was a treatment that preserved meat even in the heat of summer, however, the meat had to be salted two or three times over a period of weeks. Meat preserved by this method was salty and generally had to be par-boiled to remove the salt when it was being prepared for a meal.

The meat which was ground was usually mixed with spices and made into sausage patties. The patties were then fried, placed in a five or ten gallon crock, and covered with hot melted lard. More patties were layered in the crock and more lard added until the crock was full.

Occasionally, Mon and Dad made link sausages. However, this was a lot of work as the small intestines of the slaughtered pig had to be cleaned, scraped, and prepared. The raw ground sausage meat was then forced into the casing using a sausage press. String was then tied around

Dillard H. Gates

the stuffed casing at about six-inch intervals to form the individual link sausages. These sausages were then put into a large container, placed on the stove, and boiled for a couple of hours. After the link sausages were cooked, they were preserved in the same manner as the sausage patties.

Sometimes the loins or other cuts of meat were cut into serving size pieces, fried, and preserved in the same manner. Meat covered with lard would keep for weeks during the summer and longer if stored in the winter. When Mom wanted meat or sausage for a meal, she merely dug it out of the lard and heated it in the frying pan.

Usually the meat from the head was cooked and used to make head-cheese. The lower legs were cut into short pieces, cooked, and made into pickled pig's feet. These two foods, prepared from what some might consider scrap meat, were considered delicacies in our house. They provided the basis for wonderful snacks and sandwiches.

The final and, to me the most unpleasant task associated with butchering, was the smell of cooking the fat and rendering it for lard. Dad always liked to butcher fat hogs so there was always lots of fat to be processed. The pieces of fat which had been trimmed from the meat and that stripped from the intestines were placed into a large kettle on the stove. It was cooked until the fat was melted and separated from the non-fat materials. The hot fat was then dipped from the big kettle and placed in one to five-gallon crocks. The residue that remained following cooking was called the cracklings and contained considerable fat. These cracklings, while still hot, were placed in the lard press and all possible fat squeezed from them. The residual cracklings were utilized later in the preparation of home made lye soap. When cooled, the lard crocks were set away in the cellar or pantry. This lard provided virtually all the fat used for cooking and baking in the household.

On butchering day, the traditional supper included fresh fried liver and onions. The fresh liver and onions were a real treat, but I looked forward to dinner the next day, when Mom fried the tenderloin which was the tenderest and most tasty part of the pig.

Depending upon the weather, it normally took two or three days to get all the meat cared for and the fat rendered. During that period of time the household was, at best, organized chaos, as all of the regular activities continued in addition to the meat preparation job. But, like other jobs all members of the family were expected to help.

BEEF

Butchering a beef was similar to butchering a hog, but with some exceptions. Beef animals were much larger than the pigs and had to be handled differently. We normally butchered a beef only in the late fall or winter as the meat was more difficult to preserve than was pork. Since we did not have refrigeration, we depended on the cold weather to help prevent spoilage.

Because of its size, a higher stanchion was required from which to hang the beef carcass, so cattle were generally butchered in the alleyway of the granary. The critter to be slaughtered was roped and lead to the butchering area. A block and tackle had already been secured to a high beam extending across the alleyway. The animal was killed by a shot in the forehead from the twelve gauge shotgun, and its throat was cut immediately, and the carcass allowed to bleed. It was then skinned, hoisted by the block and tackle, and hung in the alleyway.

From that point on, the butchering process followed that of the hog. The carcass was opened down the belly and the entrails removed. The heart and liver were removed from the entrails, but since we did not utilize beef tallow the fat was not stripped from the entrails. Once gutted and cleaned, the carcass was covered with a clean sheet, hoisted high, and left to cool.

Depending on the temperature, the carcass was allowed to hang for a day or more. It was then quartered, carried into the house, cut up, and prepared for preservation. The major part of the carcass was cut into appropriate sized cuts, wrapped in a special paper for freezing, taken to Broken Bow, and placed in a rented cold storage locker. Subsequently, when Dad was in town he removed meat from the locker as needed and brought it home for family consumption.

Other cuts of meat were prepared for home preservation. Mom usually canned considerable amounts of beef by a process called cold-packing. The meat was cut into appropriate sized pieces and placed in either one or two-quart Mason jars. The meat was then lightly salted and the jar filled with water and closed with a screw-on lid. The meat-filled jars were then placed in a water bath in a wash boiler which had been placed upon the wood stove. The water was held at a full boil for over two hours. This treatment cooked the meat and destroyed any bacteria which may have gotten onto the beef during the butchering process. The jars were then removed from the hot water bath and the lids tightened. This home canned beef was mighty tasty and provided the basis for a variety of meals ranging from sandwiches to dumplings and beef stew.

SHEEP (MUTTON)

Sheep were a generally profitable enterprise on the farm, however, when I was around ten or twelve Dad got out of the sheep business, primarily as a result of dog problems. We were regularly losing sheep to predation by dogs, and friends and neighbors, even when presented with hard evidence, would not accept the fact that their friendly, loveable dogs might be pets by day but sheep killers by night.

Dad killed a few dogs in our sheep corrals at night. Others managed to escape and return home, some carrying the buckshot from Dad's twelve gauge. It became evident to Dad that the problem would only escalate. He concluded that even though sheep were a significant source of income, it was prudent to dispose of the flock. He decided it was better to forego the income from the sheep than be shot by a neighbor whose dog he had killed or to be forced to shoot a neighbor in self defense.

A sheep was a small animal with a relatively small net worth. It could be easily and quickly butchered. Mutton was nutritious and when properly prepared and cooked, and eaten hot, very palatable. As long as we had sheep Mom prepared and served mutton to the family.

There are techniques common to butchering all farm animals, however, in the case of sheep there were a few elements that differed from the others. The killing process varied from that of hogs or cattle. The sheep was led to the killing area, the shop, the box elder tree, or the granary, where a set of pulleys (usually the fence stretchers) had been suspended. A rope was secured around each of the lower back legs just above the foot. The back legs were then separated and a leg was fastened to the hook in each end of a singletree. The singletree was then attached to the hook on the hoist and the sheep was lifted from the ground and suspended by its back legs.

To slaughter the sheep, Dad grasped an ear of the sheep in his left hand, and then inserted the killing knife at a point near the base of the ear and forced it inward and upward, slicing or severing the jugular vein. The sheep bled quickly from the suspended position and the butchering process began shortly.

Even though both hogs and sheep had their throats cut while still alive, watching a sheep being slaughtered was not as traumatic an experience for me and my siblings as that of watching a hog being killed. Maybe the difference was that sheep struggled little and were relatively quiet during the entire process while pigs squealed loudly, struggled, and protested to very end.

Dad suspended and skinned the carcass taking special care to assure that the wool did not touch the skinned areas. If the wool touched the raw carcass, it tainted the meat. (There are some who might argue that it is impossible to tell if mutton is tainted or not as it all tastes bad to them.) The body cavity was than opened and the entrails removed as was the case with other animals butchered. However, the liver and heart were not removed from the sheep entrails as Dad did not consider them edible.

The carcass was cleaned, covered with a clean cloth, and left hanging overnight to cool. Depending upon the temperature and the number of mouths Mom was cooking for at the time, the carcass would be left hanging and cuts removed as required for meal preparation or taken down, quartered, then cut into appropriate size roasts, chops, etc, and placed in the coolest spot available until consumed. Mutton tended to keep well for a short period. I heard Dad say many times that it took "a sheep a week" to feed the family and two or three hired men.

A NEW BABY, JOYCE
AND MRS. GARDNER, THE HIRED LADY

In October 1934, Mom took time-out from the work on the farm. Dad took her to a mid-wife's home in Sargent to await the arrival of her eighth child, and on October 7 she presented the family with a baby girl, Joyce Mae.

The baby appeared to be healthy, but within a few days developed problems digesting Mom's milk. Dr. Fenstamacher prescribed a formula, and Joyce was put on a bottle. The formula didn't work any better than Mom's milk. The doctor fiddled with several formulas but to no avail; nothing worked and Joyce appeared to be slowly starving. At his wit's end the doctor recommended goat's milk.

Dad was able to find a farmer in the Sargent area that milked a few goats. He made arrangements to buy milk from him for a few days to see how Joyce reacted. The baby appeared to do better on the goat milk diet, so Dad decided to buy a milk goat.

He checked around the country and found a newly freshened goat for sale. The nanny was reputed to be a good milker and to have a good disposition, thus an all-white nanny goat which we named Snowball joined the barnyard family.

For a few weeks Joyce seemed to do alright on the goat milk, but then her condition worsened. Dr. Fenstamacher recommended Dad take her to a hospital in Lincoln. There her condition was diagnosed quickly. Once again her formula was changed and did not include goat's milk. The new formula worked and soon Joyce was on the road to recovery.

We bought Snowball to serve a specific need, milk for baby Joyce, but she became a permanent fixture, loved by the family, especially the kids. For years she provided part of the milk requirements for the family. Every morning and evening one of us kids would take a small pail, call to Snowball, then milk her wherever she was found. The goat had the run of the yard. She ate the flowers, she ate the rose bushes, she scavenged in the granary and the barn, and to Mom's consternation she frequently deposited goat pellets on the front porch.

It was during Mom's confinement with Joyce that Dad hired Mrs. Gardener to run the house and take care of the kids. Even though Mrs. Gardener was an experienced woman with a family of her own, she had her hands full. There were six of us kids between the ages of two and eleven. Mrs. Gardener was a strict disciplinarian, much more so than Mom, and tended to make us toe the line. Gee and Sissy were big enough to be of considerable help. Jack and I tried to stay away from her. The two little girls, Lee and Norma Jean, were under foot and demanded her attention.

While in Broken Bow attending the livestock auction, Dad bought a few bushels of pears from a truck that hauled fruit from Colorado. He brought the pears home and suggested to Mrs. Gardener that she can them. Home canning fruits and vegetables was standard operating procedure for a farm wife. Mrs. Gardener sorted the pears and the ripest ones were eaten fresh. Some were ready to can, so she took care of those. There was a bushel or so of pears not yet ripe enough to can. She set them aside to ripen and planned to can them when they were ready. Mrs. Gardener's home was in Sargent. Dad usually took her home on Friday evenings when he went to see Mom and the baby. She could have the weekend with her family and recover from the week on the farm. Before leaving our home she gave strict orders to Jack and me to stay out of the pears. She would can them on Monday after she returned.

Jack and I had a yearning for fresh pears, a fruit we didn't get often, but Mrs. Gardener's admonition was fresh in mind. Even we naive country kids had heard the phrase, "Necessity is the mother of invention." We came up with an idea we thought would allow us to consume the forbidden fruit with impunity.

When Dad came into the house we asked him if he would like to have some fresh pears. He was unaware Mrs. Gardener had cautioned us to leave the fruit alone. Dad indicated he would enjoy having a pear if some were ready to eat. Jack and I selected the best pears from the basket and brought them to Dad. The three of us enjoyed the tasty though forbidden fruit. We urged Dad to have more, while we followed our own advice.

Dillard H. Gates

Dad went to Sargent on Sunday night and brought Mrs. Gardener back to the farm. She went about her business as usual, but when we gathered around the supper table Monday evening Mrs. Gardener spoke directly to Jack and me. "I see you boys did something I told you not to. I gave you strict orders to leave the pears alone so I could can them when I returned," she scolded.

Even before she finished her comment, Dad realized he had been snookered. He knew Jack and I had offered him the pears in order to provide immunity for ourselves.

A smile spread across his face as he caught Jack and me in his gaze. "Did you offer the pears to me to get me involved in something you weren't supposed to do?" he questioned.

I dropped my eyes to avoid his gaze and responded meekly, "We just thought you would like to have some pears."

Mrs. Gardener realized she was rebuking Jack and me for something in which Dad had been involved. She quickly stated, "I guess if you wanted the pears it was alright to eat them; however, I was planning to finish the canning this week."

Dad was never one to worry about the amount anyone ate so long as they did not waste food. He chuckled and advised us that in the future we should pay attention to what Mrs. Gardener said. He then told her if there were enough pears left, she could can them; if not, we could eat them fresh.

Mom returned home in a few weeks and things around the Gates household returned to normal. In a few days Dad took Mrs. Gardener back to Sargent for the last time. We boys gave a sigh of relief as we were once again under the benevolent and lax discipline of Mom. Baby Joyce was taken to Broken Bow and placed with a practical nurse for a few weeks until she fully recovered.

ANOTHER NEW BABY, IRIS
ANOTHER HIRED LADY, MRS. OGDEN

In the fall of 1935, right on schedule, Dad once again took Mom to the mid-wife's house in Sargent. Once again he brought home another hired lady, Mrs. Ogden, to cook and care for the house and kids during Mom's absence.

Hay, Hell, Kids and Cattle

Maybe word had gotten around that caring for the Gates kids and running the household was beyond the call of duty. In any case, Mrs. Ogden was considerably different than past hired ladies. She lived in a little house in Sargent with her husband and dog, Tuffy. They needed the money and she was happy to take on the job for three dollars a week, which was the going wage for a hired woman. She was a bit old for the job in addition to having a few other odd characteristics. We kids discussed the situation and wondered why Dad hired her in the first place.

The fall months in Nebraska could be a little chilly, but were normally not cold. Mrs. Ogden dressed herself in a long dress over long underwear and long cotton ribbed stockings. She always wore at least one sweater, sometimes two. She slept in her clothes and didn't change them during the week, except maybe to put on another sweater. She apparently postponed that chore to the weekends after Dad took her home each Friday or Saturday night. Maybe she required the assistance of Mr. Ogden to get out of her clothes. Or maybe she was so modest, considering the lack of privacy at our house, she just didn't want any of the kids to see her in less than full attire.

She was a good old lady, was generally nice to us kids, and I do not recall ever playing tricks on her. But her odor was akin to that of a sour milk bucket. Those of us kids who were big enough avoided her embraces or tried to keep a few steps away from her.

Mom was a good cook, so the family was used to good, and tasty, if plain, food. Fried meat, milk gravy, and potatoes are pretty hard to mess up, but Mrs. Ogden could do it. If one of the kids reacted adversely to the taste of something, she would shrug and say, "It's alright. You can eat it with bread."

In fact, maybe that was our salvation. Surprising as it may seem, Mrs. Ogden made good bread. We ate a lot of bread. Whether the reason was to hide the taste of other food or because the bread was good, I don't remember.

Even though we did not have a refrigerator, we saved leftover food to be eaten at the next meal. If there was more than one dish of leftovers, Mrs. Ogden would just dump them all into the same bowl. The next meal the mixture would be reheated and appear on the table, sometimes as an unrecognizable hash or stew.

Table scraps, if there were any, were normally fed to ole Rags, the dog, however, Mrs. Ogden also had a dog in Sargent. The dog needed to be fed and there were not many table scraps at her home as Mr. Ogden was there by himself. Thus, all week long Mrs. Ogden accumulated table scraps in a bucket for Tuffy. On the trip to Sargent for the weekend she would hold the ripe smelling bucket of slop between her feet in the car. Sometimes some of us kids would ride along so we could see Mom and the new baby. We were accustomed to some pretty gross things on the farm, but this was appalling. I don't know how Dad was able to summon the patience to tolerate the situation, but he did. Maybe he knew Mrs. Ogden needed the job or maybe he just thought we could put up with anything for a few weeks.

On October 17 Mom gave birth to yet another baby girl, Iris. In a few days Mom and the baby were home. Mrs Ogden was retained for a while to help Mom, however, it wasn't long before Mom decided she would rather do the work herself than put up with the strange ways of Mrs. Ogden.

MISS HARRISON

Ruth Harrison (Rice) was cast from a different mold than past intermediate and primary teachers at Gates. Miss Harrison was from Broken Bow and was considered to be quite worldly by Gates school standards. Her aunt, locally known as Ma Bruggeman, operated a speakeasy at the west edge of town. It was alleged by some that Miss Harrison had been observed frequenting this evil place and, even worse, had been seen serving beer. With that kind of baggage I don't know how she was hired to teach at Gates. But she came to Gates in the fall of 1935 and stayed two years.

Miss Harrison was my teacher for the sixth and seventh grades. She was an excellent teacher, full of fun, with a great sense of humor and generally liked by the students. In the school room she was pretty strict, but during recess, breaks, and extracurricular school activities she was like one of the kids

I was in the seventh grade in March of 1937 when the school house burned to the ground. Miss Harrison provided support to the students during this unsettling period while temporary school quarters were being prepared. Modifications were made to the Gates church. In a few days it was ready to house the primary and intermediate grades until the new school house was ready the following fall.

A little later in the spring, when the snow was gone except for the north sides of the hills, four or five of us boys decided to play hooky. We had come to the conclusion that it was about time for an early spring outing. With that in mind, we decided to go down to the river a mile and a half north of Gates for our first swim of the year.

The Middle Loup River was about as cold as ice, but we took off our clothes and stood on the river bank until we could muster enough nerve to jump in. We then tried to see who could stay in the cold river the longest.

The cold swim did not last long, even for the most hearty of the bunch. We put on our clothes, tried to catch some bull frogs, ate the lunches we had carried, then messed around until early afternoon. We meandered back to Gates and then to Dad's granary, which was only about fifty yards west of the old church building that was serving as a temporary school house. We jumped in the grain for a while but soon became bored with that. For some reason we decided to stand in the granary alley, out of sight of the school, and to holler as loud as we could in an attempt to disrupt the school. We got no apparent response and soon tired of that activity too. The next great idea that surfaced was to throw dirt clods at the school house. After a barrage of dirt clods had crumbled against the school house, both Miss Harrison and the primary teacher Miss Holcomb burst outside.

I must have been slow witted even to participate in such an undertaking, but I was even slower of foot. Before I could retreat to the shelter of the granary after delivering my missiles, Miss Harrison spied me and called my name. Wondering what was going to happen, I sauntered over to where she was waiting in front of the school house.

As I approached her she reached out gently and put her hand on my shoulder, then behind my neck, and drew me close beside her. As she repeatedly asked me what I thought I was doing, so she began to rub the back of my neck and then my ears. I had no logical answer, she continued the questions and continued to rub my ears harder and harder. It felt like my ears were being torn from the side of my head, but she continued to rub, up and down and round and round. I knew I had done wrong and deserved what I was getting, but, oh my, how it hurt! I dared not try to pull away from her and was fighting back the tears when she finally stopped rubbing. She held me next to her for a few moments, then quietly told me to go inside and wait at my desk.

Miss Harrison then walked over toward the granary and called to the other boys. Chagrined and apprehensive, they abandoned their shelter and surrendered. She herded them into the schoolhouse where I was anxiously and fearfully waiting.

She talked to us about the importance of going to school and said that skipping a day of school was equivalent to skipping a day of work. She told us that our parents worked hard to provide us with an education and that we were not carrying our share of the load if we did not attend school. In addition, she told us it was thoughtless of us to disrupt the kids who were in school. She never stopped smiling nor did she raise her voice as she scolded us for our misdeeds.

She concluded that our parents could discipline us as they chose for playing hooky, however she thought we deserved some punishment for disrupting the class. She provided each of us with a notebook and instructed us to begin writing, "Noise is hard on boys." We were to spend our recesses and noon times as well as one-half hour after school every day writing until we had written the phrase one thousand times.

For the next several days the other kids in the intermediate room poked fun at us about our punishment and basked in the glory of their freedom while we stayed inside and wrote in the notebooks. Miss Harrison joked with us about our predicament, but never scolded us further about it. She had handled the situation with firmness and grace.

I didn't tell Dad about the little episode, but my sisters did. I guess Dad thought the punishment Miss Harrison had dished out was adequate. All Dad said to me about the day of hooky was, "Dill, I think it would be a good idea for you to stay in school."

Though the words were mild, the tone of the voice carried a stronger message. It was some years before my memory dimmed sufficiently to allow me to make a similar foolish mistake again.

SLEIGH RIDING AND COMMUNITY RELATIONSHIPS

We had a good sleigh-riding hill in our pasture that was relatively close to the house. In the winter on moonlit nights we occasionally had school sleigh riding parties. The parents would bring the kids and their sled, if they had one, or sometimes a scoop shovel on which to slide down the hill. Most of the parents would stay at the house and play cards or gab while the kids and the teacher were out in the snow. Miss Harrison liked to participate in the activities which generally included a wiener and marshmallow roast. The teacher always climbed the hill with us and shared the fun and stimulation of being outdoors and the camaraderie of kids having fun.

We trudged up the slippery, snow covered hill pulling our sleds, then headed down the hill for a short but exhilarating ride. This sometimes gave us a chance to select whom we wanted to ride with us down the hill. Yes, even in the middle room we had beaus. This provided an opportunity for us to sit close to the girls, and put our arms tightly around them, to keep them from falling from the sled, of course, as we sped down the hill through the snow. Even at that age, and bundled in heavy winter clothes on a cold winter night in the snow, there was something majestical about the fleeting moments spent in such close proximity to a special girl whom under other circumstances could only be admired from a somewhat greater distance.

Miss Harrison shared the task of pulling the sled up the hill and took her share of rides downhill. On one occasion when she attempted to ride a scoop shovel, she was about half way down the hill when the scoop turned sideways and she went tumbling head over heels in the snow. We kids thought it was hilarious to see the teacher in such a predicament and told her it was funny to see her "bottom side up." In good humor, she responded it might be more appropriate to use the phrase "upside down." Maybe she was reminding us of the potential sensitivity of so openly mentioning the personal aspects of her anatomy. She was always a great sport and we kids liked her all the more for it.

We generally gathered cow chips to make the fire over which we would warm our hands, dry our mittens, and roast wieners or marshmallows. We had to carry roasting sticks with us, as there were no trees or shrubs in the pasture from which to cut branches. We tried to gather enough cow chips to build a fire big enough to keep us warm and serve as an assembly point. When the fire had burned long enough to form a bed of coals, we gathered around to roast the wieners and marshmallows.

When held too close to the glowing coals marshmallows would blacken and break into a flame. Sometimes we could succeed in blowing out the fire but more often the marshmallow would melt quickly and fall off the stick and into the coals. Usually the successfully roasted marshmallows were eaten right off the roasting stick or placed between two graham crackers to create a sweet, hot sandwich. We generally held the wieners over the coals until they swelled and burst and if we were not careful until they turned black. The hot wieners were carefully eaten directly from roasting sticks or placed in a hotdog bun.

These were great times. The kids and Miss Harrison enjoyed each other and the stimulation of the cold night and the thrill of the downhill ride. It was clean, healthful fun, good for kids, parents, and teachers alike.

When the sledding was over and we were wet and cold and the cow-chip fire put out, we slouched through the snow and retreated to the house. There Mom and the other mothers had hot chocolate and cookies waiting for us. We huddled around the wood stove in the dining room to warm up and dry out as we devoured the hot treats and relived the great times we had just experienced on the snowy hills.

On several occasions during her two-year tenure at Gates, Miss Harrison visited our home and joined the family around the player piano to sing and josh and have a good time. She seemed to enjoy the unchecked energy and friendliness of the family, including all the little ones. Her great sense of humor and ability to give as good as she got stood her in good stead with Dad. My family enjoyed and supported Miss Harrison. We thought she was an asset to the school and to the community.

But, alas, despite the fact that she was a gifted teacher and well liked by the students, she could not escape the cloud of Ma Bruggeman's house. Despite her basic goodness, some of the Gates community "goodies" could not blot out the cloud or see the beautiful rays of sunshine shining through. Some were concerned about her alleged activities during her weekends in Broken Bow. Even at that early age, some of us kids wondered which of the staid citizens of District C-23 had actually inhabited Ma Bruggeman's facility and observed Miss Harrison's behavior first-hand. But rumors reign and perception can become fact.

There was a suspicion in the air that somehow these rumors, true or false, might possibly have a deleterious affect on the sweet innocence personified by the children of the intermediate grades of Gates school. As a result of narrow mindedness and self righteousness on the part of a few, the students of the middle room of Gates school were denied the benefit of a dedicated teacher and the association with a down-to-earth, caring, and concerned human being.

Dillard H. Gates

SCHOOLHOUSE FLAMES AND COMMUNITY SPARKS

It was the school house that went up in flames, but a lot of sparks flew in the Gates community before a replacement was constructed.

Dad was returning home from Sargent around 10:00 o'clock the night of March 3, 1937. As he approached Gates from the east, he saw that the school house was engulfed in flames. He quickly pulled the car to the east side of the Gates store building which was just across the road, north from the burning school. Ray and Nora Swick, who ran the Gates Store, and their two daughters Eula and Agnes, occupied living quarters in the rear of the building. Dad hammered on the door of the residence to awaken the family and told them the schoolhouse was burning. He then rousted out Ed and Tresa Russell. Ed, a brother of Nora Swick, lived across the road from the burning school and operated an auto repair garage just north of the store.

Ray and Nora were immediately concerned about the danger to their building. They were especially concerned about the gas pump located in front of the store, at a point nearest the burning school house. If the heat from the fire ignited the gas pump, it was highly probable the store building would be lost. As a safety precaution, they quickly draped wet blankets over the exposed gas pump.

In the meantime Dad looked around the burning school building to see if there was a possibility of saving anything. There was no water supply or fire protection equipment available. It was soon obvious that the building and all its contents were a total loss.

After the schoolhouse roof had fallen in and the fire continued to burn, Dad noticed that the large brick chimney at the north end of the burning building was still standing. Dad, Ray, and Ed discussed the potential problem of the chimney tipping over when people gathered around the ruins the next morning. It was too hot to approach the chimney and attempt to batter it down with a sledge hammer. They finally decided it might be possible to topple the chimney by shooting out a few bricks from the bottom. Dad had a Savage 30-caliber rifle at home and they decided to give the idea a try.

Our house was located a couple hundred yards or so west of the school. When Dad came home to get the rifle and ammunition, he awakened us, told us about the fire, and what he was planning to do about the chimney. He instructed all of us to stay home, took the rifle, and headed back to the burning school.

The family gathered in Jack's and my bedroom, located at the southeast corner of our house. After a while we heard rifle shots and knew that the effort to topple the chimney was underway. We kids huddled on the bed, peered out the window, and cried as we watched our schoolhouse go up in flames.

The next morning we were out of bed earlier than usual and rushed over to view the remains of the Gates school building. Neighbors gathered around to lament the loss, to speculate about the cause of the fire, and to wonder what we were going to do for a school. A sense of tragedy and shock prevailed.

Reactions of the spectators varied. Some students who rode horses to school actually rode by the site without realizing the building was gone. Some walked into the school yard before realizing what had happened.

Before the ashes were cool, kids and parents alike were poking through the ruins to see if anything remained. Piles of charred and burning books smoldered for hours. The metal skeletons of students' desks remained neatly in rows. The burned out remains of the pot-bellied stoves stood out as blackened snowmen among the charred debris. But everything that would burn was gone, and wisps of blue smoke wafted upward from piles of smoldering rubble.

I poked through the debris in the area where my desk had been located. I found some of the coins that had been collected from students to pay for the treats for a recent class party. I told Miss Harrison about the coins and asked her what I should do with them. She indicated that I should just keep them, as many others, adults and students alike, were scavenging through the ruins. Sometime later in the day we were instructed to stop the scavenging until the insurance adjuster had an opportunity to inspect the damage.

A few days later I went to the store to buy candy with the fire blackened coins I had salvaged from the ashes. Nora Swick, the proprietor, chided me about spending the money that had been collected to reimburse her, as the party treats had been charged at the store

One positive thing that came out of the fire was a lot of milk stools. The desks in the primary room were fastened to the wooden floors with screws. The wooden seats were attached to a metal pedestal that, too, was fastened to the floor with screws. Some sage observer of the ruins suggested the remaining pedestals would make good milk stools. Following that suggestion the pedestals disappeared quickly. We had a couple around our barn as long as we remained on the farm.

Speculation about the cause of the fire continued, but abated as years passed. Officially the cause remained unknown. Unofficially, rumors continued and years later evidence of probable cause surfaced.

REBUILDING GATES SCHOOL, A COMMUNITY DIVIDED
PLANNING

Before the ashes cooled, the people of the community were thinking about rebuilding the school. The Gates community had a history of strong commitment to the school and had met challenges before. Now it was time to start all over again. The immediate job was to prepare temporary quarters so classes could continue with a minimum of disruption for the students. This was accomplished by modifications in the old Gates church and an unused farmhouse a mile or so east of Gates.

The School Board immediately called a District meeting to evaluate the problem and consider alternatives. The vast majority of the people agreed they wanted to rebuild and continue with Gates School. They were not in favor of transporting their kids fifteen or twenty miles to surrounding towns.

There was little agreement beyond the fact that a new school building was needed. There was disagreement on the size of the new school building, the building materials, the design, the architect, on whether the new building should have inside plumbing and electricity and most of all on whether it should include a gymnasium.

With some exceptions, the lines of disagreement tended to be drawn between land owners and tenant farmers of the district. Some who analyzed the situation concluded the disagreement was more between liberals and conservatives. The argument sort of boiled down to cost and who was in favor of paying significantly higher taxes and who was not. My Dad, Alan Dewey, and John Bishop led the opposition to the higher cost-expanded version of the planned new school house.

It would be necessary to pass a bond issue to finance new school construction, and many were not prepared to see taxes increased just so kids would have a place to play indoors. Many of the farmers, including my Dad, thought there was plenty of work to do on the farm to get all the exercise needed. In his judgement, a gym was an unnecessary luxury.

Following school board meetings there were discussions at homes of the pros and cons of the various options under consideration. Understandably, kids reflected the opinions of their parents, so the arguments continued at school. Some kids found themselves excluded from what had been their peer group strictly on the basis of the known position of their parents on the issue.

TENSION TRIGGERED INCIDENT

Tension ran high in the community. Relations were strained between families who had been friends and neighbors for decades. The intensity of the feelings associated with the new school issue were dramatized when John Bishop appeared at the Gates store one evening. Characteristically, John was muttering through his teeth between which was clenched the stem of his ever present, malodorous pipe. Only this time his muttering appeared incoherent to the proprietors of the store and my Aunt Dora Robertson, who was there to make a purchase. His muttering included comments about Mary, his wife; Eddie John, his son; and members of the Gates School Board. Aunt Dora interpreted the comments as manifestations of mental instability and threats to his family and members of the school board. She decided quick action was required to prevent an impending crisis.

Leaving John in the store, still muttering, she jumped in her Model-A and headed north to the Bishop farm to check on the status of Mary and Eddie John and, if necessary, rescue them from eminent danger. Her diagnosis of John's mental condition was confirmed by Mary. Yes, John had been acting strangely, and, yes, she was concerned about his behavior. That was enough for Aunt Dora. Without informing anyone of her plans, she piled Mary and Eddie John into the car and headed toward Broken Bow. As they passed through the Gates intersection they noted John's 1928 Chevy parked by the store. They were still safe. They sped onward one-half mile south to the home of Ray Young located at the top of the Gates hill. Ray was a member of the school board, so he may have been included in the muttered comments

Dillard H. Gates

back at the store. Like Paul Revere spreading the word, she stopped only long enough to warn Ray to seek cover. Then at top speed, kicking up rooster tails of dust behind the Model-A, Aunt Dora, with Mary and Eddie John scooched down in the back seat, resumed her flight to Broken Bow.

With the potential victims delivered to a safe refuge, Aunt Dora called Ray and Nora Swick at the Gates store to check on the status of John and to inform them of the location of his wife and son. She was informed that, still muttering incoherently, John had left the store some time ago and headed in the direction of his home. She was also told that Ray had gone over to our place and familiarized Dad with the situation.

Upon getting the information, Dad told Mom and us kids that something was the matter with John. He then jumped into the old Ford and headed a mile and a quarter east to get Alan Dewey. Together they went to the Bishop farm, but John was not there. They decided to drive around the community to see if he could be located. After a period of searching they returned to the Bishop farm and discovered his car in the yard. They went to the house and found John, now armed with his twelve-gauge shotgun, mumbling that something had happened to Mary and Eddie John.

Dad and Alan concluded that John's behavior was abnormal and uncharacteristic. They assured John that Mary and Eddie John were safe and after some cajoling, talked him into surrendering the shotgun. Following an extended period of talking, during which John made many comments which Dad said should not be repeated, he and Alan agreed that John was unbalanced and needed help. Finally, in the middle of the night, John agreed to get in the car with them and go to town.

The three longtime friends and neighbors, one of who was now virtually in the custody of the other two, reluctantly drove to Broken Bow. Once in town, they rousted out the County Sheriff, Glen Fox, who was a longtime friend of the three farmers. Dad and Alan related the story of the night. After listening, Fox agreed with their contention that John needed help. He suggested that, due to the comments he had made, John should be held in custody. Though it was in the middle of the night, Fox called the State Hospital in Hastings and requested that John be admitted for treatment.

The following day Mary signed the appropriate papers and John was taken to the hospital. He remained there for a few weeks receiving treatment for his malady. When he returned home he was still our longtime neighbor and friend, but I could never completely erase from my mind the fact that he had lost his marbles and armed himself with his shotgun.

Though it was never determined if John's problem was related to the school funding controversy, many believed that it was. I don't know if the incident had an impact upon final decisions for schoolhouse construction and financing, but it did have an effect upon the community. Now in addition to the schoolhouse controversy' there was debate about whether it was safe to allow John back in the neighborhood.

FINALLY A DECISION

I do not recall the dollar amounts projected for the schoolhouse with or without the gym, but finally the lower taxes contingent won out and the decision was made to go with the no-gym configuration. The agreed upon facility was to consist of a two story structure with four main classrooms. About four feet of the lower floor was to be below ground level. The lower floor was to consist of two classrooms for the primary and intermediate grades and a furnace room for a coal fired furnace. A lean-to would be attached to the back of the building adjacent to the furnace room to serve as a coal storage area. The upper level would house two classrooms for grades nine through twelve and a room for an office located above the furnace room. The schoolhouse would be lighted by natural light through a bank of large windows in each room. The building would be constructed of brick with a glass brick wall between the two front entry doors.

Even this stripped down model sounded elaborate to those who thought the old school building was adequate and were concerned not only about educating their children but paying their taxes as well. It was considered sparse, sub-minimal, and short sighted by those committed to the more elaborate structure.

The design was completed, bids were let, contractors hired, and construction started in early summer. The contract called for the maximum use of local materials and labor consistent with acceptable construction standards.

Dillard H. Gates

CONSTRUCTION

The cement for construction of the foundation and the mortar for the bricks required lots of gravel and sand. Fortunately, the Middle Loup River was located only one and one-half miles north of Gates and there were high quality sand and gravel pits located adjacent to the river. Arrangements were made for District C-23 farmers to transport the materials from the river to the building site. Several of the farmers with suitable wagons, good teams of horses, and adequate time contracted to haul the construction sand and gravel. They were to be paid based upon the amount of sand and gravel delivered to the building site.

Transporting sand and gravel by team and wagon was slow, and the best a farmer could do was haul two loads per half-day. Thus, those who could work only half-days made only two rounds and those working all day could deliver four loads to the building site.

This arrangement worked fine until my brother Hap, who lived on a farm in the district, had a better idea. Dad had a sturdy, low bed, two-wheeled trailer with heavy duty tires. Hap had a Chevy car with a strong trailer hitch. Putting the two together, he had the equipment to haul sand and gravel much more efficiently than with a team and wagon. Utilizing this method and working very hard to load and unload rapidly, he was able to deliver at least twice as much building material to the building site as those using horses and wagons.

One of the farmers, Red Young, thought Hap was getting too big of a piece of the pie and protested, first to the other farmers and then to a relative on the school board. For the most part, other farmers thought Hap was just taking advantage of the situation. He was working very hard and delivering twice as much sand and gravel as anyone else.

Red fumed and fussed until the school board decided that since the most any farmer could deliver by team and wagon was four loads a day, Hap would be restricted to that amount. The fact that Hap was loading and unloading twice as much sand and gravel each day mattered little to Red or, for that matter, to the board. The board, like many public bodies, was more interested in spreading the work around and making it last than in efficiency. Hap characterized the situation as a local WPA project.

Hap delivered his four loads in a half day then went about his farm work. Red apparently remained content sitting on the sand in his wagon, resting and puffing on roll-your-own Bull Durham cigarettes as his team trudged the one and a half miles between the river and Gates to deliver his two loads each half day.

The head bricklayer on the construction project moved with his family to a vacant house nearby for the duration of the job. He had a son about the age of the boys who would be entering the eighth grade in the fall of 1937. The kid had spent lots of time with his father on construction sites and around construction crews. He was considerably bigger and certainly more streetwise than we country kids. He spent a good share of the summer on the building site with his dad, and most of us became acquainted with him.

When school began in the fall, the bricklayer's son was the new kid in school. He was big and aggressive and immediately attempted to establish himself at the top of the pecking order for boys in the middle room. We soon learned he could whip any one of us. He bullied us around and had his way on the playground during recesses, and before and after school. There was no doubt about it, he ruled the roost. Worst of all, several of the girls thought he was cute and flirted with him while ignoring us, their tried and true old friends and classmates.

We boys didn't like the situation. We didn't mind fighting among ourselves, but we hated being dominated by this imposter. School was being held in the Gates church, and the granary on our farm sat only a short distance west of the temporary school building. The seventh and eighth grade boys held numerous strategy meetings in the alleyway of the granary trying to devise a solution to the problem. We contemplated luring him into the granary out of sight of the teacher, then all piling on him at once; however, despite his bullying we wondered about the fairness of that approach. We considered taking him on one man (boy) at a time. If he whipped the first one then another would be waiting to take the place of the preceding defeated warrior. This would go on, one man at a time, until he was worn down and finally defeated.

But, "Who would bell the cat?" There was no consensus on which reluctant warrior would strike the first blow and likely be severely punished for the effort.

Unbeknownst to us we followed a strategy frequently used by planners everywhere. We just kept having meetings and talking about the problem and before we could find a solution it went away. In this case, the bricklayer finished his job and moved his family with him to his next construction site.

UPSETTING THE HARROW, ALL FOR A GLIMPSE OF MY GIRL

Dad went to town one Saturday in 1937 leaving me with instructions to harrow corn. The field was on the far side of our farm bordering the neighbor to the west. The hired man was cultivating corn in an adjacent field and available to help if I had a problem. It's pretty difficult to have a problem harrowing corn, but I proved that it was possible.

Mr. Woods, the farmer to the west had a daughter, Evelyn, about a year younger than me, who, at that time, I thought was about right. She often visited my sisters and I made excuses to get involved in their activities whenever I could. We were both quite shy and, as was the case with my first girlfriend, Viola Young, we probably did most of our communicating by grinning at each other rather than talking. Even so, I looked forward to seeing her whenever I could.

With the help of the hired man I hitched a team of gentle horses to a three section, spike toothed harrow. Rather than walking in the dust behind the harrow, I saddled ole Wrangler and tied the reins of his bridle to the adjustment lever of the middle harrow section. The lines from the team were long enough to reach back across the harrow to where I sat astride my horse.

The spike-toothed harrow consisted of three, four-foot sections which lay flat on the ground and were attached by eye bolts and clevises to a four by four-inch wooden timber which served as the draw-bar. The team pulled the harrow easily down the corn rows, flattening the lister ridges, uprooting small weeds, and moving soil into the furrow around the growing corn plants. The only way I was likely to have a problem was if I didn't turn soon enough at the end of the row and hooked the harrow into the fence. In the unlikely event that did happen, I could manually slide the harrow sections and draw-bar back and free the harrow.

But I demonstrated there was another heretofore undiscovered way to get into trouble with a harrow. As I approached the west end of the corn field, mounted on ole Wrangler, trailing the harrow, I stared across the fields to the west toward the Woods house about a quarter mile away. I was hoping that just maybe Evelyn would be out in her yard and I would get a glimpse of her. She might even wave at me. I pulled hard on the left rein to turn the team about.

I turned my head sharply to the right, straining my eyes to the west and continued to pull hard on the left rein. The team responded to my tug on the reins and turned sharply, too sharply. Unbeknownst to me, as my eyes and thoughts were elsewhere, instead of the harrow sliding around in a smooth half circle, the left end of the draw-bar dug into the soft soil of a lister ridge.

The team responded to my continued pull on the reins and kept turning to the left. As I stood on my toes in the stirrups, elevating my eyes as high as possible, staring to the west, I was suddenly surprised as the reins from the team were jerked from my hands. I was snapped back to reality when I looked toward the team and saw the harrow had turned completely over. As it fell back to the ground, upside down, it had torn the reins from my hands. The commotion spooked the gentle team and it headed east across the corn field at a dead run.

There I sat with no control. Ole Wrangler was tied to the harrow and galloped along behind the runaway team. I deduced the only solution for me was to jump from the horse and attempt to grab the reins that had been pulled from my grasp and now were dragging on the ground behind the harrow. I jumped and I grabbed two hands full of Custer County topsoil. The team with the harrow behind and ole Wrangler trailing left me in the dust. I followed on foot, unable to run very fast in the soft soil, wondering how I was going to explain this predicament.

The hired man noticed the team running, abandoned the Farmall tractor and cultivator, and ran over to render assistance. Before he reached the team, which had been running in his direction, they had stopped and were standing in the field panting from the exertion of the short run.

The hired man helped me get the harrow righted as I sheepishly tried to explain what happened. I climbed on ole Wrangler and went back to harrowing corn. Since there was no damage or visible evidence of the upset the hired man and I agreed there was no need to tell Dad. I did tell him about it sometime later. He was thankful I was not hurt and no damage had been done to the team or the harrow. He further told me that if in the future if I had the urge to see Evelyn, I better stop and tie the horses to the fence.

BEDS AND BEDROOMS

The number of bedrooms in our house remained static, but the demand for beds varied with fluctuations in the number of people occupying the house at any given time. There were already seven kids in the family when I entered the fray. In addition there was Mom and Dad and sometimes a hired lady and/or a hired man or two. The house may frequently have been at near capacity, but as far as I can remember there was never a time when there was not room for one more.

Sleeping arrangements for the female portion of the family were somewhat more fluid than for the men. With the exception of Dad and my big brother Hap, no one in the family had a bed by themselves. Hap occupied a very small bedroom in which there was a three-quarters size bed. Dad's bedroom had a full sized bed which he sometimes shared with a couple of the little ones who used his outstretched arm for a pillow. What a wonderful and secure place to sleep.

When we were small, three or four kids, boys and girls together, were piled into one bed. Somewhere along the line, for reasons I did not understand at the time, my brother Jack and I were diverted to a bed of our own. I was seven years old when Hap left home. Jack and I moved into the vacated bedroom and shared the three-quarter sized bed until I graduated from high school and left home.

There were two other bedrooms usually occupied by the girls. The number of girls per bed depended on people pressure at any given time. With few exceptions, when we had a hired lady she had to share a bed with one or more of the girls. Sometimes when we had a hired man the girls would be forced out of a bedroom and be required to share a bed with the other girls or with Mom. When a friend wanted to spend the night with one of the kids, which was often the case, we just had to squeeze a little tighter.

As I recall, during all the years on the farm Mom slept on a bed in the front room. The front room was separated from the dining room by large double doors which were normally removed in the summer and put back in the winter to make it easier to heat the living area of the house. There was always a kid or two in bed with Mom.

This may have been an unconventional sleeping arrangement, but it worked. I recall no kid suffering from sleep deprivation or developing a psychosis as a result of not having a room or even a bed for themselves. Nor am I aware that, despite all the stories to the contrary, any hired man, mistakenly or otherwise found his way into the bed of a hired lady or the farmer's daughter.

However, as I began to mature I became aware of a mystery which pervaded our household. When I was little, babies seemed to come along as a matter of course. Mom would go to town for a few days and come home with another baby sister. Somewhat later I began to realize that babies did not just come from town. I observed what went on in the barnyard and was aware that animals had to mate if we were going to have little pigs and calves. I finally deduced that the babies Mom kept bringing home from town must somehow be related to a similar phenomena. It was a big step in comprehension for me to transfer observations made in the barnyard to similar activities on the part of my parents.

Eventually I came to accept the biological facts. I learned where babies came from and how they got there. But a mystery remained. It was even a topic of muted discussions with my two older sisters, Gee and Sissy. Mom slept in one room and Dad in another. Mom always shared her bed with a kid or so. Occasionally so did Dad. The house was always full of kids getting up in the night for a drink of water, to use the slop pail, or to seek comfort from bad dreams. Neither my two older sisters nor I could ever recall sights or sounds indicating that either Mom or Dad made nocturnal visits to the bedroom of the other. No squeaky floors or soft calls in the darkness.

We finally concluded that since Mom seemed to be pregnant a lot of the time, circumstantial evidence proved without the shadow of doubt that more was going on than met the eye. We knew something was happening but we didn't know when, how, or where. The logistical mysteries of the love trysts remained and the babies kept coming. My youngest brother was only eighteen months old when my father died.

My older sisters have admitted to teasing Mom about this unsolved mystery up until near the time of her death at ninety-four. Neither Mom's wit or memory had failed her. She would blush and smile coquettishly as she responded, "That's for me to know and you to try to find out." They didn't find out.

A BED FULL OF SCARED KIDS

We were not latch key kids. There were no locks or keys for the doors of our house. Occasionally Mom and Dad went to town and left us home alone. As the sun went down a nervousness appeared among us. If we were still alone by dark, the nervousness turned to fear. If Mom and Dad were not home by bedtime, the fear was replaced by near terror.

All of us kids were afraid of the dark. There are sounds around the farm and our house sat only a few feet from the main road. Even common sounds translated in our minds to something sinister. We imagined tramps coming to the house and assaulting us. We worried about contemporary outlaws like John Dillinger, Pretty Boy Floyd, and Baby Faced Nelson. We were certain they were on the lam and fearful they may have selected Custer County and more specifically our farm for a hideout.

For mutual protection, we all piled into Dad's bed. Some at the head, some at the foot, stacked in like stovewood. Our imaginations ran rampant. What one could not think of, another one did. If one of the smaller ones made a sound, the bigger ones beat on them to be quiet. If a few swats didn't suffice, they were threatened with more drastic action. Sometimes we fought our fears until we were exhausted and fell asleep, a tangle of kids and blankets piled on the bed. If by chance Mom and Dad returned before we all were asleep, we would tumble out of the bed when we heard the car drive into the yard and stampede out to meet them. Then, all talking at once, each tried to tell their tale of woe and of the abuse heaped upon them by the other kids. The folks would soon get the problems solved or postponed and get the kids sorted and placed in the proper beds.

As far as I can tell the experience didn't hurt us any, maybe it even helped to stimulate our imaginations. I remember thinking when John Dillinger was gunned down by the police in front of the theater in Chicago that at least we would not have to worry about him any more.

STRAW TICKS

There were other aspects of sleeping facilities in our house that were reflective of economic over comfort concerns. In my earliest recollections, with one exception, every bed in the house consisted of a straw tick laying over a set of steel bed springs. The exception was one feather bed which no one wanted in the summer and everyone clamored for in the winter. The feather bed, when used, was also placed on a set of steel bed springs. Sometime in the mid-thirties Dad bought a regular mattress at a farm sale and replaced the straw tick on his bed.

Mom made the ticks from a blue and white ticking material purchased from J.C. Penny's. She constructed what resembled huge pillow cases the size of the beds. The ticks had a slit down the center which could be closed by several pairs of ties attached along either side of the opening. The ticking material was substantial and lasted for years; however, the straw with which the ticks were stuffed was replaced once or twice a year, or sometimes much more often if a bed-wetter was not properly padded or if there was an outbreak of bed bugs.

Stuffing the ticks with new straw was a chore, but it was also fun for us kids. We helped Mom hitch the team to a big, flat wagon, then we carried out the old ticks that needed to be emptied and refilled. We placed them on the wagon, tossed on any new ticks she had made and a couple of pitchforks. We then climbed aboard the wagon and headed for the straw stack. Oat straw was the straw of choice with which to fill a tick as it did not have the sharp, stiff beards as did rye or barley straw.

Beards were bad in tick straw as they would work their way out of the tick, through the bedding, and scratch the occupant of the bed.

Once at the straw stack, we emptied the old straw from the ticks. Then we removed the outer layers of straw from the stack and exposed clean straw with which we stuffed into the ticks.

When the ticks were filled, they were loaded onto the wagon and we headed for the house. A freshly filled tick looked more like a big, blue and white striped, semi-flattened sausage than a mattress. Before the freshly stuffed ticks were removed from the wagon, we kids (and sometimes Mom) piled on top of them in an effort to mash them down to the point where they would serve as mattresses. When the ticks were finally placed upon the beds, they were still high in the center. Sleeping on the newly stuffed ticks was a bit precarious for the first few nights until the straw packed down and flattened out. I do not recall being particularly concerned about the sleeping characteristics of the straw ticks. Like most other things on the farm, that is what we had and we made the most of it.

SECRETS OF THE SLAB CORRAL

Sex is a natural part of activities on the farm. We raised chickens, turkeys, sheep, goats, pigs, cattle, and horses in addition to all the kids. Even as a little kid I was aware that the milk cows had to be put in with the bull before they could have a calf, be freshened and provide milk for the calf and the family. I knew that Dad turned the boars in with the sows so we could have little pigs.

I observed copulation among the farm animals unaware of all the nuances, mysteries and implications of sex. I doubt I had any real idea of sex; it was what had to happen if there was going to be little ones, but I didn't know why. It was as common as the sun coming up in the morning. In fact, if you want to use the old rooster and hens in the barnyard as a measure, it was more common. The sun only comes up once a day

As common as sex was in the barnyard with the other animals, somehow horses were different. I recall the itinerant stud horse man. He periodically came to the farm, riding a horse and leading a stud. If we had a mare that was "horsin" (in heat) the man would offer the services of his stud horse for a fee.

Depending on the quality of the stud and the fee, Dad made a decision as to whether he would accept the services offered. The stud fee was based on performance. For the stud fee to be payable, the bred mare had to produce a foal that was able to stand and suck. That is, the newborn foal had to struggle to its feet and take its first nourishment from the mare before the stud fee contract was validated.

When the itinerant stud horse man rode into the farmyard, we kids knew at once that something rather mysterious was developing. Sometimes the man and Dad would have a short conversation and he would ride away leading the stallion. On other occasions we kids would be sent to the house and instructed to stay there and to not look out the windows. Like all kids I was curious and in some cases my curiosity overcame my concern for the possible consequences of not doing what Dad told me to do. Unless Mom watched us closely, which she seldom did, we kids nearly always peered out the windows toward the barnyard.

On a few occasions I slipped out into the backyard in an effort to better determine just what was going on in the barnyard that I was forbidden to see. Many times I heard horses snort and squeal and sounds of a commotion coming from the slab corral. I knew Dad, the stud horse man, one of our mares, and the stallion were in the corral, but what was going on in there was a matter for my imagination.

Dillard H. Gates

The slab corral was a holding corral attached to the front of the granary and adjacent to a larger holding corral behind the barn. The corral was made from wooden slabs sawn from cottonwood logs as the logs were squared in the process of making lumber. The slabs were approximately ten feet long and were nailed close together vertically to heavy cottonwood rails fastened between large cedar posts. This formed a strong, secure structure that was difficult to see through from a distance.

For some time during this developing and partially sheltered period of my life, Dad had an arrangement with another farmer, Frank Belders, to keep his huge, beautiful, dapple grey stallion, ole Plume. He was kept in the slab corral and for shelter had access to the large alleyway of the granary. During this period of time other farmers frequently brought mares to our place. When this occurred, we kids were sent to the house and the men and the mare disappeared into the slab corral. The noise and the commotion were then evident in the slab corral. The curiosity was heightened and the mystery deepened.

As I was coming home from school one day I heard noises emanating from the slab corral. Cautiously, I approached the corral and peeked between the slabs. It was then I learned what the commotion was all about. Dad was controlling old Plume with a strong halter with a chain bit. A neighbor who had brought over the mare was holding her by the halter. Ole Plume snorted and pranced as he approached, then mounted the mare.

I watched, spellbound, until the noise and struggling ceased and ole Plume slid from atop the mare. I suddenly realized I was watching that which Dad had forbidden me to see. Discretion overcame curiosity and I headed for the house at a dead run. From the shelter of the house, I pondered what I had just observed. The act I had just witnessed I had seen performed countless times before by other farm animals. Except for scale, I could see little difference between common and accepted farm animal behavior and the forbidden sights that I had just observed.

So much for the mysteries of the slab corral. I still tried to peek into the slab corral when there were forbidden activities underway. I am not sure why, but maybe I was developing and my prurient interests heightened my curiosity.

Eventually I was allowed to stay outside and then to observe the activities in the slab corral and eventually to help control the animals. But as long Dad lived, he sent the girls to the house when there was "activity in the slab corral."

Dillard H. Gates

THE THRESHING RUN

Sometimes it appeared the good lord saved the toughest job till last. Threshing was the final activity of grain harvest and generally took place within the period mid-July through August. During this late summer season the hot sun beat down on the stubble fields of the plains of Nebraska and temperatures often exceeded one-hundred degrees. The threshing job entailed hard, dirty work and effectively separated the men from the boys. But despite the hard work and the heat there was something about the job that tended to pull the men together. They sweat, they strained, they socialized as they labored shoulder to shoulder completing the final chapter of the grain production cycle.

The amount of grain in the bin at the end of threshing season was for many farmers a measure of their economic position. Grain yields and grain prices were key factors determining whether there would be money available to repay production loans or reduce the mortgage on the farm.

The threshing season had always been a big thing for our family. I was only four years old, but I remember when Dad replaced the old wooden threshing machine with a Case, steel, thirty-six inch machine. And I remember the huge Altman-Taylor tractor that he used to power the thresher. When these two monstrous machines were used together, under the skilled and watchful eyes of my Dad, they formed a grain threshing unit unmatched in Custer County and probably with few equals in the plains of central Nebraska.

Long before my time Dad had done custom threshing. That is, he used his threshing machine and tractor to thresh grain for other farmers. Each summer with the approach of harvest season he would establish a threshing run. This involved contracting (a hand shake) with several farmers in a community to thresh their grain in an agreed upon sequence during a specified time period. The farm community in which he made a run might be some distance from home, but the contracted farmers were located in near proximity, if not adjacent, to one another. This was necessary to minimize travel time between farms. The Altman-Taylor was very powerful on the belt and provided ample power to the thresher, but it was slow moving and took an inordinate amount of time to get from one job to another.

Threshing was a big operation, requiring more manpower and equipment than any one farmer had available. Thus, the farmers in the run banded together to help one another. The threshing operation entailed hauling the grain bundles from where they were shocked in the field to the threshing site. It was the custom for each farmer on the run to provide a bundle wagon (hayrack), a team, and a man. The wagons, teams and men would stay with the crew for the duration of the run. A farmer with a larger amount of grain to be threshed or who had some other factor adding to his share of the work might provide an extra bundle wagon or a spike pitcher. (A spike pitcher was a man without a bundle wagon who remained in the grain field and helped load the bundles).

Some members of the threshing crew competed with themselves or others in the crew to see how much work they could do. Most were willing to do their share and even a little more, but there was an occasional slacker among them who was content to let others do more than their share while he did just enough to get by. Everyone knew who the slackers were and eventually, somehow, they paid. They tended to be on the margins of the camaraderie that existed and were not fully integrated into the fellowship that permeated the threshing crew. Despite this, slackers generally remained slackers. The ostracism apparently produced less discomfort for them than the work and sweat necessary to make it go away.

Sometimes the threshing site was in the grain field and the bundles needed to be transported only short distances. In other cases, the farmer wanted the straw stack, a by-product of threshing, to be located where it was easily accessible for livestock feed or bedding. In those instances it was sometimes necessary to haul the bundles some distance. Normally every effort was made by the host farmer to minimize the distance bundles had to be hauled.

In addition to providing a bundle wagon, it was the responsibility of the host farmer to provide grain wagons to catch the grain as it came from the grain spout of the thresher and to haul it to his granary or other storage facility. A minimum of two wagons was required, as one would be filling while the other was being unloaded. If the grain was running heavy or the distance to storage was too far, an additional grain wagon or so might be required. The standard grain wagon held fifty bushels when filled level with the top.

Dad expected the grain wagons to be in place when it was time for the threshing operation to begin. I remember an occasion or two when a farmer who was habitually late did not have his grain wagon in place when it was time to start threshing, and Dad instructed the separator operator to let the grain run on the ground. When the man responsible for the grain wagon arrived, he had to scoop the grain from the ground into the wagon. The farmers for whom Dad threshed knew that he pushed hard to get the work done properly and in a timely manner. He did not look kindly on a half-dozen men sitting on their loaded bundle racks waiting while someone moved the grain wagon into place. As I often heard him say,"It does not make sense to have a dollar waiting on a dime."

Sometimes trucks or other than standard size wagons were utilized to receive the grain as it came from the thresher. In those cases, the volume of the grain box was computed and converted to bushels. This was the measure used by the farmer to determine the amount of grain he had produced and which Dad used to figure the charges for threshing. It was not uncommon for some farmers running the grain wagon to try to get a few extra bushels on the wagon for which they would not have to pay the threshing fee. They would do this by piling the grain as high as gravity would allow in the center of the wagon being loaded, or by forcing the sides of the wagon as far apart as possible. Dad was always aware of what was happening. If the cheating became too flagrant, Dad or the separator operator would step up on the side of the overloaded wagon and smooth the grain down to the point of a level load or fasten the spreader chains in the wagon box to hold the sides in the proper position. Generally after this happened a time or two the offender got the point and the cheating was reduced, if not stopped completely.

Normally threshing charges were based on a specified amount per bushel of grain. There were a few years when due to the drought grain yields were so low that Dad was forced to make an hourly charge in order to cover the costs of operating the threshing machine and tractor.

THE THRESHING MACHINE

In my earliest recollections I was fascinated by the threshing machine. It was complex with pulleys, belts, gears, bearings, shafts, cylinders, concaves, knives, teeth, straw shakers, grain sieves, elevators, feeders, blowers, conveyors, and a myriad of other components. There was a unique vocabulary associated with its maintenance, repair, and operation. I realized early on that great skill was required to properly operate the thresher.

There were only a select few men in whom Dad had the confidence to hire as threshing machine operators. The two that I remember best were Chris Peterson, a blacksmith/farmer/mechanical wizard, and Ray Harold, a farmer/threshing machine expert. Both men were longtime family friends and were honest, reliable, and trustworthy. Either man was capable of running the entire operation should the need arise.

As a squinty-eyed kid I watched Dad and the machine operator work on the thresher. I was amazed that all those belts and pulleys could be made to run in the proper direction. And I was baffled by the fact that while bundles were being pitched into the feeder, grain would come out of one spout and straw would be blown from another.

I was enthralled by the threshing machine when it was doing the job for which it was made, but the enchantment didn't end when the threshing season was over. It was an exciting and mysterious monster on which to climb and whose innards we kids explored when it was parked in the farmyard during the off season.

THE TRACTOR

The tractor that powered the threshing machine was an Altman-Taylor, model 30-60. The four cylinder motor consisted of two blocks of two cylinders laying side by side horizontally. The motor ran on kerosene or tractor fuel, but it had a small tank to hold gasoline which was used to start the engine when it was cold.

Statistics on the performance of the Altman-Taylor may be obtained from the Tractor Testing Laboratory, University of Nebraska, Lincoln, Nebraska.

Dillard H. Gates

The tractor was a powerful, steady, reliable, and imposing piece of equipment. The massive rear wheels were about two and one-half feet wide and eight feet high. Heavy steel lugs were bolted to the surface to provide traction. Large steel fenders extended over the top and inner side of the rear wheels. The front wheels were approximately four feet high and were guided by large chains connected to a steering column.

The operator's platform was located between the rear wheels above the axle. From this platform the operator had access to the steering wheel, the gear shifting mechanism, the brake, and the lever to engage the enormous drive pulley. The pulley provided power to the threshing machine through a huge drive belt that connected the tractor and the thresher. The platform also provided access to the tanks containing the oil to lubricate the immense, powerful but slow turning motor.

The radiator was located in front of the motor, above and between the front wheels. It consisted of a large, steel, horizontal, cylindrical tank with open tubes running through it. Air was forced through these cooling tubes by a large fan located on the left side of the tank. This large cylindrical radiator led some to the mistaken belief that the Altman-Taylor was a steam engine.

The machinery was protected by a rectangular wooden roof, approximately ten by fourteen feet, supported by four steel corner-posts extending up from the framework of the tractor. This roof and the tractor itself provided shade for the operator and often for some of the threshing crew as they waited to unload their bundle wagons.

I was given several jobs around the tractor and separator. The difficulty of the jobs increased each year I helped Dad with the threshing operation. The old Altman-Taylor finally wore out when I was about thirteen. Dad substituted other tractors, but somehow the romance and the thrill of the harvest season was diminished by the disappearance of the big, slow moving, powerful monster that I had watched Dad operate for as long as I could remember. It was the end of an era, on our farm and in the communities where the Altman-Taylor, the thirty-six inch Case separator, and Howe P. Gates were legend.

YOU CAN'T LEARN ANY YOUNGER, SON

By the time I was ten or eleven I had begun to accompany Dad on the threshing runs. There were several reasons for Dad to take me with him. To begin with I was fascinated with the whole operation and wanted to participate. There were many little jobs I could do around the threshing rig. I ran errands and helped keep the water jugs and buckets filled with cool water for the crew. And I believe most importantly Dad wanted me to begin learning the operation of the entire outfit. He was a firm believer in the old adage, "You can't learn any younger."

Accompanying Dad on the threshing run was tough on a kid of my age. I was ousted out of bed early in the morning, often at the crack of dawn. Mom fixed breakfast while Dad loaded the back of the 32 Ford V-8 with equipment and supplies, required for the day. We didn't have a pick-up truck to haul supplies, but the old Ford with the back seat removed served the purpose. After breakfast Dad and I crawled into the car loaded with grease and oil cans, threshing machine belts and other miscellaneous materials and headed out. It was not uncommon to drive ten to fifteen miles to where the threshing rig was located.

We picked up the threshing machine operator en route or met him at the threshing site. There were many things to be done each morning to prepare the threshing machine and tractor for the day's work ahead. If we had finished a job the night before, the first thing we would do in the morning was move the thresher to a new location.

The threshing machine had to be greased every morning, then periodically throughout the day. It seemed there were a hundred zerk grease-gun fittings. One of my first jobs around the rig was filling the grease-gun. This entailed removing the cap from the empty grease-gun, then utilizing a putty knife or a little flat piece of wood to scoop the grease from the large can into the barrel of the grease-gun. I had to take care and remove all the air bubbles or the grease gun would not function properly. If it didn't, I would be reminded that I had not done the job properly and told to correct the problem.

Once I learned to fill the grease-gun properly and had learned where at least a few of the zerk fittings were, I was ready to help grease the machinery. At first I was allowed, or expected, to grease only those points that were easily accessible. However, in a few short years I was expected to do the entire job myself, and do it correctly. An improperly greased bearing quickly heated and failed under the stress of the threshing operation. When I was able to do the job properly, the separator operator went ahead with other more complex tasks readying the machinery for the work of the new day.

All of the belts had to be removed from the separator at the end of each threshing day, stored in the back end of the machine, then put back on again before work began the following morning. This was necessary to prevent the belts from shrinking and breaking as a result of being dampened by night-time humidity or dew. There was a dozen or more belts on the separator driving the various mechanisms that did the job of separating and removing the grain from the straw. The belts were of different lengths and widths, and each fit around a specific set of pulleys. Some were put on straight; others had to be twisted. When all the belts were properly installed and tighteners set the various components of the threshing machine worked in unison.

Learning to remove the belts was easy. You just had to grab the belt in one hand and pull it toward you as you grasped and rolled a pulley with the other. The belt would practically roll itself off. Putting the belts on in the morning was another story. The first job to learn was the proper place for each belt. Generally the belts would shrink a bit during the night so installation was more arduous than merely reversing the belt removal process. A similar technique was used, but trying to force a tight belt over a pulley was more difficult, especially for a scrawny kid. But

Dad and the threshing machine operator taught me the proper techniques and eventually I was able to belt the separator by myself.

While the separator was being readied, there was also work to do on the Altman-Taylor before it was cranked to life. Dad carried fuel in five-gallon cans from the fifty-five gallon storage barrels sitting on the fuel wagon and refilled the fuel tank. The starter tank was also checked to make sure it had sufficient gasoline for starting the motor. The oil tanks had to be checked and, if needed, oil added to bring it to the correct levels. Like the separator there were many zerk fittings that had to be serviced. Normally there was less daily, routine tinkering or adjusting required on the tractor than on the threshing machine, but maintenance was important and necessary to keep the tractor running properly. Dad had good equipment and he took good care of it.

When all was ready with the separator and tractor, the separator operator helped Dad start the Altman-Taylor. Dad stood on the platform of the tractor, worked the controls, and allowed gasoline into the four cylinders of the big engine. The helper placed a crank, about four feet long into notches on the huge flywheel of the tractor and gave it a pull downward. Normally it took several pulls before one of the cylinders popped and the big motor, puffing and coughing, came slowly to life. After a few sputters and coughs it settled down into its slow, steady rhythm which continued throughout the day.

When the machines were properly adjusted and ready to work, the tractor was parked about fifty feet in front of and facing the separator. The drive belt, approximately ten inches wide, connected the drive pulley of the tractor to the main pulley of the separator. The tractor had to be placed precisely so that the drive pulley was aligned straight and square with the main pulley of the separator. Once aligned, the separator operator placed the ends of the drive belt over the main pulleys of the tractor and threshing machine. With the drive belt in place, but hanging loose, Dad backed the Altman-Taylor into the belt. That is, he backed the tractor until the belt was tight. The operator then placed a block in front of the rear wheel to hold the tractor in place. Dad then pulled back on the big lever that set the rear wheel brakes. He then moved the lever that activated the drive pulley and things would begin to roll. The pulleys of the separator would begin to turn, slowly at first, then faster. The great monster creaked and groaned and shook and shuddered as it seemed to awaken from the night's rest. The operator walked slowly around the threshing machine carefully looking and listening to make sure it was ready for a new threshing day to begin.

The time the actual threshing operation started each morning depended primarily on the moisture content of the straw in the bundles. Unless the bundles were dry, the straw was tough and it was difficult for the threshing machine to separate the straw from the grain. This was overcome in part by proper selection, installation, and adjustments of the concaves in relation to the thresher cylinder teeth. Sometimes Dad began threshing in the morning with a certain set of concaves then replaced them with another set as the straw dried during the morning.

Dad had a hard and fast rule. When the bundles were ready, that is, dry enough to thresh, the separator and tractor must be ready to go. The threshing crew was not expected to wait on the readiness of the separator unless there was a break-down beyond immediate repair. If there was a problem with the machinery at the end of a working day, Dad and the separator operator stayed late to fix it or were at the threshing site at the crack of dawn to make certain repairs were completed by the time the straw was dry enough to thresh.

As Dad and the separator operator were readying the equipment the host farmer moved the grain wagon into place to receive the grain. He also made certain that the water cans and jugs were filled with fresh, cool water and placed in the shade of the big tractor. It took lots of water to satisfy the thirst of the hard working threshing crew. Frequently, I was drafted to help with the job.

When all was ready, the bundle racks, pulled by teams of horses, were driven alongside the feeder of the separator, one on either side. Sometimes, at first, the horses were a bit skittish about approaching the noisy, shaking machine. However, after a few tries they became accustomed to the hub bub and would approach the machine without apparent fear and stand calmly as the bundles were pitched into the feeder.

FEEDING THE MONSTER, PITCHING BUNDLES

>Upon the hill
>There is a red bull
>It eats and eats
>And never gets full
>(What is it?)

So went a little riddle ditty I probably first heard during opening exercises in the primary room. The answer to the riddle is; "A threshing machine."

That was in fact an apt description of a threshing machine. All day long the threshing crew pitched load after load of bundles into the gaping mouth. But it didn't get full. It had an insatiable appetite which the men running the bundle wagons did their best to satisfy.

Running a bundle wagon on a threshing crew was a hard, hot job. Generally the man running the bundle wagons was the farmer included in the threshing run, his son, or on occasion a hired man. He had to be on the job the first thing in the morning with a load of bundles ready for the separator.

All bundle racks were not the same size; however, there was a generally accepted though unwritten rule that everyone should do his share. This meant that each man should load and pitch about the same number of bundles into the thresher each day. The smaller bundle racks, some were referred to as cracker boxes, had to be heavily loaded to approach equivalency with a moderately loaded larger wagon. If it was deemed that someone was not pulling his own weight, it was called to his attention, often in a none too subtle manner. When the bundle rack was loaded in the field, it was driven to the threshing site. If other wagons were unloading, the loaded rack was pulled into line to await its turn. The bundle pitcher would crawl down from atop the load and join others waiting in the shade of the big tractor.

Sometimes the wait was brief, but other times there would be several loaded bundle wagons waiting in line and the bundle pitcher could enjoy a cool drink, a bit of socializing, roll a cigarette and take a much needed rest. It was also a time for each of the men to make informal evaluations of the size of the loads in line ahead of them. This provided them with at least a rough measure of the relative amount of work being performed by each man. That evaluation was the basis for comparisons and comments if someone was perceived as not doing his share.

My Dad seemed to believe that bigger was better. Our hay rack, which was used as a bundle rack during the threshing season, was about half again bigger than most of the others. Thus when loaded fully it carried nearly twice as many bundles as some of the smaller bundle wagons.

One summer my older brother, Hap, still in his teens, was using Dad's hay rack as a bundle wagon. Hap was strong and husky and always willing to do more than his share. A neighbor, Red, who liked to gripe, may have had a persecution complex and may have been a bit lazy to boot, started to complain to anyone who would listen (but out of the earshot of Dad or Hap) that Hap was shirking. Hap would sometimes bring in less than a fully loaded rack or when fully loaded would occasionally fall behind in the line waiting to unload.

Red's complaints finally reached the ears of Chris Peterson, the wily separator operator. Chris decided to quietly check on the validity of Red's complaints. The next time Red came in with a load, Chris perched himself atop the separator where he had an uninterrupted view and counted the bundles Red pitched into the thresher. He repeated his count when Hap brought in his next load, a bit out of sequence.

The next time Red, sitting in the shade of the tractor with a Bull Durham cigarette hanging from his lip, began to complain that Hap had missed his turn in line and was shirking, Chris was ready. Chris was soft spoken but raised his voice to get the attention of those gathered in the shade. He then reported the results of his little study. The number of bundles in the load Hap had pitched into the thresher was only six less than twice the number of bundles in Red's load. Based on that evidence Hap was doing almost twice as much work as Red and some other members of the crew. Hap was not complaining about it, he was merely doing what he had been brought up to do. Red's face turned a deeper shade of crimson than usual as he listened to Chris tell his little story. He stopped complaining about what Hap was doing, but there was no evidence that he picked up the pace of his own efforts.

HORSEPLAY

Those waiting in the shade of the Altman-Taylor made up a dynamic group as pitchers joined the group to wait their turn or others left to unload. In addition there were normally a few other farmers and hangers-on around the threshing rig. Sometimes the separator operator joined the group. Dad was frequently there as it was a good vantage point from which to observe the operation of the entire crew and the machinery. There was a constant flow of banter among the crew. Practical jokes and horseplay were a major source of entertainment for some and a way of airing grievances for others. In general the more esteemed a person, the more he was picked on and made the butt of jokes. To a large degree, but with some exceptions, anyone outside the "in" group tended to be left alone.

Mom used to say that Dad would probably go on a threshing run even if he didn't get paid because he enjoyed it so much. He rejoiced in the fellowship and camaraderie that was a part of the threshing run. My Dad, though not a really big man, was husky and very strong. He seemed to present a constant self-imposed challenge to some of the young bucks of the crew. He frequently received good natured "threats" that he was going to be thrown in the horse tank or get his butt whipped by one or more of the young and boastful members of the crew. For the most part the "threats" remained a part of the good humored banter.

I remember one year when Dad was on a threshing run in Round Valley. Dad liked to thresh in that area because the farmers there generally paid their threshing bill promptly. There was a farmer in the area by the name of Joe Jasbra. He was a great old Bohemian: a successful farmer, hard working and honest. He had several children including two sons, Ed and Bill. Bill was the older of the two, married and beginning a family of his own. Ed was younger and bigger but still lived at home and worked for his Dad. They were both husky young men who enjoyed a special relationship with Dad. One day they decided that since neither one alone could pin Dad, they would try it together. They set up a plan which they were sure would end with Dad subdued, on the ground, and in their control.

One afternoon Dad was squatting on his heels in the shade of the tractor enjoying the chatter and comradeship of the threshing crew assembled. Ed and Bill were among them. As planned, while Dad was engaged with the others, Ed approached from the front and Bill approached quietly from the rear. On signal each lurched to grab Dad as he squatted in the shade unaware of the impending attack. Just in time, Dad reached out toward the would-be assailant in front of him. He wrapped his arms about him in a great bear-hug and rolled over onto his side. As he rolled onto the ground holding Ed in a firm grasp, he noted Bill springing to the attack from behind. Dad hooked a leg around Bill's ankles and pulled his feet from under him. As he fell to the ground, Dad wrapped his legs around his waist and held him in a scissor grip. Dad slowly tightened his grip on each of them as they squirmed and tried in vain to free themselves. He continued to squeeze until each of them in turn hollered "enough." Without uttering a word Dad released the chastened young men, picked up his hat, dusted it off, placed it back on his head and returned to his original position among the threshing crew.

"Now what was that you were saying ?" he asked the separator operator as if nothing had happened.

Red of face and still trying to get their breath, Bill and Ed climbed to their feet and extended their hands to Dad. "Darn you, Howe Gates," they muttered good naturedly. "We didn't think you could do that; we'll have to try to think of another way to get you down." I guess it was hard enough for them to live down that fiasco and they didn't have the heart to try it again.

HAZING, THE TRIBULATIONS OF "THE COLLEGE BOY"

The farmers in the area were for the most part hard working and honest but with little formal education. Many of them did not immediately accept an outsider thrust into their mist. This was especially so if the newcomer put on airs, didn't quite pull his weight, or was thought to be a smart aleck.

I recall an instance when one of the older farmers on the threshing run hired his grandson to work during the harvest season. The young man was from town, and to make matters worse was a college student. I thought he was a nice kid as he would often take the time to talk with me. Though inexperienced, he tried his best, was polite and respectful, and was willing to tackle any job given to him. He didn't put on airs or try to impress anyone with his intellect. Despite this he was considered fair game by some of the less tolerant members of the threshing crew. Right away they started to find ways to make life miserable for him. Often when he was taking a rest in the shade of the tractor, he was made the butt of crude jokes and disparaging remarks. For the most part, the kid kept his mouth shut. He appeared reluctant to return the rhetoric or respond to the off-color comments. This lack of response seemed to encourage the poor behavior of his tormentors.

The college kid wore a pair of high quality, leather work gloves. His hands were not calloused from work and needed the protection the gloves afforded. When he removed the gloves he stuck them in his hip pocket as did others who wore gloves. Occasionally one of the ruffians would jerk the gloves from the greenhorn's pocket and threaten to dip them in the oil barrel, fill them with fresh horse manure, or some other thing to despoil them. The kid would just ask the instigator to please return the gloves, which he usually did after a bit of boastful banter. On one occasion a crew member slipped up behind the unwary college kid and slipped a big gob of gun grease, which he had wrapped in a piece of paper, into the hip pocket with the gloves. When the kid removed the gloves from his pocket as he prepared to return to work, he found them and his hip pocket covered with grease. He said nothing, but walked over and picked up a grease rag from Dad's tool box, wiped the grease from the gloves and his pants and went back to work.

Before the mid-day dinner break and at the end of the day, it was clean-up time around the feeder of the threshing machine. In the process of pitching bundles into the feeder, some of the bundles and loose straw had been inadvertently dropped or missed the feeder. This debris consisting of loose straw, chaff, and bundles built up under the feeder. When the last empty bundle wagon pulled away from the separator, a few of the crew sitting around or otherwise not occupied grabbed their pitch forks and threw the material up into the feeder. The debris generally contained a lot of chaff and dust, so cleaning up could be a dirty and undesirable job.

One hot day before the dinner break the last bundle wagon pulled away from the thresher. Three or four of the crew, including the college boy, who had been sitting in the shade, grabbed their pitch forks and headed for the clean-up job. A couple of the experienced hands placed themselves on the windward side of the feeder and set to work. This forced the college boy to step to the leeward side. Thus, the dust, the chaff and the dirt tended to drift his way as he went about his job. The old hands on the windward side deliberately picked up lots of dirt and chaff and flipped it in the air so that it was blown over those working on the leeward side. The kid just ducked his head and continued to do his work. As the end of the clean up drew near, one of those on the windward side gathered up a big load of chaff and dirt on his pitch fork. He waited for the right opportunity then tossed the dirty forkful over the feeder and onto the head of the hot, sweaty, unsuspecting college kid.

The kid had reached the breaking point, but he did not snap. He merely stepped over to the man who had tossed the mess onto him and said, quietly but forcibly, "If you do not want me to help, you can do this damn dirty job by yourself." With that he strolled back to the shade of the tractor, took off his shirt and tried to brush the dirt and chaff from his sweaty body and clothes. The kid stuck it out to the end of the threshing run. He probably needed the money he was making to continue at the university in the fall. His willingness to work and tenacity gained him a modicum of respect from most of the crew. They quit picking on him, but he remained an outsider.

COOKING FOR THRESHERS

All of the hard work during the threshing season was not confined to the fields. The women folk struggled long and hard in hot kitchens preparing dinner for the crew. In fact, the harvest season was known about as much for the fabulous meals the women prepared as for the threshing operation. Conventional wisdom is right; most farm women are great cooks. During the threshing season they seemed to excel their usual high standards for quantity and quality. Cooking for threshers was not a call for the preparation of the fanciest food but rather for good, tasty, wholesome, nourishing food in sufficient quantities to quell the hunger of hard working men. Of course some of the farm wives tried to "put on the dog" and to make a statement regarding their cooking skills with the dinner they placed before the hungry and sometimes admiring men.

Many farm women considered cooking for threshers a real challenge, a challenge to provide a great meal for the threshers but also a challenge to outdo their neighbors. The women on the threshing run helped one another prepare. When it was time for them to prepare dinner at their own place however, each wanted to outstrip those meals they may have helped their friends and neighbor women prepare.

Every day on the threshing run the crew was presented with a dinner that could only be described as a feast. In most cases it was comparable to Christmas or Thanksgiving dinners, but without the festivities. The dinner often consisted of fried chicken caught, killed, cleaned and cooked the morning before the dinner. It also normally included mashed potatoes, milk gravy, vegetables from the garden, homemade rolls, breads, butter, and jellies. A heavy dessert followed, often consisting of fresh baked pies and cakes and sometimes topped off with homemade ice cream. Drinks for the hot and thirsty crew usually included iced tea, lemonade (fresh squeezed lemons), coffee, and, of course, cool water.

There were probably more fryers caught, killed, and consumed during the harvest season than during all the remainder of the year. Fryer chickens were home grown, quickly available (an additional one or two could be caught and prepared quickly if the crew turned out to be bigger than originally expected) and relatively cheap. Most people liked home fried chicken and the mashed potatoes and milk gravy that went with it. However, sometimes the crew did get a little tired of it if it was served too many days in a row. Beef or pork roasts, also accompanied by potatoes and gravy, were staples frequently set before the threshers.

Dillard H. Gates

The mid-day break was not for the men alone. It was also a time to give the horses a break. Teams were unhitched from the bundle racks, brought to the stock tank to drink, tied to a bundle rack, in the shade if possible, and given some hay and grain. The horses were cared for before the men came to the house to wash up and eat.

The place for the crew to wash before dinner generally consisted of several wash basins and soap, sitting on benches or tables placed in the shade near the house. A few buckets of cold water and a dipper sat on an adjacent table. Several drying towels were hung on tree branches, fences or tables nearby. There was usually a mirror hanging on a tree or wall in the area and big combs available so the more fastidious of the crew could see to comb their hair which had been thoroughly wetted in the washing process. There were always some single men on the threshing crew and often there was an unmarried gal or so helping to prepare and serve dinner to the threshers.

When the crew gathered around the heavily laden table, the banter continued, cleaned up somewhat out of respect for the women folk. Eating was a serious business, but there always seemed to be enough energy remaining in the hard working men of the crew for practical jokes and horseplay.

AN ATTEMPT TO UNSEAT THE BOSS

On one occasion all the crew, including Dad, was seated at the dinner table exchanging pleasantries and concentrating on the feast before them. The women in the kitchen apprehended a couple of kids, yet too young to be regular crew members, trying to sneak through the kitchen and into the dining room with a rope in their hands. Upon closer inspection they spotted two additional boys just outside the kitchen door holding on to a two-hundred pound calf with the other end of the rope tied around its neck. The boys and their rope were quickly hustled out of the kitchen.

Following some interrogation by the their captors, the boys divulged the scheme, the implementation of which had been interrupted. It was revealed that they and Dad were constantly in a good-natured battle of wits. The kids had about exhausted their bag of tricks. In their desperation they came up with an idea that, if it worked, was certain to really place them one-up on Dad. Consequently they had taken one of the bucket calves (a calf that had been born to a milk cow but had been trained to drink milk from a bucket) from the barnyard, put one end of the long rope around its neck and brought it to the kitchen door. Two of the boys, with the end of the rope, intended to sneak up behind Dad as he was sitting at the table. They hoped that since practical jokes were a common thing their secret would not be revealed even if other crew members spotted them creeping up on Dad. Their intent was to tie the end of the rope onto the leg of Dad's chair then spook the calf so it would run and pull the chair from under him. They figured that the sight of Dad suddenly sprawled on the floor by the table would get a laugh from the entire crew, and it probably would have.

    The cooks in the kitchen refused to be accomplices to the proposed escapade. The boys were sent back to the barnyard to release the calf. Dad knew nothing of the incident until dinner was finished and the women informed them of the aborted attempt to unseat him. I guess this was additional validation of the old adage, "The best laid plans of mice and men often go astray."

Dillard H. Gates

MRS. COPP

    I began the eighth grade in the fall of 1937 still in the old Gates church building but with a new teacher Mrs. Copp. She had been hired from outside the Gates and Lillian communities and was a stranger to all of us. The fact that she was divorced was alleged to be a matter of concern for some of the good folks of the district. However, despite this obvious short-coming, she came with good recommendations and maybe the school board thought it would be the Christian thing to do to give her a chance. I guess the school board backed into the correct decision. I thought Mrs. Copp was a good teacher and a gracious lady.

    She was a small woman with red hair. Naturally we kids assumed she would be strict and have a temperament to go with the hair color. Mrs. Copp also had a young daughter who attended primary school. They lived in a small house located adjacent to that of John and Mary Bishop north of the school.

    Mrs. Copp was firm but not strict with the students, nor did her temperament reflect the color of her hair. She did have her hands full though as there were several boys, me included, in the seventh and eighth grades that, to say the least, were a bit mischievous and operated on the edge of acceptable behavior.

THE INK SPOTS

    One cool, fall day Mrs. Copp, as usual, arrived at school well ahead of class time to fire up the pot bellied, coal burning stove so the room would be warm when the students arrived. The stove had a chrome plated, decorative dome-like fixture on the top, which may have helped radiate heat but whose primary function was aesthetics. A piece of the cast metal from which the decorative fixture was molded had been broken off exposing a small area of the top of the stove.

    Some of the students had arrived early. Most of the girls had taken their seats, but some of the boys were just milling around in the back of the class room waiting for class time. A seventh grader, Donald Douglas, had heard somewhere that if small pieces of chalk were shaved into a partially empty ink bottle and heated to a boil, it would explode with extra force. Unbeknown to any of the other students or the teacher, Don had prepared an ink bottle, slipped it through the hole in the decorative fixture, set it on top of the stove and pushed it back out of sight. He then told me and some of the other boys what he had done.

Mrs. Copp called the classes to order. The freshly stoked fire burned strongly and the stove became hotter. Innocent students, not in the know, bent over their notebooks preparing for class. Others of us whom Don had brought in as co-conspirators bent over our notebooks but our minds were not on academics.

For some reason Mrs. Copp called Don to the back of the room to discuss something with him. As they stood together near her desk, he could hear the now hot bottle of ink bouncing on top of the stove under the decorative dome. He sort of maneuvered around to get Mrs. Copp between him and the hot stove with the bouncing bottle. As quickly as he could, he finished his business with the teacher and headed for his desk in the front of the room.

When Don was about half way to his desk, the chalk charged bottle of ink exploded. Hot ink sprayed over Mrs. Copp and several students sitting in the vicinity of the stove. Don didn't miss a step but hastened on to his desk. Mrs. Copp's dress was covered with ink. The dark ink splattered on her face contrasted sharply with her red freckles. Momentarily stunned, she recovered quickly and realized that an ink bottle had been set on the stove and it had exploded.

Her first concern was for the students. She was quickly assured that no one had been injured by flying glass. The faces of some of the students sitting near the point of explosion were as speckled as a turkey egg, but the speckles were black. The ink spots didn't show much on the blue overalls which most of the boys were wearing, but they were all too apparent on the dresses of a few of the girls.

As soon as Mrs. Copp had restored some semblance of tranquility, she called the class to order and asked, "Who did that?" No explanation was required for everyone in the class to know what "that" meant. All was quiet. She repeated her question in a somewhat louder voice and sharper tone.

Don, reflecting his honesty and integrity turned slowly, stood by his desk, and with a red but otherwise clean face and spotless clothes responded, "I did."

"You, you did it," retorted Mrs. Copp. "Was that why you moved around back here so that I was between you and the stove?"

"Yes," Don admitted. "I didn't know what would happen if the ink bottle exploded, and I wanted to get out of the way."

Mrs. Copp assigned Don the lead role in cleaning ink from the floor, desks and walls. Luckily no serious damage was done. The affected girls were angry and some of the boys were a bit miffed about ink on their clothes.

I don't remember the punishment that Mrs. Copp dished out to Don, but I doubt it was very severe. He was not sent home nor was he expelled. In a few days things were back to normal at Gates Intermediate School. But on the walls and floor in the back of the room, near the pot bellied stove, traces of ink spots remained.

For the most part, the eighth grade was an uneventful year. Sometime during the fall we moved from the old church building to the new school house which had been built to replace the old torched structure. The rooms were bigger, it had lots of windows, it was nice and clean and we kids thought it was wonderful. But like the old, the new school building had neither electricity nor plumbing. When nature called it was still necessary to hold up your hand and get permission to make the trek to the outhouse.

SEVENTH AND EIGHTH GRADE EXAMS

Gates School was not accredited and so was under the administrative jurisdiction of the Custer County Superintendent of School. It was the duty of the Superintendent (or maybe he just wanted to get out of his office) to periodically visit each of the schools under his jurisdiction.

From the time I started to school through the eighth grade, I believe the County Superintendent was Harry E. Weekly. To me at least, he was an imposing and very important person. As I recall he was a rather large man with an officious manner. He combed his well-oiled hair straight back in what we referred to as a pompadour. His complexion was very white, almost pasty. He wore dark, horned rim glasses. He was always dressed in a freshly starched and ironed white shirt and a three-piece, dark blue suit with a light pin stripe. The clothes alone were enough to impress and intimidate we grubby kids dressed in baggy overalls, hand-me-downs, and flour-sack dresses. If his intent was to impress the kids at the schools he visited, he was successful, with me at least.

The teachers always seemed to know when Mr. Weekly was to pay a visit and would make certain that the "house keeping" was done and the school room ready for his perusal if not formal inspection. I doubt the teachers were as impressed with him as were the students, but they did seem to strive for his approval. When making a call the Superintendent would visit the classes in each room. I think he wanted to make certain that each student had the opportunity, in person, to observe his majestic presence.

It was the responsibility of the Superintendent of Schools to certify that all students in non-accredited schools reached a certain level of scholastic achievement before they were advanced from the seventh to the eighth grade and from the eighth to the ninth grade. To demonstrate this measure of scholarly progress, all students in the seventh and eighth grades were required to pass exams prepared by the Superintendent's office.

The two-day exams covered all subjects we had been required to study during the preceding year. As might be expected, the seventh and eighth grade teachers spent a disproportionate amount of time preparing us for the exams. We crammed, we drilled, we reviewed until we could at least answer correctly all the questions and solve the problems that had been included in exams in previous years. All of us were stressed, some more than others depending upon the level of confidence each had in his/her ability to pass the exams. Most passed the exam, but it was a put-down for those few who did not. The exam was given only once a year, so failure meant falling behind your peers and long-time class mates.

There were many one room, non-accredited, schools in Custer County that offered only grades one through eight. Generally schools selected to administer the exams offered classes through high school, and Gates was designated each year. Teachers from other schools were selected to help proctor the exams.

On the fateful day, students migrated to Gates school to take the qualifying exams. An atmosphere of anxiety, nervousness, and trepidation permeated the exam rooms. We sat with strangers, listened to instructions, and waited for the exams to be distributed. The excitement escalated as the exam papers were placed face down upon the desks in front of us.

The words, "You may now turn over your papers and begin," ended the period of anticipation but interjected new emotions of fear, confidence, doubt and self-reliance as we quickly scanned the exam papers and began to work. The exams were all administered under strict time limits. There were sighs and groans as students, under pressure, squirmed in their seats and with an eye on the clock tried mightily to put down the correct answers within the time allotted. There were sighs of relief and squeals of delight as the better students completed their exams quickly and with an air of confidence signaled the teacher that they were finished. This act alone contributed to the nervousness and stress of other students searching their memories for elusive answers.

The end of the torment or the challenge, depending on the individual situation, came when the teacher uttered, "Your time is up, please lay down your pencils and turn your papers face down on the desk." Papers were picked up and sealed in an envelope. When all tests were completed the sealed envelopes were forwarded to the office of the Superintendent to be corrected and graded. Results of the exams were returned to each school in a couple of weeks and the students informed of their scores. Those students who had done well were elated, others relieved that they had survived the ordeal. Those who failed were probably not surprised but had retained a glimmer of hope until they received the final grades.

EIGHTH GRADE GRADUATION

Students successfully completing the eighth grade exam were invited to attend a ceremony in Broken Bow, the county seat, where each would receive the Eighth Grade Graduation Diploma. Diplomas were presented to the students by the County Superintendent himself. In most cases local schools also held a graduation ceremony to honor students who had earned the "rights of passage" from intermediate to high school.

This was a special occasion for most of the rural students. We were going to Broken Bow to be recognized for our accomplishments. Intermediate school was now behind us: We were growing up and were being declared ready for high school. Even so there was a bit of nostalgia as we realized we were exchanging the high status of an eighth grader in the intermediate room for that of a lowly high school freshman.

For some of us the opportunity to attend the graduation ceremony meant that we had to acquire appropriate clothes. Somehow an old shirt, a clean pair of overalls and work shoes, which had served as our usual dress attire, was not the proper dress for such an occasion.

I wanted very much to participate in the eighth grade graduation ceremonies, but my wardrobe was limited to the standard garb. Money was short, but I conjured up enough courage to ask Dad if he would buy me clothes suitable for the graduation exercises. I was elated when he pursed his lips, laid his hand on my shoulder and assured me, "Sure, we'll go to town one of these days and take care of that."

The following Saturday Dad took me with him to Broken Bow. When the livestock auction was over and he had completed his other business I followed Dad to "Ayers Clothiers" on the south side of the square. The store was considered the best men's clothing store in town and allegedly was stocked to accommodate the most discriminating buyers in Custer County. Dad informed his old friend, Hank Ayers, that we were looking for clothes appropriate for me to wear to the graduation exercises.

In record time Mr. Ayers had several options spread out on the table before us. I was overcome by the selection offered and too unsure of myself to make a choice. Previous choices for selecting my attire had been limited to whether I would wear my overalls again or put on a clean pair. Dad finally selected a dark blue, wool, three piece suit that Mr. Ayers assured us was the best buy in the house. It must have been a good suit for the price was $14.00. That was almost a half month's wages for a hired man. Under the tutelage of Mr. Ayers, Dad then selected a shirt and tie and a pair of black shoes and socks to go with the suit. In my mind Dad's stature increase enormously that evening. I was proud of what he had done for me.

We headed home with my new wardrobe secured in Ayers Clothiers' boxes wrapped in brown paper. I could hardly contain myself as I showed my new purchases to Mom and my siblings. I was so happy and puffed up about the new clothes that, had I tried to put them on right then, they would have been four sizes too small. And I could hardly wait to display my new bib-and-tucker at the Gates School and Custer County graduation exercises. The new suit was more than just a suit to me, it was an expression of Dad's love and concern for me. I was somewhat deflated by the fact that Dad did not accompany me to either of the graduation exercises. In many ways he was a generous and supportive father, but he consistently refused to attend or participate in the school functions of any of his kids.

HOLIDAYS ON THE FARM

Holidays were more than just a day in our family. Christmas and Thanksgiving were the culmination of a holiday season and both carried a meaningful significance. The Fourth of July was recognized for its significance for heralding the beginning of our country, and even when we could not take time off from work to celebrate, we were always aware of the true meaning and significance of the day.

The birthdays of presidents Washington and Lincoln, though not celebrated as were the other three major holidays, were considered to be significant, meaningful and important events. Dad had a strong sense of country and considered it important for us to know and appreciate the contributions these men had made toward the development of our democracy.

Certainly ours was not a pious family; in fact there were probably some in the community, who hiding behind their own religiosity, may have considered us irreligious. We belonged to the First Christian Church at Lillian. Church attendance for Mom and us kids was intermittent at best. I do not recall Dad ever attending church though he encouraged our attendance. I was aware that in the past he had been a regular member of the congregation and supporter of the church.

CHRISTMAS

Christmas was recognized as the primary religious holiday at home, at school, and at church. During the Christmas season we were taught about the birth of Christ in the manger in Bethlehem. We learned about the three wise men and were constantly reminded of the true meaning of Christmas.

School lessons included stories of the first Christmas, what it meant to us and its relevance to the world. We decorated our class rooms with pictures, cut-outs, and other icons of Christmas. During the month of December we learned and sang Silent Night, Holy Night with the same off-key enthusiasm as we sang *Santa Claus Is Coming To Town*. We learned about Santa Claus and his sleigh pulled by reindeer bringing gifts for the good little kids at the same time we were learning about Mary and Joseph traveling to Jerusalem on the backs of little donkeys bringing joy to the world. Christmas programs for all grades, one through twelve, included religious songs, skits, and other activities. We drew names and exchanged small gifts at school, but the emphasis was on Christmas as a season of special importance for Christians.

If there were objections to mixing religion into the school curriculum and activities, they were never voiced. In the Gates School and neighborhood, people believed in the family, in God, and in our country and fully supported the amalgam that reflected the values, traditions, and ideals of the community.

At home the Christmas season, while recognized for its religious significance, also carried an aura of excitement and mystery. School activities carried over into the home. The kids were busy making Christmas decorations and presents for siblings, friends and teachers. The mostly barren and dull walls of the house came to support Christmas pictures, cut-outs and other adornments.

Dillard H. Gates

We kids spent countless hours huddled around the dining room table in the dim, yellow light of the kerosene lamp, cutting out strips of red and green paper and pasting them together to form chains with which to decorate the Christmas tree. We popped popcorn, strung it like beads and hung it on the tree for decoration. There was no electricity for lights, and because of fire danger, candles were not permitted on the Christmas tree.

Other forms of decorations were cut from paper and fitted with short strands of yarn by which they could be attached to the branches of the tree. In addition a large star was cut from a piece of cardboard and covered with tin foil garnered from chewing gum wrappers or cigarette packages. This was the crowning element of the decorations and was placed at the very top of the Christmas tree.

Hay, Hell, Kids and Cattle

Trees, like money, were a scarce commodity on the plains of Nebraska, and sometimes it was difficult to find a suitable Christmas tree. With the exception of cottonwoods most of the trees had been planted as a part of a tree claim when the land was homesteaded or as windbreaks around farmsteads. There were no pine or fir trees in the area. The only evergreen trees growing on our farm were a few junipers (we called them cedars) interspersed among the deciduous trees in the grove (the original tree claim) and an occasional volunteer growing in the grassy right-of-way between the pasture fence and the dirt road.

Cedars were scarce and Dad was reluctant to let us cut one down, even for a Christmas tree. Generally, following a lot of begging and kids providing him reasons why a given, small, cedar tree was more important as a Christmas symbol than just being a tree, he would relent. Most often the trees were not large, probably not more than four or five feet tall, but standing in the front room of our home loaded down with hand-made decorations, they looked beautiful. When the house got warm, the pungent smell of juniper permeated the air. It was a nice sight. It was a nice smell. It was comforting to be a part of the family at such a wonderful time. We did not have much money to spend, but in the ways it really mattered we were certainly not poor.

When it came to gifts and general treatment, there were no favorites at Christmas time. We were all treated alike; that is none of us received very much in the way of non-essential presents. We kids were considered lucky if we received one store-bought toy for Christmas. We all received sufficient, good, practical clothes and shoes. And there was always more good food around than could be eaten and plenty of fuel for the wood-burning stove. Despite the scarcity of material goods, we were alright. We were occasionally reminded of that fact with the admonition to think of the poor, cold, starving children in China.

Dad did not buy a specific present for each of the kids. That would have involved a bigger investment than he was prepared to make. However, he generally bought big bags of hard Christmas candy and various kinds of nuts. Sometimes he bought the goodies a few weeks before Christmas and hid them in the barn or granary where he thought they would be safe from snooping and searching kids. Occasionally he was successful. On those occasions we kids were disappointed as we feared there would be no special treats at Christmas time.

Dillard H. Gates

During the weeks just prior to Christmas each of us kids became more diligent in our observations of the behavior of both Mom and Dad. If they were spotted doing something that was a bit out of character or seen slipping into the granary or barn when it was obviously not chore time, we became mighty suspicious. Frequently our suspicions led to the discovery of the cache of Christmas treats. Then the challenge for the discoverer was how to keep the secret from the rest of the kids while discretely sampling the lode. Sometimes the results of repeated sampling was discovered by Dad and without comment the treasure moved to another location. Then the search began again. This cat and mouse game would continue until Dad officially brought the remaining treats to the house a day or so before Christmas so they could be shared by all, not just the one(s) who had found the treasure trove.

The last days leading up to Christmas were exciting for us kids as we tried to complete our various projects and anxiously awaited Christmas morn. It was an exciting time for Mom as well, but it was an awful lot of work. The everyday work of running the house continued as preparations were made for Christmas dinner.

It might be cold outside, but she wiped the sweat from her brow with the back of her hand as she scurried about making pies, cakes, cookies, rolls, and bread: her tasks interrupted only by the need to change the baby's diaper, wipe snotty noses, stop kid fights, fix the regular meals, clean house and stoke the cook stove.

On the day before Christmas she prepared the turkey and dressing. There were no refrigerators or freezers available, so perishable foods had to be prepared not earlier than the day before they would be used. When possible Mom took advantage of the weather and set food, in various stages of preparation, out in the unheated hall to hold for a day or so.

We always spent Christmas at home. As far back as I remember we were joined by the older kids coming home, uncles, aunts, and other relatives or friends. Everyone who came for Christmas dinner brought food. But regardless of how much food Mom expected others to bring, she seemed to have an obsession to prepare enough for everybody.

Despite its significance and the weeks of preparation, Christmas day began like most other days except with a higher than usual sense of excitement. The little kids tumbled from bed in the unheated bedrooms, grabbed some clothes and headed for the dining room where Mom had long ago started the fire in the heating stove. We huddled around the hot stove as we hurriedly dressed. We hustled about as we attempted to see what was under the tree. The little ones, who still believed, looked to see if Santa had filled the stockings they had dutifully hung before going to bed the night before. Except for the little ones with filled stockings, we had to wait until guests for the day arrived so all could participate in the gift opening ceremony.

The livestock knew nothing about the holiday, so before we could begin to celebrate Christmas day the chores had to be done. The cows had to be milked, the hogs and cattle fed and hay pushed into the mangers for the horses. We hurried and tried our best to cut corners, but the work had to be done. When finished we were free for the day, that is until it was chore time again in the evening.

On Christmas day the significance of Christmas was not obliterated but was pushed into the background as we kids concentrated on the Christmas tree, the presents beneath it and later in the day the stacks of food Mom had prepared. It was with a mixture of joy and sadness that I would open a package to find a pair of long, brown, ribbed, cotton stockings or a pair of long handled underwear. The joy of knowing the clothes would provide protection against the cold Nebraska winter wind was dampened by the disappointment of not receiving a toy that I had pointed out in the Sears and Roebuck catalogue.

The house became a literal mad-house as relatives and friends arrived to share our Christmas bounty. The bedlam was intensified if bad weather kept the kids inside. On occasions when there was sufficient snow, the kids, big and little, grabbed the sleds and headed for the sleigh-riding hills in the pasture. There they stayed until the cold forced them back to the warm house or their internal signals told them it was time for Christmas dinner.

The dining room table in our house, huge by most standards, was loaded with food prepared by Mom and the other women. The adults and kids too small to help themselves generally sat at the table. Others filled their plates and sat on extra chairs or on the floor. The noise level escalated as adults tried to converse over the shouts and laughter of the kids. It mattered little as there were no thoughts of serious conversation. For the most part we concentrated upon the bounty set before us. The supply of food seemed endless as dishes emptied were quickly refilled. The food over which the women had worked so hard and long disappeared almost as fast as the corn fed to the hogs during the morning chores.

When the meal was over, the kids disappeared, the women folks did the dishes while the men who smoked, and most did in those days, had a cigarette and offered solutions to the weighty problems of the world. Generally the dishes were done before the problems of the world were solved. The women then joined the menfolks and they gathered around tables for a few hands of Rook.

As the day waned the kids and big folks alike wandered back to the kitchen to partake of leftovers from the midday meal. Following this second stomach stuffing of the day, the guests began to gather up their kids and prepared to head for home. As the last guest or relative took their leave, the house settled back into some semblance of normalcy. Once again it was chore time and soon thereafter time to get the little ones ready for bed. The bigger kids sat around the table, reexamined their gifts, read books or relived the events of the day. Dad leaned back in his big chair at the head of the table and read an ever present book, generally with one of the little kids on his lap. There the child would lay with its head on Dad's chest, listening to his watch tick, until they fell asleep and someone carted them off to bed.

It was not long before we bigger kids and Dad headed off to bed. Mom took another turn around the kitchen to make sure everything was put away for the night before she blew out the kerosene lamp and called it a day. In some respects this was a typical day for her: first up in the morning and last to go to bed at night. Tomorrow would be another day. And with the coming of the morning her routine would be repeated.

While Christmas is a time to celebrate the birth of Jesus Christ and to recognize his mother Mary, it also seems appropriate to pay homage to and ask God's blessings on all the mothers who do so much to assure that Christmas remains a meaningful, joyful and happy day.

THANKSGIVING

Thanksgiving had a long tradition at the Gates home. It was not just a day at our house, in the Gates community, or I suspect in most of rural America. It was a season and I now realize that it was a significant period of learning. It was a time when basic concepts and ideas about the making of and the meaning of America were planted in our open and fertile minds. Thanksgiving was a special season, but not the only season, when we were made aware of what it meant to be an American and to be thankful for the privileges that went with it.

Our ancestors came to America long before there was a United States of America. In 1637 my grandfather, many times removed, and his family arrived in New Ipswich, Massachusetts, aboard the ship Diligent outbound from England..

Thanksgiving season began at school in early November when the teacher began talking about the pilgrims and why they came to America, about Plymouth Rock, John Smith, Pocahontas, the problems of survival in the new world, the scarcity of food and about the first Thanksgiving day. We were taught the lesson attributed to John Smith: that is, if you want to eat then you have to work.

In addition to reading and being told stories about the first Thanksgiving, the teacher had us draw and color pictures of the pilgrims, the harvests and of course turkeys. We learned and sang songs about the Thanksgiving season. "Over the river and through the woods" was then and still is a favorite of mine. I now sing it to my three grandchildren, but I don't think it is as meaningful to them as it is to me. You see, they have not had the privilege of growing up in an environment where scarcity was the normal situation and abundance of material things virtually unknown.

At home we repeated many of the things we did at school, and Mom and Dad talked, but not much, about Thanksgiving when they were kids. At night, gathered around the table, by the light of the kerosene lamp, we drew, colored and cut out pictures of pilgrims, Indians and turkeys to show our parents and to decorate the house. We brought books home from school to read about the first Thanksgiving.

Thanksgiving was a season, but we all looked forward to Thanksgiving day. Every meal at our house was a job for Mom as there were seldom less than ten pairs of feet under the dining room table. Nevertheless, we looked forward to an even bigger meal on Thanksgiving day. We knew that Mom would fix a turkey and all the trimmings and that many family members and friends would join us for the day and the feast.

I'm sure Mom also enjoyed the Thanksgiving season, but I am equally certain that she viewed it from a different perspective than the kids, or Dad. It was up to Mom and the older girls to prepare most of the food for Thanksgiving dinner. Everyone who came for dinner brought food, but it seemed that the bulk of the work fell upon Mom. Dad would kill and dress the turkey, but the rest of the preparations for dinner were up to her.

As I recall, we always had turkey for Thanksgiving dinner. However, the source of the turkey varied considerably. Some years we raised turkeys and killed and dressed one of our own. In some cases Dad would buy a turkey, but more often he would win a bird at a "turkey shoot."

Turkey shoots were held a few days before Thanksgiving and Christmas. This provided Dad with the opportunity to win a turkey for dinner if he could shoot well enough.

A turkey shoot was usually sponsored by a civic or charitable organization as a fund raiser. They were also important social affairs where people could get together to swap stories, brag about their shooting abilities and engage in fellowship. The sponsor provided the turkeys and sometimes ducks and hams as well, the blue rocks (some people now call them clay pigeons), the facilities and the officials. Sponsors also had shotgun shells available for sale to the contestants.

Normally a lunch stand was provided by the sponsor or a local church group, where hamburgers, hot dogs, or pie could be bought for a dime and coffee or pop for a nickel.

Alcoholic drinks were not sold as it was the general opinion that shotguns and alcohol were not a good mixture. However, it was evident from sight and smell that this general rule was often broken. Some of the spectators, and shooters as well, made frequent trips to their cars for a slug from a bottle stashed under the seat or slipped around a corner out of sight to take a swig from a flask secreted in their hip pocket. Within limits such behavior was tolerated, even expected of some.

I do not recall any serious problems resulting from these encounters with John Barlycorn. However, a good old fashioned fist fight was not necessarily considered unacceptable behavior in Custer County in the decade of the thirties. I do recall, on a occasion or two, I asking my teetotaling Dad what was the matter with some guy who was bleary eyed, stammering, boisterous and maybe not tracking too well. Dad responded something to the effect that some guys could not handle liquor and would probably be a lot better off if they did not use the stuff, but instead spent the liquor money on their families. He told me he knew of no situation where drinking solved problems but lots of cases where it led to trouble.

Each "shoot" consisted of five shooters. Each shooter paid an entry fee, the amount varied from $0.50 to $2.00 depending upon whether he was shooting for a turkey, a duck or a ham. That was a lot of money to risk when a good man could be hired to work for $1.00 a day.

The shooters stood in a line some distance behind a pit where the blue-rock thrower was located. When ready shoot the first shooter hollered "pull" and a blue-rock was shot into the air by a spring loaded machine operated by the man in the pit. The shooter had one shot at the blue-rock as it sailed through the air. An official kept score of hits and misses. Following the first shooter the process was repeated down the line until all five shooters had shot. This process was repeated five times until each shooter had shot five times from his position. The shooters then moved down one space to change shooting positions. The shooter on the end of the line moved to the head of the line each time. This process was repeated until each shooter had shot five times from each position, a total of 25 shots. The shooter with the highest score (most blue-rocks broken) was the winner of the prize for which they were shooting. In the case of a tie the tied shooters were allowed five more shots, one from each position. If this did not produce a winner, the process was repeated until a shooter finally missed.

Generally the potential shooters paid their entry fees and were randomly assigned to shooting groups. As expected, there was oftentimes jockeying by some shooters to get assigned to a group where they thought they would have an advantage. It was also common toward the end of the shoot to arrange a shoot-off among some of the best shooters of the day. The shoot-offs seemed to enhance the gaming spirit, so bets were placed on favorites and money changed hands at the end of the shoots.

Dad was pretty good with the old Browning 12-gauge automatic and always came home with at least one bird for Thanksgiving dinner. I was proud of my Dad and liked to see him shoot but recall standing around shivering in the cold, with a runny nose and wanting to find a place where I could get warm. I warmed up more quickly if Dad gave me a dime so I could go to the lunch shack and get a hamburger while I waited.

While the preparation of the turkey was a big job, it was certainly not the only job connected with the preparation of the Thanksgiving dinner For days before Thanksgiving the smells of baking bread, cakes and pies permeated the house. The smells were great but none of us kids gave a thought to, or maybe didn't understand, the hard work Mom put in to prepare the Thanksgiving feast for the family. All of the baking was done "from scratch" as there were no prepared foods available at our house. Breads and rolls were made from a bread starter that Mom cultured in the kitchen. Making bread was a process that took lots of time as the starter was prepared, the dough mixed, allowed to raise, kneaded down, allowed to raise again, patted into loaves of bread or buns or rolls, allowed to raise again then baked in the oven of the wood burning stove.

For several days before Thanksgiving day, Mom allowed bread to dry for use in the dressing that would be used to stuff the turkey. It took a lot of dry bread to make the amount of dressing required to satisfy the group that was expected around the dinner table.

On the night before Thanksgiving, Mom made final preparations on the turkey. She washed it, inside and out, chopped the giblets for the stuffing, then set the bird out on the enclosed porch to keep cool until morning.

On Thanksgiving morning Mom was up even earlier than usual to fix the stuffing for the turkey. This required mixing the chopped giblets with the dry bread and other ingredients. I don't know the ingredients or how they were mixed, but I do remember the smell of sage and pepper. She then packed the empty cavity of the turkey full of the stuffing. She always made more stuffing than the body cavity of the turkey could accommodate as she had learned from experience that demands were heavy for the dressing. The extra stuffing was placed in a large baking pan and made ready to go into the oven with the turkey.

When all was ready while most of the family was still sleeping, the turkey and the extra pan of stuffing were popped into the oven. It seemed to take all day for the turkey to get done. Soon the smells of the sage and the baking turkey were wafting throughout the house. Mom had no temperature gauge on the oven, meat thermometer or timer. She opened the oven door occasionally to take a peek or to baste the cooking bird, and in so doing would release a surge of the wonderful smell of stuffing and turkey cooking.

It required a lot of stove wood to keep the oven hot, so the kids were called frequently to keep the woodbox full. I don't suppose we liked to carry in wood any better on Thanksgiving day than any other day. However, the smells from the oven and the promise of the roast turkey and dressing may have tended to lighten the imagined burden.

Dillard H. Gates

Once the turkey was in the oven Mom could begin her regular day; that is, get the kids out of bed and dressed then get breakfast for the family. Breakfast on Thanksgiving day was no less of a breakfast than on any other.

On the farm things did not shut down because it was a holiday. There were chores to be done, cows to be milked, hogs to be fed and hay hauled out and fed to the cattle. If we had corn pickers they might even hitch up the team and shuck a load of corn in the morning. Corn pickers were paid from two to four cents a bushel for the corn picked and did not earn money setting around waiting for a turkey to cook.

As the day progressed and between peeks into the oven and stoking the stove, Mom and the girls or women present peeled, it seemed, a half bushel of potatoes and prepared other vegetables that would be cooked as the baking turkey approached the done stage. All the while, depending upon the number of family members and relatives that had come home, the house was full of people. Kids were underfoot and adults filled the remaining space. It was hectic; it was noisy; it was fun for us kids at least. It was home, and there was a great sense of family.

As turkey-done time approached it became even more hectic; the potatoes had to be boiled and mashed and the other vegetables cooked. At the appropriate time the turkey was removed from the oven, the stuffing scooped into serving bowls, the turkey cut up (we didn't carve the turkey; we just cut it up, though I suppose the results were about the same) and gravy made from the juice that had accumulated in the bottom of the roasting pan. The food was placed on the table, and it was time to eat.

Generally the space around the table was taken up by the adults, and sometimes there was not enough room for all of them. In that case the women folks and extra adults fixed their plates and sat in the kitchen or on the floor to eat.

If a table could feel, I am sure our table groaned under the weight of the food piled upon it. If it could hear, I am sure it was overwhelmed by the sound of clanking dishes and eating utensils, calls for another helping, the chatter and laughter and likely some unmuffled burps. If the table could talk, it would probably tell stories, maybe some almost unbelievable, about the huge amounts of food consumed by some of those gathered around. It might repeat some of the praise it heard about the good food or the requests to Mom or one of the other cooks for the recipe for a special dish. Or the table might even marvel at the fortitude, the strength, the courage and the happiness of the people grouped around it despite the drought, the depression and the hard times. For on this day the bad times were pushed to the back of the mind and thanks were given for what we had and for family and friends.

When the meal was over, the dishes were cleared and the leftover food put on the kitchen table. We had no refrigerator, and besides some people would continue picking at it for the remainder of the day. Mom and the other women washed the dishes and sort of straighten up the kitchen. The men folks gathered around the heating stove in the dining room to ruminate until the women were finished in the kitchen. The men who smoked pulled out the makins and rolled a Bull Durham cigarette, or some of the more affluent might displayed a pack of tailor-mades. Depending upon the weather the bigger kids played outside, in the barn or somewhere inside the house but made every effort to stay away from the adults. The little kids remained underfoot or were on the laps of some of the adults, either napping or just enjoying the attention. Sometimes a game of Rook was started among the adults and went on until it was time to eat again or someone had to head home. Looking back at the amount of food that had been consumed just a few hours before it was amazing that anyone could eat again, but they did.

The holiday ended when the guests went home and the evening chores had to be done. Mom and the girls once again washed and dried the dishes, put the food away and straightened up the kitchen for the final time that day. Tired kids were put in their pajamas and sent off to bed. In some instances the little kids lay down on the floor next to the stove where it was warm, and went to sleep. It was a bit of a chore to put pajamas on a sleeping kid, but it was done and they were carried to bed.

Finally another long and tiring day was over. It had been a day of hard work, of family and friends, of joy and happiness and thankfulness. Eventually the big kids and Mom and Dad called it a day. The kerosene lamp was turned down low or blown out. Thanksgiving day was over, and tomorrow morning a new day would begin on the farm.

THE FOURTH OF JULY

We kids always knew that the Fourth of July was the day the Thirteen Original Colonies declared themselves free of England and formed the United States of America. We knew it was Independence Day, but to us it was The Fourth of July.

Unlike Christmas and Thanksgiving which fell during winter and fall slack work periods on the farm, The Fourth of July fell right in the middle of an extremely busy season. In the normal course of things there were two or three important farming activities happening about this time.

"Lay it by, by the first of July" was the ditty associated with the final cultivation of the corn. If the corn had grown as expected, it was necessary to perform this final operation before the plants were tall enough to be broken over by the cultivator. Also, at this stage of growth the corn plants shaded the ground sufficiently to restrict growth of ever present weeds. Lay-by time was critical, and Dad was reluctant to take time off from the field work, even to celebrate The Fourth of July.

There were several years I recall during the thirties where due to drought the corn hardly reached the "lay-by" stage. In some cases the drought-stunted corn was plowed under and some variety of sorghum planted as a substitute. Sorghum was more drought tolerant and would usually make some grain or forage even during the driest years.

The Fourth of July also signaled the beginning of the small-grain harvest season. Like other farm crops the stage of development of the small grain was greatly influenced by weather. We worried about there being enough rain to produce a crop of grain. If we had a good crop as it approached maturity, we then worried about hail. Severe hail storms were common on the plains and in minutes could reduce a good stand of grain or corn to a field of shredded stems or stalks. When the grain was ready to harvest, it was prudent to get it cut and in the shock as soon as possible.

The thirties were pre-combine days. Most of the grain was harvested with a binder which cut the grain, tied it in bundles and dropped them in piles forming windrows. The bundles were then picked up by hand and placed in shocks. Shocks were formed by first standing two or three bundles upright and propping them together with the heads up. Additional bundles were placed around this core to form a shock. A shock normally consisted of a half-dozen to a dozen bundles, depending on the density and distribution of the bundles in the field. This allowed the grain to dry and cure until time for the threshing operation.

Cutting, harvesting, or binding were all names used to describe the process. Regardless of what it was called, the job was done with a machine called a binder pulled either by horses or a tractor. I remember our horse drawn binder which was pulled by a six-horse team. Cutting grain was a hot, dirty, frustrating job as the operator had to put up with the horses as they fought the sweat bees and horse flies as well as contend with the machinations of the complex machine, the grain binder.

I remember when the six-horse hitch was removed from the front of the binder and a tractor hitch installed for the new rubber-tired F-20 Farmall. From the standpoint of power this was a great improvement. However, replacing the horses with a tractor did nothing to improve the inherent problems of the binder designed to be horse-drawn and dependent on the bull-wheel to drive all of the mechanisms. These mechanisms included the cutter bar, the rollers which drove the platform and elevator canvases, the compacting forks, and the intricate mechanism that wrapped the bundles with twine then tied the twine in a knot to hold the bundles together. I recall Dad lamenting the fact that pulling the binder with the tractor seemed to compound the mechanical problems. And sure enough the fast and unrelenting pace of the tractor soon strained the old binder beyond its design limits.

It wasn't long before Dad parked the old horse binder in the machinery graveyard behind the shop and replaced it with a McCormack-Deering binder from Fred Bates Implement Company in Broken Bow. For years Dad had done custom binding, first with the horse drawn binder, then with the tractor drawn horse binder and now with the new power binder. Custom binding involved cutting grain for farmers in the community who did not have the right equipment. He contracted with individual farmers to harvest their grain on a certain schedule. The harvesting runs were generally arranged to get the jobs done in the proper sequence with the minimum amount of travel and back-tracking. Somewhere in the sequence he had to cut his own grain.

In addition to the pressure of getting the corn laid by and grain harvested, there were also times when the second cutting of alfalfa was coming on. Sometimes the system was about overloaded with the demands on machinery, manpower and time. To complicate the situation there was always a big Fourth of July celebration planned in one of the surrounding towns.

As June was drawing to a close, we kids began to query Dad about the possibility of attending one of the Fourth of July celebrations. Dad was generally non-committal. We were reminded of the amount of work to be done, of the pressure being put on him by client farmers and the ever present desire to get the grain cut before it was hit by a hail storm. By the first of July we kids were really getting antsy as we wanted a commitment from Dad. If he couldn't take time off from work, maybe he would allow Mom to take us to a celebration.

During this period of uncertainty and stress, Mom was noncommital in response to our questions about going to a celebration. However, if by about July third we kids had not extracted a firm answer from Dad, Mom exerted herself to the point of telling him she had to know what he planned. If we were going, food, and lots of it, had to prepared. No consideration was given to buying food from the vendors at the celebration as the cost of filling all the bellies and satisfying the appetites would have been too great. Mom normally went ahead and prepared some food. If it was not used for the picnic dinner at the celebration, it would be eaten as a part of our regular meals. It would not be wasted.

Mom would catch a few fryers with a chicken hook or have some of the kids chase them down. She would wring off their heads, scald, pluck and gut them in short order. It was a quick trip from the farmyard to the frying pan.

When I was big enough, I suppose at ten or so, I inherited the job of decapitating the chickens destined for the frying pan, roaster, or stew pot. I usually accomplished the job with a quick blow from the axe as the

Hay, Hell, Kids and Cattle

chicken's neck was stretched across the chopping block. An alternative method, equally quick and effective, was to lay a stick across the chicken's neck just below the head, place a foot on each end of the stick, grasp the bird firmly with both hands and pull upward sharply popping off the head. In either case the headless body of the chicken was laid aside to bleed for a few minutes.

Even in cases where Dad responded in the affirmative to Mom she was unsure of his final plans. He would generally spend at least part of the morning cutting grain, cultivating corn, stacking hay, or whatever he thought most needed to be done. Only when he finally came into the house and told us to get ready were we certain we would be going. From that moment on it was hectic around the household as Mom finished her work and the bigger kids helped the little ones get dressed. Finally Dad, Mom, the kids and the food were packed into the old Ford V-8 and we headed for the town we had selected for the celebration.

The Fourth of July was more than just a holiday; it was Independence Day. My Dad was a patriot, believed in, and loved the United Sates of America and supported the Constitution, even though he believed it was being systematically ravaged by Roosevelt.

From an ethnic standpoint the ancestry of the people of the Gates community was primarily western European, English and Irish. However, there were surrounding communities dominated by Poles and Bohemians or others of eastern European origin. Some of them did not speak the English language very well, but they, or their ancestors, had left the old country for a myriad of reasons and migrated to the United States. On this day we were all Americans and together we celebrated our freedom and Independence Day.

Most of the cars headed for the celebrations were adorned with American flags of various sizes attached to the radiator ornament, the headlights, or the radio antenna (for the few that had radios in their cars). We were flag wavers and proud of it.

Upon arrival at the celebration site, we kids burst from the car like a covey of quail, anxious to see what the place had to offer. Generally the offerings were limited to a parade, which may have been over by the time we arrived, stands selling fireworks, a few food booths sponsored by local churches or civic groups, a soda pop and ice cream stand and, most popular of all, the fireworks stand.

Dillard H. Gates

Normally there would be a ball game or so scheduled for the afternoon. Occasionally there would be a short speech by a local politician or other self-appointed, self-promoting, blow-hard. Their words, profound or otherwise, were generally drowned out by the sound of fireworks nearby. Little did the kids know that the sound of their fireworks was saving their parents from having to listen to the drivel being offered by the fat man with the big mouth and the bull-horn.

There was little direct talk about Independence Day, but the people there knew what they were celebrating. The main attraction was the opportunity for the people to get together, relax, socialize and talk. The kids played in the park, shot fire crackers and cap guns and generally enjoyed being kids.

One of the first things we kids did after arrival at the celebration site was to beg Dad for money to buy fireworks and soda pop. Even though money was short, Dad tended to be generous with the kids' requests. He had agreed to bring us to the Fourth of July celebration and accepted the fact that we needed a bit of money in order to participate in the goings-on. Under the circumstance, being generous amounted to giving each kid a quarter. Later in the afternoon, when we had blown our first draw, we would try to locate Dad again and put the bite on him for another quarter.

He was generally responsive to our plea, "Please Dad, can I have some more money?" The twenty-five to fifty cents may not sound like too much money, but even we kids could add. The distribution of that amount of money to each of a half-dozen kids added up to be the equivalent of a day or two wages for the hired man. Viewed from that perspective it was evident to that, in total, the change Dad handed out to us represented a significant amount of money.

Following a quick circuit of the grounds, we kids would congregate back to where Mom had the picnic lunch spread out on a table if available and if not on blankets on the grass. Following the quick demise of the fried chicken, buns, potato salad, fruit salad, boiled eggs, cake, pie, and maybe home-made ice cream, the kids set out once again, this time to indulge in the fireworks and other offerings of the day.

We had been warned about buying the big firecrackers that could blow off a finger, put out an eye or do other serious injury. We were instructed to light the fire crackers then get back quickly until it went off. We were further cautioned not to approach and try to relight a firecracker that had failed to explode. It might be that the fuse burned slowly and it could explode in our face as we bent over to attempt to light it again.

As proof positive of the need for caution, Dad had shown us a small scar on his chin resulting from a cut he received as a boy when he was hit in the face with an iron skillet. He had placed a large firecracker under the skillet to see how high it would go when the firecracker exploded. When the firecracker didn't go off in the expected amount of time, Dad bent over the skillet with the intention of relighting the firecracker. The firecracker exploded and the skillet hit him square in the face gashing his chin. He had learned his lesson the hard way and hoped his offspring might learn from his experience.

I do not know if we learned or were just lucky. None of the many kids ever received an injury more serious than slightly burned fingers.

Mom usually hung out at the picnic table or the site where she had originally spread the midday meal. She and other mothers tended to occupy and protect the home sites as there were generally little ones to watch and care for. In addition, it was a refuge, site even for the bigger kids to retreat to if they became hungry or tired or if faced with a situation for which they needed parental input. By the end of the afternoon most of us kids trickled back to once again raid the food box and to get revitalized.

Dillard H. Gates

If there were fireworks planned for after darkness we normally stayed to see the display. If not, Mom and Dad herded the kids together, loaded the old Ford and we headed for home. Before we were around the first turn, the little ones were asleep and the bigger ones yawning as they recounted the day's activities.

By the time we made it home it was past bedtime, for the little kids at least. But bedtime or not, there were still chores to be done and Dad helped get the cows milked and the livestock fed. Only when the chores were done could we call it a day.

We were exhausted by the activities of the day and glad to finally get to bed. The Fourth of July was a time for celebration, but the next day was just other day on the farm, with crops and livestock to tend and much of the harvest still ahead.

THE HOG PEN,
A LIFE EXPERIENCES LABORATORY

In addition to hay, hell, kids and cattle, my Dad also raised pigs. In fact pigs provided a significant part of the income to the Gates household.

Our hog pen was about a quarter of a mile northwest of the farmstead located in what remained of the tree claim established when my great grandfather, Stillman Gates, homesteaded the farm back in the 1870s. The old tree claim was called "The Grove." In addition to serving as the hog pen, it was also the source of much of the wood used for fuel. It also served as shelter for the cattle when cold winds and snow swept across the plains of central Nebraska..

The advantage of the hog pen being far from the farmstead was that the strong odors and the flies associated with raising hogs were away from the house. The disadvantage was that it was some distance away and the hogs had to be fed twice daily during most of the year. The hogs also required vaccinations to prevent cholera and other diseases as well as some veterinary services.

Feeding or caring for the hogs was a part of both morning and evening chores. Each morning after breakfast but before school began one of us kids, depending upon age, would jump on Ole Wrangler, ride down to the grove and feed the pigs. This might entail scooping out the required amount of corn or other grain from a wagon parked in the hog pen or dumping a prepared ground grain and water swill into troughs, then preparing a new batch for the next feeding. There was a windmill and pump in the hog pen so there was water available at all times. However, each time we fed the pigs it was necessary to check and make certain the well was working properly. In the winter it was frequently necessary to break the ice in the troughs so the hogs could drink.

Caring for the hogs was an important job and had to be done by someone regardless of the weather. If the weather was really bad in the winter, Dad often gave us kids a reprieve and either he or the hired man took care of the job.

I learned a lot in the pig pen. Dad taught me the importance of providing proper care to the animals and how to provide that care. I learned to respect the pigs, especially the mother sows and the boars, but not to be afraid of them. I learned to control my fear of the animals and to behave as Dad expected, maybe out of a greater fear of what I thought he would do if I did not do as I was told.

LEARNING TO STAND MY GROUND

It was frequently necessary to provide treatment to baby pigs when they were only a few days old. Mother pigs, old sows or whatever you want to call them are very protective of their babies, and seem not to understand the good intentions of those wanting to provide help. Sometimes when providing treatment to the little pigs Dad moved the sows into another pen separating them from their pigs. However, there were times when, I guess, Dad thought that separating them was too much bother and he crawled into the pen with the sow and pigs. He picked up the pigs from under or around the sow and provided them the necessary treatment. The frightened little pigs generally squealed loudly and the sows became agitated and excited.

Dad always maintained that the sow would not bite if you just held your hands up out of her reach and stood perfectly still. Many times I watched as he stood in a small pen with the little pig in his hands with an excited sow snapping her teeth and rushing toward him. Sometimes the sow put her snout against his leg but I never saw one bite him.

Watching Dad handle the pigs was exciting. It became even more exciting when I was big enough and Dad told me to crawl into the pen and hand the little pigs to him.

Even though I had seen Dad do the job literally hundreds of times, and he had coached me well on how to behave, I suddenly realized that watching something happen and talking about it was not the same as doing it. I knew I had to do the job because Dad told me to. I wanted to believe what Dad had taught me and what I had seen, but I was terrified of that old sow. After a split second of reflection I knew I was more scared of Dad than I was of the sow. I slowly and reluctantly crawled over the fence and into the pen with the sow and her pigs.

Under the watchful eyes of my Dad and the old sow, I moved slowly and deliberately to pick up one of the little pigs. The pig remained quiet until I straightened up and started to hand it to Dad. Then it let out a squeal like I was trying to kill it and I think the sow believed the message. She snorted and rushed toward me with her mouth wide open. Some may think that a pig does not have a big mouth, but that is proof they have never been in a small pen with an excited and protective old sow. My on-board computer made a lot of rapid calculations and analyses based upon stored memory and real time information being provided. Dad was telling me to stand still, but I was having a difficult time getting that information to my feet because they wanted to get me out of that pen.

I guess the coaching paid off for even under the stressful circumstances I was still more afraid of Dad than I was the old sow. I stood still and held my hands up out of reach and the sow rushed to me, put her nose against my leg and stopped. She did not bite. After a brief stand-off I handed the pig to Dad and he did whatever he had to do with it and set it down outside the pen so that it would not get mixed with the untreated pigs. The process was repeated until all the pigs in all of the pens had been treated. I could then walk side by side with my Dad knowing that I had done my job and that what he had taught me about doing the job was true. I had learned something about hogs, but in so doing I had also learned that if you keep your head you can still do a pretty good job even while scared.

CASTRATING THE PIGS

Dad generally took care of the health problems of the pigs himself. He did most of the vaccinating, castrating, or other jobs that needed to be done. He did not use a vet much as the cost of the vet was probably more than the value of a pig needing treatment. He did on occasion call a vet for a sick cow or horse, but only as a last resort. Some of the larger animals might be worth more than the vet's bill.

Dad castrated (cut) our pigs himself when they were a couple or so months old. When I was big enough I had to hold the male pigs while Dad performed the surgery. I learned to hold the pig in the correct position and over the years watched Dad cut hundreds of them. It was not complex surgery and eventually under his supervision, Dad let me try it myself.

Dad usually went to town on Saturdays to attend the livestock auction, buy a few groceries, get a shave and visit with other farmers. He generally left us kids home with instructions to get certain jobs done. There was always fence to fix, barns to be cleaned, animals to be fed, weeds to be hoed or a myriad of other jobs.

On one particular Saturday when I was around thirteen and was in town, my younger brother, Jack, and I decided there were several pigs in the pen that were ready to be cut. We further made the decision to help Dad and take care of the situation ourselves. We ran some of the pigs into a pen and proceeded, unaided and clumsily, to remove the nuts (testicles) from several of the male pigs. After we had cut ten or fifteen pigs we began to have second thoughts about what we were doing and to wonder what Dad would do when he observed the results of our handiwork. In fact, after a bit of thought, if we could have put all those pig nuts back where they came from we would have been glad to do so.

On Sunday morning Dad decided to look over the pigs, as he did on occasion, just to see how they were doing. My worst fears had come true. I had hoped that a few days would pass before Dad ventured to the hog pen and by then the results of our Saturday activities would not be so obvious. Despite the fact that I could virtually feel the kick in the butt I expected to receive and hear the questions about just what I thought I was doing, I knew that I had to go with him to the hog pen.

After checking the well and feeding the hogs he strolled through the herd. The results of Jack and my Saturday activities were clearly evident. We walked among the pigs and Dad grunted as he noted the affects of the recent surgery. The anticipation of expected punishment became almost unbearable.

As we walked back toward the car Dad grunted again and commented, "Dill, it looks like you were pretty busy yesterday."

"Yes," I responded meekly, steeling myself for what I was sure would come next.

"It looks like you did a pretty good job." he responded, "but next time maybe you better wait and let me help."

I breathed a sigh of relief. The incident was over and I had lucked out. My first venture into the field of swine surgery turned out alright. None of the castrated pigs died and all healed satisfactorily.

I cut lots of pigs after that, but for some time it was always under Dad's supervision.

MUD SOLD FOR THE SAME PRICE AS PORK

Dad sold pigs at different sizes, depending on the market price, the number of pigs he had to sell, and his need for cash at any given time. Sometimes he trucked the pigs to Sargent or Broken Bow and sold them at auction. Other times a hustler, speculator, or representative from one of the auction yards would come out to the farm and negotiate directly with Dad to reach a selling price for the pigs.

I remember, on several occasions, sitting in the hog pen with Dad and the potential buyer listening to them trying to arrive at a mutually acceptable selling price. I didn't understand how they could haggle so long over whether the pigs would be sold by the head or by weight, the significance of one-half cent per pound, or whether the pigs would be weighed following a feeding or after an overnight shrink. There were also discussions about payments and point of delivery. If the pigs were sold on the farm, by the head, then the buyer paid for the transportation and payment was made before the pigs left the farm.

On one occasion when I was around thirteen, Floyd Pulliam from the Sargent auction yard came to the farm to buy feeder pigs. Pulliam was a speculator and his intent was to buy hogs on the farm at a price he deemed favorable to him. He intended to take the pigs to Sargent and run them through the auction ring or sell them directly to a hog buyer. In either case he expected to sell the hogs for more than he paid for them. He was taking a risk, but he knew hogs and the market and expected to make a profit. I'm sure he generally did, as he seemed to me to be the picture of success. He was the head honcho at the Sargent Auction Yard, always drove a new car, smoked a big cigar and did a lot of back-slapping.

In this case Dad and Pulliam arrived at a price for the hogs based on their weight across the scales in Sargent, and Dad was to pay trucking costs from the farm to the point of delivery. A local trucker came to the farm, loaded the hogs and delivered them to the auction yard pens in Sargent where they were to be put across the scales. Dad and I got in the old Ford and accompanied the hogs to the sale yard in Sargent where we met Mr. Pulliam.

It didn't rain much in central Nebraska during the thirties, but there had been a good rain in the last day or so and the unloading pens at the auction yard were a sea of mud. The day was warm and the hogs were hot from the truck ride. Dad and I climbed into the receiving pens to push the pigs across the scales as the trucker moved them out of the truck and down the unloading chute. When the hot pigs landed in the muddy pens, they immediately began to wallow in the mud. I was intent on doing a good job and began to poke the pigs and chase them toward the scales. Dad called to me not to be in such a hurry, so the pigs wallowed in the mud for some time before we pushed them across the scales.

I was of the age where Dad thought I should be learning something about the business of selling hogs. He instructed me to take the weight of the hogs from the scales and based upon the selling price compute how much Pulliam would have to pay for the hogs. I was then to deduct the cost of the trucking and determine the net amount he would receive from the sale.

I checked the scale weight and multiplied it by the price per pound. When I arrived at a figure I showed it to Dad, but I was sure I had made an error as the amount seemed so large. Dad told me to compare my figure with Pulliam's, and I discovered it was the same. It was hard for a kid used to seeing only pennies, nickels and dimes to realize the value of the pigs and the amount of money Dad received from the sale. I had no idea if the amount Dad received from the hogs paid for the cost of producing them. All I knew at the time was that it seemed like a heck of a lot of money.

On our way home I was still wondering why Dad had told me not to be in a hurry to move the pigs toward the scales when they were wallowing in the muddy pens. In response to my question Dad replied that a lot of mud was sticking to the wallowing pigs and the additional weight of the mud was probably enough to pay for the trucking costs.

Hay, Hell, Kids and Cattle

Pulliam had been there helping with the pigs, observed everything and appeared unconcerned. I concluded that the technique was all right, or at least within the acceptable bounds of hog-selling procedures. It was considered pretty hard to get the best of an auction yard buyer or speculator. I am sure Pulliam's bid on the pigs included sufficient cushion to cover the cost of the mud.

FIRE CRACKERS IN THE HOG PEN

Firecrackers were a big part of celebrating the Fourth of July. When I was around eleven years old I had some firecrackers left over from the celebration. The fire crackers were not the really big ones, probably only about one and a half inches long. My brother, Jack, and I had to go down to the grove and feed the hogs on July fifth so we took some of the fire crackers and matches with us. As we walked along the sandy trail toward the grove, we shot off a few just for the fun of it. After all, that was what firecrackers were for.

We called the pigs, ranging in size from weaners to feeder pigs and sows, and scooped grain from the wagon. We wondered how pigs would react to firecrackers, so we lit a few and tossed them into the pen as the hogs were eating. They jumped a bit but appeared unconcerned. A hog eating is not easily distracted. Watching an unconcerned hog eating was not very exciting, so I searched my mind for a way to take the fun to a higher level.

After about ten seconds of serious consideration, I decided to stick a firecracker in the hind end of a couple of the sows and light them off, just to see what would happen. The hogs were fairly gentle and not disturbed as Jack and I moved among them, firecrackers in hand, to select the pigs that were to be a part of our experiment. However, the pigs did not stand still as we attempted to strategically place the firecrackers. After a few missed tries we managed to install a couple of firecrackers into the orifices under the tails of a couple of sows.

As it turned out placing the firecrackers, even in such unlikely positions, was much easier than lighting the fuse. The process of lighting a match near the rear end of a moving sow and bringing the flame in contact with the firecracker fuse was a bit tricky. However, after several tries I managed to bring the flame and the fuse together. The selected sow continued to concentrate on the feed oblivious to that little wisp of smoke wafting upward from beneath her wiggling tail.

In the brief time it took the spark to devour the fuse and move toward the base of the sow's tail, I had began to wonder if what I thought was great fun a few seconds ago was really such a good idea after all. Too late, the firecracker exploded, the sow let out a squeal as her rear feet went off the ground. Like a rocket out of control, she made a couple of high-speed loops around the pen then with head-down crashed through the boards of the closed gate and disappeared into the grove. Jack and I stumbled through the trees trying to follow her in a vain attempt to observe the results of our action. We found that a two-hundred pound sow with an exploded rocket in her ass could outrun both of us.

To complicate matters, the second sow with unlit firecracker tucked firmly in her behind also ran through the broken gate and out into the grove. Both Jack and I now began to wonder about the possible consequences of our escapade. We pondered if the exploding firecracker had left sufficient evidence that Dad might see it the next time he came to the hog pen. And if there was visible evidence, how would we explain the hog with hemorrhoids?

We were also concerned about the second sow that escaped into the grove. Would the firecracker fall out? If not, and Dad happened to see it, how would we explain it's presence to him? A firecracker protruding beneath the tail of a pig was hardly a natural phenomena. The fear of what Dad might do was almost as bad a the butt kicking itself.

Luck was with us. Forensic evidence, if any existed, never came to Dad's attention. Jack and I learned how a hog responded to a certain stimulus but decided that henceforth we would use a bit more discretion in the placement of firecrackers.

CASTRATING THE OLD BOAR

Dad raised high quality Hampshire hogs. He bought good boars and disposed of them at appropriate times to avoid inbreeding, as we generally raised our own breeding sows.

I can't remember the circumstances as to why, but once we had an old boar that must have weighed over four hundred pounds. He had tusks two or three inches long and a bad disposition. He had not threatened any of us but had slashed a couple of steers in the feed yard

Hay, Hell, Kids and Cattle

where they were being fattened for market. It was a common practice to run hogs behind cattle being fattened as the undigested grain in the cattle manure was utilized by the hogs and provided a low-cost source of feed.

When Dad saw the slashes on the sides of the steers in the feedlot, he immediately decided the problem had to be dealt with. The tusks and the testicles had to go.

Dad could have taken the boar directly to the auction but it had little value either for slaughter or as a breeding boar. It was common knowledge that old boar meat was tough, strong smelling and tasted as bad as it smelled. However, if an old boar was castrated and fed for a few months the quality of the meat was somewhat improved. The stag could then be marketed for slaughter and would bring a better price.

Castrating a big old boar is not an easy job. Even when the operation is a success, the patient sometimes dies. Dad decided to do the job, so he sharpened his knife picked up the lariat and we headed for the hog pen.

The boar was not wild, just cantankerous, so catching him was a relatively easy job. Dad put feed in the trough, and while the boar was eating he managed to slip a small loop of the lariat around the lower jaw, behind the large tusks. We then hazed the boar out of the pen toward a nearby tree. Dad wrapped the lariat around the tree as I poked the boar with a stick and urged it forward. Dad took up the slack in the lariat as the boar moved toward the tree until its snout was snuggled against the trunk. The lariat tightened around the boar's jaw as it roared and pulled back.

The first thing Dad wanted to do was to get rid of the big tusks. As the boar continued to pull back and roar Dad took a big pair of pinchers and cut each tusk off at the gum line. Removal of the vicious tusks provided assurance the boar would not be slashing anymore cattle, if he survived the planned surgery.

Holding the sharp knife in his hand Dad moved behind the boar and felt the large, thick-skinned scrotum enclosing the testicles. The boar roared in pain and anger as Dad's knife slashed through the scrotum, partially exposing a huge, white testicle. With another cut or two the testicle was out and the cord severed. The boar roared, as only a boar can roar, pulled back and sat on his haunches protecting the remaining, still intact, testicle. Dad grabbed the boar's tail and tried unsuccessfully to lift him to his feet. The boar was big, strong, hurt and angry and would not budge. He threw his head from side to side as he tried to free himself and continued to pull back on the rope. In the violent struggle the boar threw himself onto his side. Using the loose end of the lariat Dad secured the legs of the boar to prevent it from regaining its feet. As he lay on his side snubbed to the tree and roaring Dad removed the remaining testicle. Dad washed the gaping wound and saturated it with turpentine, the all purpose disinfectant.

Dad removed the rope from the tree and from around the lower jaw of the hog that had been a boar but was now a stag. He then removed the rope that secured the legs and quickly stepped back putting the tree between himself and the enraged stag. The stag struggled to his feet, shook his head, snapped his tuskless jaws and with tail held high exposing a bloody behind, headed for the shelter of the grove.

The stag showed up for feed the next morning. He was gaunt and his back end was swelled larger than the original scrotum, but there was no excessive bleeding. In a few days the swelling had subsided and the stag was on the road to recovery.

The stag was fed with the rest of the hogs for two or three months until Dad thought he was ready for market. The four-hundred pound stag was then sold to a farmer who lived back in the hills east of Gates.

Like Dad, the buyer had a big family and a limited income but a different philosophy regarding the feeding of his family. He related to Dad that he preferred to buy stags to butcher for the family's meat supply as, "The meat was just as nutritious as other meat but was tough and strong smelling and the kids didn't eat as much."

HOG STEALING, A HIRED MAN GONE BAD

One summer, when I was about twelve, we had an exceptionally good hired man by the name of Wilson Shelton. He was hard working, reliable, a self-starter, got along well with the kids, and was considered completely trustworthy. He was working for a dollar a day plus room and board and seemed happy to have the job.

During the previous several months Dad had developed a severe pain in his abdomen and had been unable to get relief from the local doctors. My older sister, Gee (Virginia), also had been complaining about a side ache which had been diagnosed as appendicitis.

Sometime during the summer, after the hay was put up, Dad loaded Gee into the Ford V8 and they headed to the Mayo Brothers Clinic in Minnesota. He figured they would be gone a couple weeks or so and left Wilson in charge of the farm work. It was understood that we kids were to help as we could and take care of the chores. In addition, my older brother, Hap, was living on a farm about four miles away and was available to help if necessary.

As far as we knew at the time, things went well on the farm and the work was done as expected. Dad returned home with the diagnosis of kidney stones and Gee minus her appendix. When the summer work was finished, Dad let Wilson go.

But apparently the summer on the farm had included some clandestine activities that had gone unnoticed. The hired man, Wilson, had a friend, Ed Reynolds, who farmed in the hills six or eight miles northeast of us. Ed, and sometimes his wife, had frequently come to see Wilson while he was working for us. If he was in the field they would drive out to where he was working. Ed's car, an old Chevy coupe with a rumble seat, was a familiar sight on the farm.

Orville Reynolds, the father of Ed, had worked for Dad intermittently over the past few years. Thus, he was familiar with the farm, he knew our family and he and we kids learned to tolerate each other. He was a dirty old man, and unbeknown to Dad had a vile mouth around us kids. We didn't trust the old codger, but we made the best of it.

Early in the fall following Dad's return from the Mayo Clinic, Orville came to the house and asked to talk to Dad in private. He confided that his son and Wilson had stolen some pigs from our pig pen while Dad was away at Mayo's Clinic. He reported that Ed and Wilson had loaded three or four weaner pigs into the back of Ed's coupe and taken them to Ed's farm. Orville was snitching on them because he of a falling out with his son and he wanted to get even with him.

This was an unpleasant situation for Dad as he held Wilson in high regard but did not trust Ed Reynolds. He was extremely disappointed to hear that, if what Orville had said was true, one whom he had considered trustworthy had betrayed him.

Dad loaded Orville in the old Ford and headed to Broken Bow to see the Sheriff, Glenn Fox. Orville repeated the story of the stolen hogs to the Sheriff. The Sheriff informed Dad that he could swear out a warrant and have them arrested. However, Dad was still a bit reluctant to charge Wilson with the crime. Following more discussion they decided to have a talk with Ed and Wilson.

They located Wilson at another farm where he was working and took him to the farm of Ed Reynolds. Sure enough, there were pigs in the pen, now several months older and much bigger than when allegedly taken from our farm. Hogs of a given breed tend to look alike, and Dad did not try to specifically identify the hogs.

The Sheriff told Ed and Wilson what they could be charged with and what the likely outcome would be if convicted. Dad still did not want Wilson to face a jail term. Following some agonizing, Dad told them that if they admitted their guilt and returned the stolen pigs to our farm he would not press charges. Fox agreed that was an acceptable resolution, and he and Dad returned to Broken Bow assuming that the pigs would be returned and the case would be closed.

The following day, Dad was away from the farm. We kids saw a pickup truck drive across the lower part of the farm and into the grove. The pickup left shortly and drove back across the farm to the road and headed north in the direction which Reynolds lived.

As soon as the pickup disappeared, Jack and I jumped on ole Wrangler and galloped to the hog pens. As expected we saw four hogs confined in a small pen. However, to our surprise two of the pigs were Hampshire and two were spotted Poland China. Dad raised only Hampshires.

When Dad returned home that evening, Jack and I told him about the pigs which had been delivered to the pig pens. The next morning Jack and I went down to the grove with Dad to confirm what we previously related to him. Dad took a look into the pen, grunted in disgust, and told us to get in the car. We too headed up the road north to Ed Reynold's farm.

When we located Ed, Dad informed him in no uncertain terms that he and Wilson had returned some of the wrong pigs. Ed appeared perplexed and insisted the hogs were the ones stolen from Dad, and, if not, he just couldn't understand where they had come from.

The matter was finally settled when Dad said to Ed, "Listen, I raise only Hampshire hogs. They are black with a white belt, not spotted. You admitted stealing hogs from me. Now return Hampshire hogs to me.

If you don't know where you stole the spotted pigs, how do you expect me to know where they come from."

The following day the pickup again drove across the farm to the hog pens. It left again shortly. This time when we went to the pig pens we found that the two spotted hogs had been replaced by a couple of Hampshires.

Even though Dad was never sure that it was our hogs returned to us, the case was considered officially closed. Dad remained reluctant to accept the fact that Wilson had violated his trust, and I am certain forgave him for his lapse of judgement. However, he did not work for us again.

Neighbors told us later that Ed Reynolds had related to them that he thought he had gotten a bad deal. Ignoring the fact that Dad had not pressed charges and he had thus avoided a jail term, he complained that Dad should have reimbursed him for the cost of the feed consumed by the pigs between the time he stole them and when he returned them to our hog pens. However, he did not voice his complaint to Dad.

RUNT PIGS AND A POWER WASHING MACHINE FOR MOM

Anyone who raises hogs knows that runt pigs are just part of the operation. There are many reason for runts. Some pigs are born smaller than others in the liter. Some are unable to find the sow's teats and so do not get enough milk. Some get stepped on or otherwise injured. Runt pigs are generally a nuisance and not worth keeping.

Runts were usually disposed of by knocking them in the head and throwing the little carcass onto the trash heap. Occasionally one was brought to the house and taught to drink milk from a nipple or suck on an improvised nipple made by forcing a piece of cloth through a hole poked in the bottom of a shallow pan. This method was a lot easier and quicker than feeding a little pig with a bottle. It wasn't long before the pig drank milk from a pan without the cloth nipple.

Sometime in the mid-thirties one of the big, old sows gave birth to an extremely large litter. She had more pigs than teats so some of the piglets were destined for the trash heap. My younger brother, Jack, and I asked Dad if we could take a couple of the pigs to raise. We agreed that when the pigs reached market size we would sell them and use the money to buy Mom a new power washing machine to replace the hand-operated monster she had been using for years.

Dillard H. Gates

Dad selected a couple of pigs from the litter. We took them to the house, fixed a little pen and proceeded to teach them to drink milk from the pan with a cloth nipple. Things went well with the pigs, but Mom probably did most of the actual feeding when the pigs were small. Kids frequently start projects that moms finish.

The pigs soon out-grew the little pen and a bigger one had to be constructed. When they were big enough to eat grain and make it on their own, we notched their ears for identification purposes and put them in the pen with the other hogs. They were somewhat smaller than the other pigs but eventually reached market size.

When it was time to take the pigs to the auction, Dad, Jack and I loaded them into the stock trailer pulled behind the old Ford V8. We picked up Mom at the house and headed for town. Jack and I proudly watched as the pigs were brought into the auction ring and the auctioneer began to sing. We were thrilled when we went to the auction yard office to pick up the check from the clerk. Neither of us had ever held that much money in our hands.

Dad, Mom, Jack and I assembled at the Gamble store to select a new washer. The selection process was simple as there were few models from which to choose. Mom soon selected a Coronado, single tub machine with wringer, powered by a one cylinder Briggs and Stratton motor. I don't remember the cost of the washing machine, but Jack and I were thrilled that the check from the sale of the pigs covered the price of it.

We loaded the washing machine into the stock trailer that had carried the pigs to town, took it to the farm and unloaded it into the back hall. From then on Mom washed clothes in the hall instead of the kitchen as the exhaust pipe of the washing machine motor had to be out of doors. It was a noisy contraption but a great improvement over the hand-operated washer.

Mom was proud of her boys for buying the washing machine for her. This, despite the fact that she probably did more work raising the pigs than we did. Maybe the old adage, "It's the thought that counts," was valid in this instance.

CATTLE

Cattle were a major asset on our farm and Dad liked good quality cattle. His concern was for body conformation and performance. Blood lines and breeds were of less importance to him than what he considered quality. However, over the years our herd was made up mostly of Herefords, Shorthorns or Hereford-Shorthorn crosses. Colors ranged from typical Herefords to red white faced and solid reds. Dad preferred polled cattle (without horns). But for the most part our cattle were naturally horned so dehorning was an annual task.

Our beef herd varied in size between fifty and one hundred head during the period of my recollection. However, before my time Dad and his father, Bert Gates, had run large numbers of cattle on more than one ranch in Custer County. During the drought and depression of the thirties, livestock numbers varied according to available feed and prices. The attempt to balance cattle numbers, available feed and prices resulted in a constant struggle in which the banker played a significant role. It was not an unusual occurrence for Old Joe Haumont of the Security State Bank in Broken Bow to come out to the farm to look over the stock on which he held the mortgage.

In addition to the beef cattle, we also had enough milk cows to provide milk for the family. These were not dairy cows as such but were shorthorns that had been selected from the beef herd because they had a large udder and looked like they would be good milkers. Once selected, they generally remained milk cows as long as they gave enough milk to make it worthwhile. Some of the milk cows were around for several years and were given names and treated sort of like pets.

In the summer the milk cows grazed in the pasture with the other cattle but at night were brought to the corral and barn for milking. They were kept in the corral over night, milked and returned to the pasture the following morning. Bringing in the cows in the evening and turning them out again in the morning was another routine job that had to be done by the kids.

Dillard H. Gates

CARING FOR THE CATTLE

Caring for the cattle was a primary undertaking on the farm. They required feed, shelter, water and some veterinary services, which were usually provided by Dad. The cows also had to be bred, calves delivered, male calves castrated and all calves branded and vaccinated. In addition horned calves and horned cows that may have been acquired during the past year had to be dehorned. There was a continuing need to move cattle from one area to another to assure an adequate supply of available feed.

There was always fence to fix, both to confine our stock and keep out the neighbors'. Dad did not mind if a neighbor's cow somehow got into our pasture and mixed with our herd. The amount of grass she consumed was relatively insignificant However, he became disturbed if the neighbor's scrub bulls got through the fence and bred one of our cows. There was sort of a gentlemen's agreement between neighbors with a common boundary line that each had the responsibility for maintaining a certain section of the fence. But as might be expected, the disparities in what neighbors considered a satisfactory fence were as great as what they considered good cattle. On occasion this led to disagreements between neighbors and in some cases became a chronic, festering sore.

Like all other jobs on the farm, when the kids were big enough to help care for the livestock they were expected to do so whether they wanted to or not. What a kid wanted to do had little relationship to what he or she did if there was work to be done.

FEEDING THE CATTLE.

Our farm included two hundred acres of native grass pasture. This was not enough to provide forage for all the cattle even for the regular grazing season, especially during drought years when the grass was short or during times when the size of the cow herd increased. Alfalfa hay and sorghum fodder were grown on the farm as alternative forage sources. In addition, the cattle grazed the corn stocks and other farm residues following harvest. For a few years Dad rented pasture from my older brother, Hap, who had leased a ranch southwest of Dunning but did not have enough cattle to stock it fully. Hap's ranch was about fifty miles, as the crow flies, northwest of our farm. By the roads it was about seventy miles away.

Taking care of the feed requirements of the cattle during the summer and fall months was a relatively simple job, assuming there was feed available. We simply moved the cattle from one pasture to another or to fields where they could utilize crop aftermath. It was during the cold winter months that feeding the cattle became a real chore.

There were sometimes problems associated with grazing crop aftermath. Under some conditions cattle bloated when feeding on corn stocks in the fall and winter and while grazing alfalfa regrowth in the fall. Dad could sometimes save a bloated cow by sticking a knife blade between her ribs thereby relieving the gas pressure. As the gas rushed out through the puncture hole in the cow's side, it made a whistle sound like air rushing from a large balloon. The late summer and fall regrowth of some sorghum varieties formed prussic acid which, when consumed, could kill a cow almost as quickly as a shotgun blast between the eyes.

We had a large barn on the farm with a couple of sheds which could accommodate all of the cattle during extremely cold periods or blizzard conditions. We also had a big feed rack adjacent to the barn where hay or fodder was stored. These facilities were only used during weather emergencies; otherwise the beef cattle were kept out in the fields during the entire winter. Cattle do very well outdoors during Nebraska winters if they have adequate feed and a windbreak. Providing the cattle with feed in the winter was a demanding and ever present job. As a little kid I remember Dad and my older brother, Hap, bundled in sheepskin coats and Scotch caps going to the barn, hitching a team to the big hay rack and heading to the field to fetch a load of alfalfa hay for the cattle.

If there was a shortage of alfalfa hay or if Dad planned to sell some, he sometimes relied on sorghum fodder for cattle feed. The hay or fodder was loaded into the hay rack from the stack where it was stored and transported to the cattle. Dad liked to feed the cattle in the fields as the manure and hay residues added fertility to the soil and provided ground cover which helped reduce wind erosion.

When I was around eleven or twelve years old, I was considered big enough to help Dad haul hay to the cattle in the winter. It was a cold hard job which I hated. Except for the few occasions when blizzards struck and the cattle were brought into the barnyard corrals, hauling hay to the cattle was a daily job regardless of the weather.

Dad usually had the team hitched to the hay rack and was waiting for me when I got home from school shortly after four o'clock. I put on warmer clothes, crawled into the hay rack with Dad, and with the ole dog, Rags, following we headed for the hay stack. The hay stacks were about one-half mile north of the house. I often complained to Dad about the cold before we were out of the barnyard but received little sympathy. He merely told me to jump up and down and swing my arms hard around my body to keep warm. Regardless of the temperature Dad seemed immune to the cold. Dad considered my complaints about being cold as a manifestation on my laziness, and in some instances he may have been correct.

The alfalfa hay had been stacked in the field in fifteen to twenty ton stacks. Dad would pull the hayrack against the leeward side of the hay stack, tie the reins to the hitch-pole at the front of the hayrack and crawl onto the hay stack. I heard him say many times that he thought the coldest place in the world was on the top of a hay stack when it was twenty degrees below zero and the wind was blowing forty miles an hour. But the cold did not deter him from the work to be done. I was down in the hayrack somewhat protected from the wind but always cold.

Dad then pitched the hay from the stack into the hayrack. My job was to load the hayrack. I had to place the hay properly, that Dad pitched into the rack so that we could get the maximum amount of hay on the load. Sometimes I stumbled around half-blinded by tears, pitchfork in hand, trying to get the hay into the proper place. I would try to convey to Dad how cold I was, and he would merely tell me to get to work and I would warm up. Apparently that worked for him, but it didn't seem to work for me. I never ceased being cold.

When the hay rack was loaded, Dad crawled off the stack onto the top of the load with me. By then it was dark and darkness always seemed to make it colder. Sometimes when I was exceptionally cold Dad tossed ole Rags on top of the load and placed him across my lap. Sometimes he didn't smell very good, but he was a warm blanket. The hayrack creaked under the heavy load as the team strained at the tugs and pulled us slowly homeward.

When we arrived back at the farmstead we pulled the load to the front of the barn and unhitch the team. The horses were watered after the ice was broken in the stock tank so they could drink and put in their stalls in the barn. Dad unharnessed the horses while I put grain in their feed boxes and pitched hay from the haymow into their mangers. After the horses were properly cared for, we headed for the warm house where Mom was preparing supper.

The following morning Dad hitched the team to the loaded hayrack and pulled it to field where the cattle stood with humps in their backs and tails to the wind waiting to be fed. As the team walked slowly Dad pitched the hay onto the ground scattering it so that all the cattle would have access to the feed. When I got home from school that night, Dad would have the team hitched to the hay rack again and the process would be repeated.

I didn't like cold weather on the farm, and I still don't. The cold Nebraska winters were a primary factor in my decision to migrate to a region of milder climate. The only place I like to see ice now is when it is cooling a tall drink.

BULLS

In order to raise good cattle it was necessary to have good bulls. Occasionally due to economic circumstances, meaning there was not enough money available, Dad would select a high quality grade bull calf from our herd and keep him for breeding purposes. However, he usually went outside and purchased a good grade Hereford or shorthorn bull. He

Dillard H. Gates

would keep the bull for a couple years or so, then take it to the livestock auction where it was sold for breeding purposes or hamburger.

SHOWING DAD TO THE BULLS

It is alleged that one year Dad was shopping for a herd bull. In the process he went to see a stockman who raised Hereford bulls and had several ready for sale. Dad drove into the farmyard, met the owner and told him he was in the market for a good herd bull. As Dad outlined his needs to the stockman, their chat turned to exchanging pleasantries.

After a short interval the conversation turned to their families. Following an exchange or two the bull seller asked, "Mr. Gates do you have a family?"

"Yes, I guess you could say I have a family," Dad responded.

"How many children do you have?" the stockman continued in his friendly manner.

"Fifteen," Dad responded proudly.

The man with the bulls for sale grabbed Dad by the arm and rushed him toward the corral where the bulls were confined. "You don't need to be in such a hurry," Dad retorted as he was hastened across the farmyard, "I have plenty of time to look at the bulls."

"I don't care if you see the bulls or not," the bull breeder replied quickly, "I just want to make sure my breeding bulls see you!"

MISCHIEF THE EIGHTH

On one occasion Dad splurged and purchased Mischief the Eighth, a registered Hereford bull. The bull had been raised for show and was accustomed to being handled. Mischief was big and gentle, and, in addition to doing his duty as a bull, he was a real pet. He was completely approachable, in the pasture, the corrals or barns. In fact, if he was nearby, unless he had a cow on his mind, he would mosey over and rub you with his horns until you scratched his back. All of the kids played with him without fear, and the bigger kids crawled all over him. We tossed the little ones onto his back and he never seemed to mind. That bull was Mischief in name only.

Dad kept Mischief a bit longer than he usually kept bulls, in part because he was such a pet, but it eventually became time for him to take the trip to the auction yard. It was a hard time for all of us, little and big kids alike. When ole Mischief was loaded into the stock truck, we kids didn't know if he was destined for greener pastures filled with happy heifers or the hamburger joint filled with giggling girls and french fries.

PUTTING BLINDERS ON THE BULL

We once had another big Hereford bull whose behavior was much different than that of old Mischief. He wasn't mean but had an independent streak and little respect for fences. If he decided he wanted to be on the other side of the fence to smell the posies, because the grass was greener, or for any bull-only-knows reason, he lowered his head, walked up to the fence and keep walking. The fence creaked, a post or two snapped, the wires separated and the bull was where he wanted to be. There was always fence to be fixed on the farm, but that bull compounded the job.

He was a good quality bull, and Dad didn't want to get rid of him but did not relish the thought of continuing to fix the fences the bull tore down. Dad devised a workable solution even though it turned out to be difficult to implement. He decided to hang a blind from the horns of the bull that would cover his eyes when he held his head in the upright position. When the head was down the blind would tilt forward and the bull would be able to see to graze and drink. The blind would not interfere with his nose, which let him know the time and place for him to perform his primary duty.

For the blind, Dad removed a seat from an old implement setting in the farm machinery junk yard. Dad and the hired man put the bull in the barn, placed the lariat around his horns and secured him to a snubbing post. I was a curious bystander. This was an exciting event for me but the bull was not happy. When Dad began messing with its horns and head, the bull became agitated.

The bull thrashed around until the lariat broke. He stormed around the shed in the barn with the seat fastened to one horn, hanging over the side of his head covering one eye. Before Dad was able to restrain him, the bull had broken through a wall separating the shed from the horse barn and jumped into a hay manger where he became stuck. The bull kicked and struggled, blew snot and bellowed but could not free himself from the manger.

Dad was able to get another rope around the bull's horns and secured the head again, this time to a stanchion supporting the manger. Dad decided to complete the task of fastening the cover to the horns before trying to extract the bull from its predicament.

Finally, with the blinder in place, the big job was to get the bull out of the manger. Dad decided it would be simpler to lift the bull out than to dismantle and rebuild the manger. He and the hired man rigged a block and tackle to barn timbers above the manger. They managed to place ropes under the chest of the bull forming a sling which was then attached to the block and tackle. Utilizing the block and tackle they lifted the bull enough so that he could extricate himself from the manger. The bull was not free; he was still in the barn, but he was out of the manger. However, now when he held his head upright, the blinder covered his eyes and restricted his vision. With a bit of maneuvering, Dad managed to get the sling and remaining rope off the horns of the irritated if somewhat subdued bull.

The bull was returned to the herd with the implement seat, now bull blinder, hanging over his eyes. The procedure worked, and the bull seemed little the worse for wear. The blinder did not interfere with his primary duties, and he stopped walking through fences. I don't remember if Dad had a problem removing the blinder when the bull eventually headed for the hamburger plant via the auction yard.

SCRUB BULLS

Technically speaking, any adult male bovine creature with testicles intact could be called a bull. However, for someone interested in producing quality cattle, that definition leaves much to be desired. Some of the neighbors with pastures adjoining ours seemed to think that anything that could impregnate their cows was an acceptable bull. Dad's idea of what constituted a breeding bull was certainly not in agreement with theirs.

Dad had no problem with the quality of the neighbors' bulls as long as they stayed on their own side of the fence. However, if a scrub bull somehow got into our pasture when a cow was bulling (in heat) and bred her then that was a different matter.

We had neighbors whose pastures bordered ours on the south. They were good neighbors, but their ideas concerning quality cattle apparently differed greatly from Dad's. On several occasions their bulls, which Dad considered scrubs, showed up in our pasture. A cow in heat is a mighty strong attraction to quality and scrub bulls alike. A sniff of the breeze sometimes resulted in the scrub bulls breaching a fence that otherwise would be considered adequate. When a scrub bull was discovered in our pasture, one or two of us kids would get on the saddle horses, separate the ardorous, single minded critter from the herd and push it back into its own pasture. This was sometimes a difficult job as even a scrub bull responding to natural instincts can be difficult to handle. I remember two occasions when Dad tried alternative solutions to keep those bulls from our cows.

THE HIKEY SOLUTION

Dad always kept a bottle of "hikey" in the barn. Hikey was a foul smelling sulfuric liquid (carbon di-sulfide) that produced a severe burning sensation when applied to the hairy skin of an animal. The affect was short-lived, probably only a half minute or so, but properly administered would cause a rather violent reaction by the animal to which it was applied. The hikey did no permanent damage and except for a slight odor of sulfur was not detectable a few minutes after its use. Dad kept the hikey around mostly to put on stray dogs, but it also had other uses.

Dillard H. Gates

In one instance the neighbor's scrub bull had gotten into our pasture a couple of times, and we had pushed it back through the fence. The next day it was back so Dad grabbed the hikey bottle, mounted old Wrangler and headed to the pasture where the bull was courting a cow. He rode along side of the bull and poured a stream of hikey along its back. In a few seconds the scrub bull let out a mournful bellow and bent its body sideways almost into the form of a "U". It straightened out, continued to bellow and headed south. Only this time it did not head for the gate. Rather it hit the closest fence, head down at a dead run. Wires squeaked and posts snapped as the bull crashed through the fence trying to shed that fiery serpent from his back. Dad had a bit of fence fixing to do but that was the last time that bull breached the fence to smell the flowers in our pasture.

A SHOT IN THE SCROTUM SOLUTION

One Sunday Dad took Jack and me out to the pasture to look at the cattle and shoot a few prairie dogs. Dad had a little 22-caliber Remington automatic rifle that he always carried in the car. Dad taught both of us boys gun safety and how to shoot with that rifle. After we finished plinking a few prairie dogs, we drove on to see the cattle.

When we got to where the cattle were grazing there was another neighbor's scrub bull fraternizing with one of our cows which was in heat. This neighbor had similar quality standards for his cattle as did the owner of the hikeyed bull. We kids had returned that bull to its proper pasture several times in recent weeks, so Dad was slightly miffed when he saw it with our cows again. Dad had the rifle laying across his lap, with the barrel sticking out the car window, as he drove around the pasture.

Impulsively, Dad decided to subject this bull to a treatment that would make his stay in our pasture unpleasant but memorable. The size of a bull's scrotum is not a reflection of the quality of the bull. In this case a scrawny red bull had an exceptionally large bag hanging down from where it grew. Dad drove slowly through the cattle until he was in the correct position. The bull was standing still. The scrotum was fully exposed and no other animal was in the line of fire. Dad carefully took aim with the rifle and placed a 22 long rifle bullet directly in the testicles of that bull. The scrub bull stamped its foot like it had been bitten on the bag by a huge horse fly, let out a bellow and charged around through the cattle. After rushing around for a few minutes, it settled down but kept stamping its hind legs as if the pesky horse fly was continuing to bite.

Later in the day Dad saddled up old Wrangler, went out to the pasture and once again put the bull back through the fence where it belonged. I don't know if the shot in the scrotum dampened the bull's ardor, but he didn't come through the fence and into our pasture again.

MAKING A DEMOCRAT OUT OF A BULL

For a few years my older brother Hap lived on a farm up the river three or four miles northwest of us. He farmed, milked cows and raised a few beef cattle. He did have a few cows to breed but not enough to justify an investment in a bull. One solution would have been to transport our bull to Hap's farm when one of his cows was in heat. However, loading and transporting a big bull can be quite a chore even if the bull is gentle. So the decision was made to bring the cows to the bull.

Dad had a low-bed livestock trailer built to be pulled behind a car. When one of Hap's cows came in heat, he loaded her into the trailer and brought her to our bull. He pulled the trailer into the pasture where the bull was grazing, unloaded the cow and led or hazed her toward the bull. If the cow was ready, the bull took over and quickly did what he was supposed to do to earn his board and keep. Sometimes this would be accomplished shortly and Hap would load the cow back into the trailer and take her home. Other times, if the cow was not quite ready to take the bull, more time was required. Hap would leave the cow in the pasture then come back and pick her up later.

This procedure was repeated several times, and the bull apparently got the notion that anytime a car came into the pasture it was bringing goodies for him. He would come running over to the car looking for his "lady for the day." If a car was in the pasture even without a trailer, the bull followed it around, moaning low as if complaining about not getting that which he had come to expect.

After observing this phenomena a few times Dad told Hap that he was making a Democrat out of the bull. He went on to explain that the once hard working bull had become content to "stand around and bawl" until someone brought it to him rather than get out and hustle for himself.

COWS

Our cattle were reasonably gentle as they were handled often and were accustomed to people, little and big, on foot or on horseback. Dad was never concerned that the cows, or bulls for that matter, would bother us kids in the corrals or the pasture. The possible exception was when a cow had a new calf; she might threaten then if an intruder got too close to her calf.

THE WILD COW

Contrary to his usual procedures Dad bought a cow, from a local auction, that didn't meet his usual standards for cow behavior. The cow, a horned Hereford, if not wild was at least high-spirited. She didn't bother anyone out in the pasture where she had plenty of room, however, when confined in a corral she became down-right threatening.

Dad always said, "When an animal threatens, just stand still and it will not bother you." The advice may have been sound, but as a thirteen year old it was sometimes difficult to follow. The stand-still technique seemed to work alright for Dad, but then he had the courage of his convictions.

Hay, Hell, Kids and Cattle

One day we had around fifty head of cattle, including the wild one, in the slab working-corral. Dad was culling out non-productive cows to take to the livestock auction.

Dad moved through the herd on foot trying to separate the barren cows from the other cattle. A hired man, Cap Ward, and I were in the corral between the herd and the partially open gate. Dad selected a cow from the herd and then pushed it past Cap and me and out the open gate. As the cattle milled around in the corral the wild one would occasionally find her way to the edge of the herd. If Cap or I was close-by, she would stop, lower her head, stamp her feet and blow snot. Her actions seemed a lot more threatening to Cap and me than to Dad.

Noticing our concern Dad would call out, "Stand still, don't move and she won't bother you." After a brief stare-down, the wild cow would give up or be jostled by the other cows and rejoin the milling herd.

This freeze and look-um-in-the-eye technique worked on several occasions. Cap and I listened to the guidance provided by Dad and managed to stand our ground. Then the wild cow moved to the edge of the herd again. I don't know if my courage left me, or if I was suddenly reminded of the old adage, "Discretion is the better part of valor."

Even a full bucket can be emptied by a continuous slow drip. My courage bucket had about dripped dry. My feet would no longer stand still. I panicked, whirled, and took off, my body trying to keep up with my feet. I was only a step ahead of the wild cow as I passed through the partially open gate and lunged aside. The wild cow, followed by the rest of the herd, poured through the gate into the barnyard. I lay on the ground where I had fallen, watching the cattle rush past, contemplating what Dad was going to say. I pondered the alternatives. After the fact I wondered if a butt by the cow have been any worse than what I expected from Dad.

Dad followed the last cow through the open gate. The running cattle had blocked me from his view and he was concerned about my welfare. Dad saw me prostrate on the ground, covered by dust kicked up by the running cattle but otherwise unharmed.

I rolled over and wiped the dust from my eyes as he questioned gruffly , "Are you alright, Dill?"

When I replied in the affirmative, he grabbed me by the arm, stood me on my feet, gave me a boot in the seat of my pants, and retorted, "You're lucky this isn't the head of that cow hitting you in the butt. One more step and she would of had you. You can't outrun a cow. Next time do as I tell you. Now get on the horse, round up the cattle, and put them back in the corral."

I got on ole Wrangler and headed after the cattle relieved to have gotten off so easy. Certainly Dad's kick in the rear end was not as bad as what I could have gotten from the cow. But maybe if I had heeded Dad's advice, if I had stood my ground, I would have received neither. As I kicked Wrangler in the sides with my heels and guided him around the cattle I felt lucky but also that I had let my father down.

It wasn't long before the cattle were back in the corral. Dad pulled my saddle off the horse and replaced it with his own. He grabbed his lariat and crawled on Wrangler. He rode into the herd, selected a barren cow and dropped the loop over her head. As he eased her from the herd, Cap swung the big gate open. Dad half pulled, half herded the cow from the corral into the barnyard, then slipped the rope from her neck and released her. The process was repeated until all the cull cows were separated from the herd.

I peered through the rough boards of the slab corral, away from the wild cow, and watched as Dad skillfully sorted the cattle. I marveled at Dad's confidence as he guided Wrangler through the herd and the apparent ease with which he dropped the lariat over the head of each cow selected. Dad wasn't a cowboy. He didn't even wear boots, but he was a good stockman and he knew cattle.

I stood on the safe side of the fence, and I continued to mull over the message Dad had implanted into my mind and reenforced with the toe of his shoe to my behind, "Stand your ground, Dill, don't run." I didn't realize it at the time but Dad was not only teaching me how to handle cattle, he was preparing me for the realities of life far beyond the cattle corral.

THE WILD COW AND THE BILLY GOAT

The wild cow had to go. Dad finally accepted the fact that she might hurt someone and decided to take her to the auction. The herd of about fifty head was run into a corral so the wild cow could run through the cutting gate and be isolated. She was to be held in the smaller slab corral until she was loaded into the trailer for the trip to the slaughter house.

During this same period, "Snowball," the nanny goat, needed to be bred if she was to continue giving milk. A neighbor, Jesse Swick, had a billy goat which we borrowed as needed to breed Snowball.

The billy was a long-haired, smelly, brown goat with two big curled horns. He was gentle and was no bother to have around as long as he remained downwind. Since the neighbor had no particular use for the billy goat, we sometimes did not return him promptly after he had finished his billy goat duties. Despite his smell Snowball seemed to enjoy having another goat for company. Dad had decided to return the billy goat to Jesse and had put him in the slab corral until one of us kids could take him home.

The billy goat was standing in the middle of the corral when we ran the wild cow in and closed the gate. The billy and the wild cow saw one another about the same time. The cow hesitated for only a moment then lowered her head and charged. The goat met her with lowered horns and they collided, head to head, in the middle of the corral. The impact sent him rolling.

The old billy probably weighed no more than one hundred fifty to one hundred seventy-five pounds. The wild cow probably weighed around one thousand pounds. The billy goat was outweighed, but he had spirit. The cow backed off, blew snot, stamped her feet, shook her head and charged again. The goat once more met her head on and this time remained on his feet. The billy goat held his position in the center of the corral. The cow circled then charged again. The billy was doing well despite his weight disadvantage and held his own for several charges.

We were peering through the fence and all cheering for the goat. We were hoping that despite the odds somehow he would defeat the wild cow that had been nothing but grief to us. However, on a final charge they again met head to head and the impact broke off one of the billy goat's horns right at the juncture with the skull. The rancid smelling old warrior with the fighting heart must have decided that if he was to live to fight another day he had better seek refuge. He backed away from the fracas and jumped into the feed rack in the corner of the corral out of reach of his oversized, enraged and undoubtedly confused opponent.

Animal fights were a diversion from kid fights, and we encouraged them whenever we had a chance if Dad wasn't around. Despite the size differential in the combatants, this was one of the best fights I had ever witnessed. I wonder if that wild cow was still trying to figure out what that stinky, hard headed thing in the corral was, right up to the time she was struck down by a blow from the poling axe in the slaughter house.

THE PROTECTIVE COW WITH THE NEW CALF

Mother cows are not necessarily ornery but may become very aggressive in defense of a perceived danger to their calf. There was a large oat-straw stack about a quarter mile south, plainly visible from the farmyard. Dad had been feeding the cattle hay in the forty acre field during the late winter, early spring period.

One wet, cold, misty morning Dad looked across the field to the south. He spotted a cow with a hump in her back standing in the shelter of the straw stack. The cow was one he noticed was heavy with calf while feeding the cattle the previous day. He called to Jack and me and told us to walk down to the straw stack to see if she had calved and if she was alright.

The weather was miserable. Jack and I pulled on our overshoes and bundled up in heavy, warm coats and headed across the muddy, slush-covered field to do Dad's bidding.

As we walked around the straw stack, we spotted a calf lying in the litter with the cow standing nearby. The cow spotted us about the same time we saw her and without warning lowered her head and charged. We both managed to side-step the cow. Her charge carried her past us about ten yards before she stopped and turned about. The cow faced us with head down ready to charge the first one that moved. There Jack and I stood, eyeing the cow, both aware of Dad's past admonitions to,"Stand still and she won't hurt you." We were both sure the cow would charge if we moved. After a few moments hesitation, I told Jack I would make a move so the cow would charge me. Based upon my performance a few moments ago, I was confident I could dodge her again. When the cow charged me Jack was to run a few steps in the direction of the house then stop and stand still.

I took a step toward the house and the cow charged. Once again I side-stepped the cow, and as planned Jack ran a few steps and stopped. Now it was Jack's turn to attract the charge of the cow and my turn to run a few steps toward safety. It worked. Jack also safely avoided the charge of the cow.

The cow's bloodline was not that of a Spanish fighting bull nor were Jack and I matadors, but we were playing a serious game. Jack and I were alternately attracting then dodging the cow, leap-frogging our way homeward. The cow remained defiant, but appeared to be tiring. Jack and I wondered how long our luck would hold. After what seemed ages to us we saw Dad coming across the field with a team and wagon. He drove the wagon between the cow and us and we climbed aboard.

Dad related to us that he had been watching the performance for some time but had waited to see how we would solve the problem. He praised us for doing a good job but added, "If that cow had not been so weak from calving you may have not been so lucky."

Dillard H. Gates

HORSES

My dad liked good horses. The decade of the thirties was a transitional period on the farm during which horses were being replaced by tractors as the primary power source. However, as tractors were being phased in there was a continuing need for horses. In fact it was not uncommon to utilize horses to pull out a tractor that had become stuck in the mud, sand, or snow.

As a little guy I recall that although we had a Farmall tractor horses were an essential source of power for feeding cattle, threshing, picking corn, fixing fences, cultivating corn, transportation, feeding cattle and a myriad of other jobs. In the summer most of the stalls in the barn were full of work horses. What a wonderful experience it was to walk down the alleyway of the barn and see, hear, and smell the horses in their stalls with mangers full of hay and grain in the feed boxes.

This changed gradually, and by the time my father died in 1941 we had only a couple teams of horses, plus a saddle horse and ole Wrangler. As the number of horses on the farm declined, Dad's concern for quality seemed to increase. If he was to have only a team or so, at least they were going to be good ones. His teams were well broke and he liked to drive and show them off at every opportunity.

BREAKING HORSES

Dad was an excellent horseman. He took great pride in his ability to take a wild or green horse, break it to work and teach it to pull. It took skill, time and patience to break a horse to perform the many and varied jobs expected of it. It was especially difficult to teach a horse to pull a heavy load without balking.

Time permitting, Dad was deliberate in his approach to breaking horses. He would first break it to lead with the rope, then the halter. He would tie it in the barn for a day or so where there was a manger full of hay. While the horse was tied, he would begin to slowly and carefully rub his hands over the horse's body from head to tail, from the back to the fetlocks. As the horse became accustomed to this treatment, Dad would break out the curry comb. Over the course of a day or so he would curry and brush the horse repeatedly. The horse would normally respond positively to the handling. Soon it would allow Dad to touch it anywhere and liked the attention and the currying. Depending on the amount of time available, Dad then liked to place the harness on the horse and let it stand tied in the barn or outside for a day or so. In this way the horse became accustomed to the feel and the noise of the harness.

The next phase was hitching the unbroken horse to the wagon. The green horse was always first hitched with an older experienced horse. For several years we had a old mare, Brownie. She was big, gentle, reliable, experienced and a good teacher of young horses. When Brownie was hitched with the horse to be broken Dad knew she would control the colt.

When a green horse was first hitched to a wagon, Dad's technique was to let them run if it wanted to, and most of them did. Thus, Brownie and the new horse would be hitched to our flat wagon out in the field where there was room to run. Normally Dad would have my older brother, Hap, or a hired man help control the colt and get the horses hitched.

Once the horses were hitched Dad would climb aboard the flat wagon with the reins in his hands. He would holler to whomever was holding the bridle of the colt, "Turn um loose."

Usually the green horse took off on the run with Brownie hitched beside keeping pace. Most of the time the new horse didn't run far before beginning to tire. As it tired Dad would snap it on the rear end with the end of the reins, urging it to run more. Dad would also urge ole Brownie to keep going, sometimes practically dragging the now tired and reluctant colt. Generally, after the colt had time to get its breath back it would make another attempt to run. Each time Dad let it run then whipped it on the butt end when it tired and wanted to rest.

Usually after about a half hour of this run and stop exercise, the new horse was covered with lather and ready to settle down, walk beside ole Brownie, tighten the tugs, and begin to pull the wagon. After an hour or so, when the new horse was about exhausted, Dad would stop the team for a rest. After a few sessions on the wagon under the tutelage of ole Brownie, the new horse was ready to be hitched to a piece of machinery and go to work. If hitched with good experienced horses, the green horse learned quickly and within a day or so became a productive member of the team.

Dad especially liked to take his time if the horses being broken were destined to become his personal team. However, on many occasions time was short and an additional horse or two was needed. In such cases the horse-breaking procedure was cut short. For the horse it was sometimes a quick transition from green pastures and running free to the harness, a heavy load, sweat, and discipline.

Sometimes a wild or green horse would be roped, snubbed down, harnessed, and hitched directly to the flat wagon with ole Brownie or another experienced lead horse. Often this turned out to be somewhat of a wildwest show as the green horse fought against his tormentors every step of the way. We kids watched the exhibition from the safe perch of a hay rack or other piece of equipment setting nearby.

As a little boy I found breaking horses was thrilling. In addition, whenever possible I liked to get involved. On several occasions while Dad was getting the green horse and ole Brownie hitched for the first time, he would tell me to climb up on the flat wagon, sit down, and wait. When he climbed onto the wagon with the reins in his hands and braced himself in preparation for the run, I clambered to my feet, put my arms tight around his leg and held on for dear life. It was a rough and bumpy ride as the wagon bounced across the field with Dad hollering and urging the horses on. I was exhilarated as I stood there holding on tightly, with my cheek pressed against the rough denim overalls. I felt safe and secure because I was with Dad.

DAD'S PERSONAL TEAMS

BUNK and TRAP

When I was eleven or twelve we were in need of an additional team of horses. Dad attended livestock auctions, and visited individual farmers with good, young, unbroken horses for sale. He finally found, at different locations, two steel-grays, a mare and a gelding, that looked like they would make a great matched pair. The gelding seemed to be a bit more spirited than did the mare, but Dad thought the disposition of each was acceptable. Dad liked short, distinct names for his horses so he called the mare Bunk and the gelding Trap.

They were still too young to break so Dad kept them around the barnyard for a few months. During that period he worked with and handled them as often as possible. He broke them to lead and to the halter. He rubbed, combed and curried them until they were completely gentle. He harnessed them in the mornings and let them stand in the barn for days with the harness on.

It was anti-climatic when it was finally time to hitch them to the flat wagon for the first time. There was no show; they did not run. They thrashed about a bit until they determined what was expected of them, then settled down quickly.

After each had a short session with ole Brownie in charge, they were hitched together as a team. From then on, it was just a matter of continuing to teach them what to do. They were gentle, dependable, good workers and became a great team.

While Bunk and Trap were Dad's team, they were also an important part of the power source for the farm. They were the main team used for most of the routine chores around the farm. The word got around about the great team of matched greys owned by Howe Gates. On several occasions a potential buyer would stop by the farm and ask Dad if the team was for sale. Times were tough and money was short, but Dad said, "No, not for the price offered."

When the horses were being worked, they would be brought into the barn, fed grain and hay after the work was finished. Depending on the season and the weather, they would be turned out to the pasture in the evening. One of the pastures frequently used for the work horses was just across the road south of the farmyard.

In the evening after the horses had cleaned up their grain and had a chance to get at least a partial fill of alfalfa hay from their mangers, Dad would send us kids down to turn them into the pasture. We untied their halter ropes from the manger stanchion, led the horses across the road to the pasture, removed their halters, and released them. This procedure worked well for us kids until Trap began to display some of his spirited disposition. When we had the horses through the pasture gate and reached up to unsnap the throat-latch of the halter Trap would throw up his head, spin and take off on the run, jerking the halter rope from our hands. With halter rope dragging Trap would race to the backside of the pasture. Generally when we rounded up the horses the following morning, the halter rope would be trampled to shreds.

This went on several times with my older sisters, Gee and Sis, and with me. Dad thought it was just kids and was getting tired of replacing halter ropes. One evening Gee asked Dad to watch from a distance as she took the horses to the pasture. Sure enough, when Gee reached up to undo the halter, Trap pulled the same old trick and left her standing there gaping as he charged across the pasture. That convinced Dad it was the behavior of his prize horse, not that of the kids, causing the problem. He thought he had a solution.

There was a roll of one-inch rope in the barn remaining from times past when a hay fork was used to store hay in the mow. The next day Dad took about seventy-five feet of the rope and secured one end to the base of the gate post leading into the pasture. He formed a loop in the other end that could be easily slipped over Trap's head then quickly tightened. That evening, accompanied by Dad, I lead Bunk and Trap across the road to the pasture gate.

As I opened the gate Dad gently slipped the loop around Trap's neck and secured it snugly high on the neck next to his head. With Dad at my side I reached up to release Trap's halter. As usual, Trap threw up his head, whirled and started to run. Dad slapped him on the back and let out a yell as he passed by with the halter rope dragging and the big rope uncoiling behind. Trap was going at full speed when he came to the end of the rope. The rope pulled taunt and he let out a moan as he was jerked from his feet, stretched full length and landed full on his back. For a moment he lay there dazed then scrambled to his feet. Dad slid his hand along the big rope and approached Trap. He took him by the halter rope and led him back to the gate. Once again he told me to try to remove Trap's halter. Once again Trap bolted and hit the end of the rope, but this time with less force than the first. Again Dad led Trap back to the gate and the process was repeated. After the third or fourth run, Trap had enough. When Dad led him back to the gate again, the subdued horse let me remove his halter and in addition refused to move. Dad finally removed the rope from around Trap's neck, but still he wouldn't move. We finally took the halter and rope back to the barn and left him with head down, standing by the gate. I don't know how long he stood there, afraid to move, before he joined the rest of the horses.

The next morning when the horses were brought in from the pasture we noticed that Trap's neck was swollen and bruised from the rope. Dad was now concerned that he may have done serious and maybe permanent damage to one of his prize horses. From then on when taken to pasture, ole Trap stood gently until his halter was removed before making any attempt to walk away. The horse had learned a painful lesson. As it turned out the lesson turned out to be temporarily painful to Dad as well.

A horse buyer, who had previously made an unsatisfactory offer for the team, returned and said he was now prepared to meet Dad's asking price of four hundred dollars. The offer now was contingent upon the dissipation of the swelling on the neck and the complete recovery of Trap.

After a couple weeks the swelling in Trap's neck disappeared completely. One day the horse buyer showed up at the farm to claim his purchase. With a feeling of sadness we all bid the team farewell. Financially the sale had been a good move. However, without a prize team around Dad was as nervous as a bull Durham smoker with an empty tobacco sack. In a few days Dad was back in the market looking for another pair of young horses he could build into a team.

Dillard H. Gates

PET and FOX

Dad once again was fortunate enough to find two steel grays that appeared to have the potential for becoming the kind of horses he coveted. This team also consisted of a mare and a gelding. Consistent with his naming criteria he called them Pet and Fox.

Dad utilized the same slow, deliberate training process for Pet and Fox as he had with Bunk and Trap. They were beautiful animals, gentle, docile, and easy to handle. When fully trained they were unsurpassed in the community as pullers. They would lean slowly into the traces and move loads that would leave other teams floundering.

Like the other team, Pet and Fox made up the primary team for routine chores around the farm. When pulling heavy loads, Dad would stop the team periodically to let them blow and have a short rest. Then with a cluck of his tongue and a shake of the reins followed by, "Gidup," they would tighten the tugs and move on. The team became spoiled and sometimes even when pulling an empty or lightly loaded wagon would stop for a breather. Dad humored the team and most of the time as they would rest only a brief period and then, without coaxing, move on.

One wintry Saturday afternoon when I was thirteen or fourteen Dad and I hitched Pet and Fox to the hay rack and headed up the road toward the hay field to get a load of alfalfa to feed the cattle. A neighbor, Henry Worth, lived about a half mile north of Gates on the east side of the road. His house was just a short distance from the gate into the alfalfa field to which we were heading. As we came broadside of Henry's house, he has standing in his yard. He called to Dad to come in for a few minutes as he had business to talk about. Pet and Fox were broke to stand so Dad pulled the hay rack to the side of the road, stopped and wrapped the lines around the hitch-pole in the front of the rack. We climbed down from the rack and crawled through the fence into Henry's yard. Since it was chilly Henry suggested we step into the house.

What Dad had intended to be a few minutes turned into a better part of an hour. When Dad and I left the house we noted that the horses and hay rack were gone. Dad figured the team had rested a few minutes and then without urging had gone through the gate into the alfalfa field and over to the hay stack where Dad had gotten several loads of hay before. The ground was frozen so tracks of the horses or the hay rack were not readily evident.

Dad told me to run over to the hay stack to see if by chance the team and rack were out of site behind the hay stack. I climbed through the fence to the hay field and jogged over to the stack. The horses were not there so I headed back to where Dad was waiting for me, but this time I planned to exit through the gate rather than climb back through the fence. As I approached the gate I noticed what looked like wagon tracks in the alfalfa stubble. It appeared the tracks went through the gate, made a big circle and then back through the gate. Once back on the hard frozen road the tracks disappeared.

Dad looked at the tracks and concluded I was correct. He then assumed the horses had rested sufficiently after we left them standing and moved on. They had successfully pulled the hay rack through the gate into the field and back again from the field into the road. From there the team must have gone back up the road toward home.

Henry suggested we get in his car and he would help us locate the horses. He drove us back to our place and sure enough there stood Pet and Fox in front of the barn waiting patiently. There appeared to be no damage to the horses or to the hay rack. It was getting late in the afternoon by then, but Dad and I crawled into the hay rack and headed back to the hay field. Dad pitched on enough hay to feed the cattle

Sunday morning and in the dark, with a short load, we returned home. Dad concluded that this was a team that took care of itself.

The following summer Dad was doing custom threshing in a community several miles east of Gates. For some reason one of the farmers in the threshing crew was short a team and bundle rack. He asked Dad if he could borrow Pet and Fox and a bundle rack for a few days. Normally Dad would not have loaned his prize team to anyone. However, in this case he knew Temp Wycoff was a good horseman and would handle the team properly.

There was a small creek separating the grain field and the threshing machine site. It was not a problem, but the loaded bundle racks had to be pulled across the creek to get to the thresher. On his first trip with Pet and Fox, Temp loaded the bundle rack, climbed on top of the load and headed for the thresher. As the team crossed the creek the bundle rack surged forward slightly and momentarily stopped with the front wheels in the bottom. The team moved ahead but as the traces tightened they stopped. Temp's first thought was, "My God, this is Howe's team and I have balked them." He sat on the load for a minute and decided he better call Dad before any damage was done to the team. He wrapped the lines around the hitching-pole and prepared to climb down. As he swung his legs over the front of the bundle rack, Pet and Fox leaned into the traces and without a sound from Temp moved the load on across the creek and up the trail toward the thresher.

Temp was amazed but delighted. What he had at first thought was going to be a bad situation turned out to be no problem at all. Ole Pet and Fox apparently thought they had picked a good place to rest. Following their usual procedure, after a short breather they moved on without urging.

When Temp reached the thresher and was waiting his turn to unload he related the incident to Dad. He said he had trained a lot of horses but that was the first team he had driven that selected its own time-outs and then ended them without goading.

Pet and Fox continued to be Dad's pride and joy around the farm for a couple of years. Then as was the case with Bunk and Trap, a horse buyer came along looking for a well-broke team of matched grays. He had an order from a client in the east who wanted such a team for his showplace farm. Following a period of negotiation, the buyer agreed to the price of five hundred dollars for the team.

Once more we all watched as a prized team was loaded into a stock truck and disappeared down the road. We hoped they would have a good home and be as special to the new owner as they had been to Dad. We were saddened but realized this was the way things were on the farm. We raised animals to use, for food, and to sell. Even so, in the process some of the animals became more than economic assets. But we lived and learned. Even members of the family did not stay with us forever.

OLE DUKE, THE WEAK LEGGED STALLION

Dad's love for good horses was not limited to his working teams. Maybe if resources had been available he would have been a horse collector, so that he could be surrounded by, train and admire the beautiful creatures.

It was around 1938 or 39 that Dad attended a horse sale in Broken Bow and saw a young, strawberry roan stallion he could not resist. We didn't have enough mares to justify the costs and problems of keeping a stallion around, but to Dad's eyes this was a beautiful animal with the potential to develop into a great stud horse. Maybe Dad envisioned lots of strawberry roan colts in the neighborhood. Regardless of the rationale, Dad brought the young stallion home.

The stallion was still too immature for stud service. We kept him in the barn or barnyard corral where he was curried, rubbed, combed and broke to the halter. As he matured he was also trained to respond to the special halter used to control a stud horse. Ole Duke soon developed into a real pet. We kids, even the little ones, would crawl all over him. We rode him around the corral and the barnyard. He would follow us around and nuzzle us with his nose attempting to get someone to rub him behind the ears. In addition to developing into a big, beautiful animal he became a favorite of the family. As Duke matured he too was kept in the slab corral. He was used to breed our mares, and Dad put him up for stud and he serviced a few mares in the community. By this time I was considered big and mature enough to assist in the process.

Handling a stallion in contact with a mare in heat and intent only on what comes naturally is a difficult job. Handling the mare is less difficult, but she too must be controlled properly to prevent injury to either of the animals. Dad always assumed the responsibility for handling the stud and my job was to control the mare. Sometimes, as the horses became excited in the heat of the moment, it was difficult for a scrawny fourteen or fifteen year old kid. My incentives for doing the job were two-fold. First I wanted to demonstrate that I could do the job. I was also fascinated by the breeding process of these two large animals.

As Duke matured and demands for his stud service increased, problems developed. The first symptoms were that Duke seemed to have problems supporting himself on his rear legs. Sometimes as he reared to mount a mare, his back legs would buckle and he would fall to the ground. The problem increased and ole Duke would sometimes stumble backwards and end up setting on his rear haunches like a dog. The local vet diagnosed an incurable back problem. A stud horse that cannot support himself on his hind legs is to paraphrase Mom, "About as worthless as a whip socket on an automobile." Duke's days as a stud horse were over.

The condition of ole Duke was paradoxical. He was now worthless as a stud, or anything else, but he was a big loveable pet. Dad knew Duke's condition would continue to deteriorate. While he agonized over the fact, he could not bring himself to destroy the animal that by now had captured the hearts and sympathy of the entire family. This was surprising as normally Dad was pragmatic, if not cold or dispassionate, in his analysis and solution of problems, especially those involving animals.

While Duke was having his health problems so was Dad. Maybe that had something to do with his feeling toward ole Duke. In the late summer of 1940 he made arrangements to go to the Mayo Brother's Clinic for a check up and treatment. Just before he got in the car to head for Rochester, Minnesota, he called me aside. As he looked me in the eyes, he said to me in an almost apologetic tone, "Dill, take care of ole Duke before I get back."

Uncharacteristically, Dad had shifted an unpleasant burden from his shoulders to mine. Maybe it was his way of testing me to determine if I was capable of carrying out a difficult task. I didn't know why he left the job for me. I only knew that somehow I had to get it done.

A few days after Dad left for Mayo's, I got out the 12-gauge automatic shotgun, put a couple of shells in my pocket and asked Jack to accompany me as I headed for the barn. I was familiar with the gun as Dad had instructed me how to use it properly. I recalled my enjoyment as Dad had taught me to shoot and my elation when I was finally able to bring down a pheasant, but I was not elated now nor did I anticipate enjoyment from the task before me. I propped the shotgun against the side of the barn and with some hesitation entered ole Duke's stall. I untied the halter rope from the hitching post and lead him slowly outside to the front of the barn.

Jack was doing his best to keep back the tears as I handed him the halter rope and asked him to try to hold ole Duke's head still. I reluctantly inserted a shell into the chamber of the 12-gauge and took my place directly in front of the unknowing and trustful friend that had brought pleasure to me and others in the family. He was condemned, not for anything he had done but as a result of an unknown and incurable malady.

I had seen Dad shoot old, emaciated or injured horses before, but for the most part they were animals to which I had no emotional attachment. I knew what had to be done and how to do it, but this was different. Jack grasped the halter rope as he stood beside me and I laboriously raised the 12-gauge to my shoulder. This time it did not feel like the light, well balanced, instrument which on previous occasions I had quickly brought to my shoulder and easily swung toward the target as a pheasant flushed from the weeds. That shotgun now weighed a ton. Ole Duke's head loomed above me. I sighted up the barrel to a spot on his forehead where imaginary lines extending from the base of each ear to the eye on the opposite side of the head would cross. The intersection of the imaginary lines fell in the center of a white blaze that adorned the forehead of ole Duke. I took a deep breath and held the gun on target as steady as possible. As I squeezed the trigger I prayed that somehow ole Duke would understand.

As the gunshot echoed from the side of the barn Ole Duke crumpled to the ground in front of my brother and me. Jack stood there still grasping the halter rope in his shaking hand as tears rolled down his cheeks. I propped the shotgun, smelling of gun smoke, against the side of the barn and slumped down beside it. We had little time to reflect on our sorrow or our misery. Ole Duke was on the ground before us, but our job was not finished.

We had been raised to not waste or discard anything of value. A good horse hide was worth a few dollars, and dollars were scarce. Actually we were not sure whether we would sell Duke's hide or have it tanned. We had two or three horsehide robes on beds in the house. These robes were a source of comfort in cold weather and reminders of other horses which had served the family well in the past.

Jack and I sharpened the knives and began the laborious job of skinning Ole Duke. It was a difficult task for us. We both were emotionally drained and not big or strong enough to handle the massive carcass of the fallen stallion. We had both helped Dad skin animals before but this was the first time for us to do the job by ourselves. We got the skin off one side and then utilized the Farmall tractor to turn the carcass over so we could get at the other. When the skin was removed we stretched it out on the ground and salted it thoroughly. We then rolled it, secured it with binder twine and put it in the granary to await Dad's decision for disposal. We later tied a chain around the hind legs of the carcass, hooked it to the Farmall and dragged it the quarter-mile to the hog pen. Ole Duke's final, but inglorious, contribution to the welfare of the family was to serve as feed for the hogs.

This was an ignoble end for what had been a true and faithful friend. It was also a difficult and stressful undertaking for two scrawny boys, thirteen and fifteen years old, who inadvertently were being forced to shoulder the mantle of men.

SADDLE HORSES

Saddle horses were an absolute necessity around the farm. It would be more appropriate to refer to them as riding than saddle horses as kids and adults rode bareback as often as with a saddle. A primary characteristic of a riding horse around our place was gentleness. The horse had to be even tempered and tolerant of kids, but in addition it had to perform effectively under a myriad of conditions. Depending upon circumstances it served as a cutting horse, a roping horse, a race horse, a recreational vehicle or merely a form of transportation. And it had to have the ability to adapt quickly. Dad might step down from the saddle following a spirited and quick paced session cutting out cattle, grab up one of the kids standing nearby and plant it firmly in the saddle with instructions to carry out a menial chore requiring a calm and gentle horse.

All of the kids liked to ride. With only one or two riding horses and lots of kids around, the horses were kept busy, especially during the summer months. Our riding horses, with kids stacked on their backs from the neck to tail, were common sights around the Gates community.

Dad tossed my brothers and sisters, while still in diapers, onto the back of the riding horses in front of one of the bigger kids as they learned to ride. As the kids got bigger they sat behind, with arms clutching the more experienced rider in front of them. By the time we kids were three or four, we were accustomed to riding alone. In another couple of years we were assigned riding jobs. We brought in the milk cows, took the water jug to the men in the field or ran errands for Dad or the hired men.

And we rode just for the fun of it. Riding a horse was second nature to all of us. It was about as common as walking, a skill most of us learned subsequent to our first having forked a horse.

A major problem to overcome when I was a little kid was how to mount a horse. If an adult was around he might grab me up and slap me onto the horse's back or when I was a little bigger he might grab my foot and give me a boost. Otherwise it was necessary to find some object, such as a wagon, a box, or a wooden gate I could crawl upon and from that scramble onto the horse's back.

I wondered if I would ever get big enough to get on the horse by myself. I remember grasping the mane of the horse and trying to pull myself up so I could throw my right leg over the back of the horse. Finally I was able to jump up, hook my left elbow over the horse's neck, then swing my right foot up and over the horse's back. Then using a few crab-like moves I was able to struggle aboard. Being able to get on the horse unassisted was a "right of passage" which gave me an additional sense of freedom. With this new found skill I could now move on to more advanced stages of testing my wings.

Dad had a full sized-saddle he generally used when riding. However, he thought it safer for kids to ride bareback so we could not get tangled in the stirrups or straps that were part of the saddle. In addition, the big saddle was too heavy and cumbersome for little kids to lift to the back of a horse.

When I was around ten Dad brought home a nearly new kids' saddle which he had purchased at auction. From then on, except for short rides, we used the saddle a good share of the time. A problem of riding bareback, especially on hot days or for long distances, was the horse's sweat. After riding bareback for a while, we would be wet with sweat and covered with horse hair from the seat of the pants to the knees. The sweat was accompanied by the smell of the horse. We kids did not notice the smell of the horse and sweat, but some others did.

Dad or one of the other adults rode the riding horses on occasion when the job demanded it. However, for the most part riding was done by one of the kids. There were kids of all ages around, and Dad did not discriminate between boys and girls. When there was a job to be done, he signaled the most visible kid, that was big enough, and told them to get at it.

OLE SNORT

Ole Snort was the first riding horse I remember. He was a big bay with a white blaze. Snort was a dual purpose horse. That is that he was broke to work as well as to ride.

Snort had been around for some years prior to my earliest memories. Dad liked to ride him as Dad was a big man and Snort had the size to carry him. Mom didn't ride often, but she thought Snort was about the best horse ever to put his nose in a feed box.

Despite his size, he was very gentle and good with kids. Reputedly, if someone fell from his back he would freeze in his tracks so as not to step on them. My older sisters, Anna, Alice, and Gee rode him regularly. Undoubtedly I had been tossed on his back in front of one of my sisters while I was still in diapers.

I remember Gee learning to ride standing on Snort's back, even at gallop. She was a good and daring rider. She fell off occasionally as she was learning but was never injured.

Snort remained on our farm for years after we had acquired another riding horse. He continued to be used for both work and riding until, against the protests of Mom and the older girls, Dad sold him to a neighbor, Temp Wycoff.

OLE WRANGLER

I could have been no more than six years old when I first saw ole Wrangler. Anna and Alice were still at home, and they didn't run off until the summer of 1932 when I was seven.

At the breakfast table one Sunday morning, Dad was telling about a new, green-broke riding horse he had bought at the livestock auction in Broken Bow the day before. He had a neighbor truck the horse home the night before and it was now tied in a stall in the barn. He said the horse was called a hot-blood, then went on to explain what the term hot-blood meant.

In the thirties the horse calvary was still a part of the U. S. Army. The calvary was always in need of good horses. Thus, it had a program of making hot-blood stallions available, with no stud fee, to breed mares meeting certain quality and size requirements. The hot-blood was a spirited horse similar in size and conformation to the quarter horse. They were not big horses but were tough and reported to be intelligent and easy to train. The offspring of these matings were to provide a pool of high quality horses from which the calvary could select and purchase replacements as required.

He further related to the kids around the table that we should stay away from the new horse until he had time to gentle it to the stage where children were safe around it. Dad then noted that Anna and Alice were not present at the breakfast table. He asked Mom if she had seen the girls this morning. Mom related she had heard them earlier in the morning but didn't know where they were now.

After breakfast Dad took us down to the barn to have a look at his new purchase. When he swung open the barn door he saw that the new horse was gone and his halter was hanging from the hitching rack. The bridle used for saddle horses was gone from its peg on the wall, but a milk bucket was hanging on another peg nearby. It was then Dad realized that not only was the new horse gone but Anna and Alice were gone as well. Dad was not the excitable type. He decided the best thing to do was to wait awhile to see if the girls and the new horse showed up.

Before very long the new horse with Anna and Alice astride, riding bareback, came galloping around the corner of the granary and into the barnyard. With legs and arms flopping and hair stringing in the breeze, they were urging him on. Dad uttered a sigh of relief as they pulled the horse to a stop in front of him.

Out of breath and both talking at once, they tried to tell Dad what had happened. As it turned out, after getting out of bed they decided to slip out to the barn and milk the cows before breakfast, something they rarely did without urging. They saw the new horse in the barn and not knowing it was unsafe had slipped on the bridle, led him from the barn and climbed aboard. They related he had pranced around a bit at first but they soon had him under control and out on the road. They then headed west and rode the four miles around the square.

The square was a section of land (640 acres) bounded by county roads and in local vernacular was known as the square. Our farmstead was located near the south-eastern corner of the section.

One of the girls had just finished reading a Zane Gray novel in which there was a hero horse called Wrangler. She thought Wrangler would be a good name for the newly acquired steed. The name was too long to suit Dad, but he agreed if that's what they wanted he would go along with it. Wrangler became a permanent, reliable, and loved part of the Gates barnyard family.

Needless to say, Dad did not have to spend much time gentling the horse. The older girls and my big brother, Hap, rode Wrangler to gather the cattle, do chores and for recreation. He soon allowed kids to be piled on his back from head to tail.

Dad worked with Wrangler and trained him to cut cattle and serve as a roping horse. Wrangler was a horse of many talents. He could carry Dad into a herd of cattle, sort out a selected critter and move it from the herd. With the rope around the saddle horn he could drag a calf to the branding or working area. He would also put up with the kids on his back or under his feet. I guess he was a horse of the moment. He met the criterion of being able to adapt quickly from a hard working, spirited cow-horse to a gentle and docile kid-horse.

A LOOSE CINCH AND A CACTUS PATCH

Sometimes when Dad was in town Jack and I liked to engage in activities we would not have considered had he been present. One Saturday afternoon we decided to play cowboy.

I saddled old Wrangler and headed for the pasture. My intent was to single out a calf, give chase, and try to drop a loop over it's head as we raced across the pasture. Jack and I were then going to try our luck at throwing and hog-tying the calf. I successfully separated a calf from the herd and at full gallop was doing my best to get into position to toss the loop. The calf made a sharp turn and as a good cowhorse should, Wrangler followed. I didn't. As Wrangler made his sudden move, the saddle turned and I found myself clawing the air. When I connected with the earth, it was right in the middle of a big cactus plant.

My cowboy bravado disappeared as I tried to extricate myself form the spiny trap. I rolled over and it seemed that half of the cactus plant was sticking to me. Jack, who had been watching from a hilltop nearby, came running in response to my anguished cries.

I lay on the ground with cactus spines stitching my pants to my flesh from my butt down to my knee. I begged Jack to run to the house and get the hired man, Ab Myers, to come and pull the cactus out of my butt and legs.

I was writhing in pain when Ab arrived with a pair of pliers. He stood me on my feet, unfastened my overalls, then with one pull jerked them down to my knees. Some of the spines remained attached to the pads and were pulled from my butt and legs as my overalls were pulled down. But many spines had been broken from the cactus pads and remained imbedded in the lower extremities of a now totally subdued wantabe cowboy.

A drop of blood appeared at each spot where a spine had pulled out when my pants were jerked down. Each spot burned like a hot needle was being thrust into my flesh. I felt like I was on fire and Ab had not yet begun the tedious and painful process of removing the remaining cactus spines. He laid me on the ground, rolled me onto my belly and began his work. My continuous moan was interrupted by a yelp of distress with the removal of each spine. All the while, with saddle askew, ole Wrangler stood nearby munching grass with no apparent concern for the tragedy unfolding before him.

When Ab finished the spine pulling task, he helped me to my feet. Jack caught Wrangler, and supported by Ab I walked the quarter mile or so back to the house. Mom prepared a potion of baking soda and spread it over my painful, sore, and swelling rear end and leg.

When Dad returned home and was told of the incident, he grunted and confirmed that I was not seriously hurt. He then advised, "You saddled ole Wrangler and you set the cinch. If you are going to play cowboy you'll have to learn to check your own riggin."

By the next morning most of the pain and swelling were gone. However, for the next several days little infected places appeared where a spine had broken off and remained under the skin. Mom or Dad using a big needle or the point of a sharp knife dug out the infected pieces of cactus spine and dabbed the spot with turpentine.

A BARBED WIRE CUT

All horse owners live with a lurking fear of barbed wire. Accidental encounters with barbed wire has diverted many horses from potential greatness to the rendering plant.

Such was the fate of Ole Wrangler. His effectiveness as a cow horse was ended by a bout with a barbed wire fence.

The farm my brother, Hap, was renting was located along the Middle Loup River. He and the landlord, Bill Books, agreed to cooperate in blasting a drainage ditch about five hundred feet long through a piece of land near the river. The land through which the ditch was to be blasted was bordered on the north by the river and the south by a steep bank about forty feet high leading to the plain above. If the ditch functioned as planned, several acres of fertile land would be brought into production.

On the day selected to carry out the activity, there was lots of help available. Most people in the neighborhood had never seen a blast of the magnitude planned to form the drainage ditch. Hap had hired a man experienced in handling explosives to supervise the blasting project. Under his direction and with the willing help of neighbors, sticks of dynamite were placed in holes which had been made in the soil along the intended blasting route. With the dynamite in place, all except the explosive expert climbed the bluff and joined others who had gathered on the plain overlooking the field below. The expert placed the caps in the dynamite sticks, attached the wires and joined the spectators.

Several cars which people had driven to the area were parked near the bluff as were a couple of teams hitched to wagons. I had ridden Wrangler to the area and had tied him to a post in a barbed wire fence nearby.

When all was ready the explosive expert attached the wires to the blasting box. He called to see that the blasting area was clear and plunged the handle down. In an instant my ears were filled with a deafening noise, and what appeared to be a wall of earth rose in front of me and thundered skyward. The mud and dirt went so high it seemed to be towering over me. I was terrified and turned to run from the area on which I was sure the flying material would land. Before I had gone many steps, a few pieces of mud splattered down on me, the other spectators and the plain. As expected by the expert the bulk of material blasted from the ditch fell onto the field below. .

The ditch had not cleared properly in a few places. The explosive expert placed a few more sticks of dynamite in strategic places and set them off. Finally the blasting was completed, the excitement over and people began to leave for home.

I headed to where I had tied ole Wrangler. I intended to ride to Hap's house and then the four miles home. I noticed Wrangler was down the fence from where I had tied him. His right front foot was hooked over a strand of barbed wire and he was thrashing back and forth along the fence while the barbs of the wire cut like a saw into his pastern.

I was scared by the sight of the cut, the blood and the obvious predicament of my horse. Wrangler was struggling and fighting the wire, and I was afraid to go near him. I ran to get Dad to help me with the terrible mess.

Dad rushed to my assistance, calmed Wrangler and freed his foot from the wire. Wrangler's pastern and foot were severely injured. Dad deduced that the blasts had startled Wrangler and he had lunged into the fence, catching his foot over the barbed wire. He had then pulled back breaking the reins with which I had tied him to the post. Frightened by subsequent blasts he had struggled against the wire as it cut into his pastern

Dad debated with himself as to whether he should immediately put Wrangler out of his misery. He was sure that even if the wound healed, the horse would be severely crippled. I believe, in deference to my feelings of guilt for the accident, he decided to spare Wrangler for the moment. Dad obtained some salves and ointment from the supply in Hap's barn, doctored Wrangler's wounds the best he could, then turned him into a small pasture by the river. Wrangler hobbled over to the shallow pool and stood in the cool water to soothe the injured foot. Dad told me later he would not have been surprised if Wrangler had died that night.

Wrangler spent the rest of the summer in the pasture by the river. The wound healed slowly and it was evident he would be left with a club foot. With the coming of fall we brought Wrangler home and turned him into the pasture where we could watch him. The healing process continued through the winter, and by spring he was getting around reasonably well, walking on all four legs but with a pronounced limp.

We brought Wrangler back to the barn and we kids began to ride him again. Slowly at first, but as time passed the size of the club foot decreased and the limp lessened. Wrangler's days as a working cow horse were over, but he continued to serve a useful purpose as the kids rode him to do chores and for fun. He remained a good and faithful friend until he was sold at the dispersal sale following the death of my father.

Though ole Wrangler carried the blood of a hot-blood, he never served in the Calvary for which he was bred, but he served, long and well. He was a valuable and useful asset and provided years of service to the Gates family. During those years he displayed the heart, the stamina, the intelligence, the patience, the devotion, and the

Dillard H. Gates

dependability which would have reflected credit to the Calvary had he been called to duty.

    Dad bought other saddle horses to replace Wrangler for the more difficult jobs of working cattle; however, the other saddle horses didn't replace Wrangler. They were just horses which were needed to get a job done.

HELL

"Some folks say
There ain't no hell
But they don't farm
So they can't tell"

So began a ditty I first heard as a child. It was repeated many times as my family struggled through the vicissitudes of life on the farm during the drought and depression.

According to historical accounts, life on the plains of Nebraska has been a sort of hell since homestead days, especially for the women. I recall reading an early account that described it this way. "The prairies of Nebraska are great for cattle and men but hell for horses and women." A sort of hell prevailed during the drought and depression of the thirties. As real and pervasive as it was, this may not have been the extent of the hell Dad alluded to in his response to the sophisticate in the hotel lobby in Rochester, Minnesota.

As I remember there was an pervasive but intermittent undercurrent of hell being raised around our place. We kids got into things we shouldn't have and did things we weren't supposed to do. We played practical jokes on each other, our folks, the neighbors, or anyone who happened to fit the situation at the time a devious thought entered our minds. We didn't discriminate, but I suppose on occasion we exerted some discretion, to protect our own behinds. "CYA" was a concept we well understood. We just didn't call it that. There were loosely defined behavioral boundaries that had evolved over time, which changed as we aged but tended to set parameters for the hell raised within the family and the community.

CUSSING MRS. THURMAN

In the fall of 1929 I was four years old. The Gates School District hired a new Superintendent, Mr. Gerald Thurman, and his wife to teach the high school grades. Mr. Thurman was a great joker and always pulling something on one of the kids. Mrs. Thurman was a pretty, exuberant, always smiling, gushy lady full of sweet talk, especially to little kids.

She smothered me with her mushy talk and tried to give me a hug every time she saw me. I don't know why as I must have been a grubby little waif and she was always immaculate . She didn't favor me; she treated all little kids the same way. Some may have liked, it but I didn't. I would squirm or duck and try to avoid her embraces, usually unsuccessfully as Mom would admonish me, "Now Dillard, be nice to Mrs. Thurman."

I finally told Mom, "I don't want Mrs Thurman to do that to me, if she does it again I'm gonna cuss her."

"Never, ever say bad words to Mrs. Thurman," were Mom's emphatic and strict orders.

The next time Mrs. Thurman came to see Mom I was playing outside and tried to avoid her. When she was about ready to leave, Mom called me into the house to say, "Hi," I reluctantly shuffled into the hall as Mom and Mrs. Thurman were coming outside. As I approached, Mrs. Thurman reached down to embrace me while exclaiming, "Oh there you are, sweetheart. I was afraid I was not going to get to see you."

I squirmed, trying to avoid her embrace, looked up at Mom and threatened, "Mom, I told you what I was going to do."

"You better not," Mom entreated as Mrs. Thurman bent over and pulled me against her bosom .

That gesture triggered the response which Mom had warned me against. I pulled away from her and unleashed all the swear words in my not so limited vocabulary. Profanity was forbidden in our home, at least within earshot of Dad, but this had not stopped me from acquiring some proficiency from other kids and hired men. I didn't know the meaning of the words but their use certainly caused a reaction.

"Oh my", she gasped, "You are being a bad boy, aren't you?"

I escaped her grasp and fled into the backyard leaving both Mom and Mrs. Thurman aghast standing in the hall.

After Mrs.Thurman departed, Mom scolded me about my behavior and lamented, "Son, I was never so mortified in my life."

To the best of my memory the only consequence of my outburst was that from then on Mrs. Thurman stayed her distance. She did not try to embrace me and the sweet talk was curtailed.

SOME MORE CUSSIN

Cussing was not tolerated in our household. Mom reprimanded us if she heard us use bad words, but we normally didn't take it seriously as her bark was worse than her bite. We received frequent warnings that we would get our mouth washed out with soap if we didn't stop swearing. When Dad was not around, cuss words occasionally slipped into our vocabulary, but Mom's threat was never carried out.

We nearly always had hired men who sometimes inadvertently, sometimes deliberately, taught us new and colorful swear words in English, Polish and Bohemian. When we were little we didn't know any better than to use the new words. As we got bigger we probably thought it was kinda smart to be able to swear, even if we didn't know the meaning of the words being uttered.

As kids we were subjected to religious training and admonished not to not take the Lord's name in vain. Our school teachers provided warnings about the consequences of using bad words. I sat wide-eyed in church and listened to fire and brimstone sermons detailing the repercussions of not following the words of the Lord. Even though somewhat scary, the sermons were more entertaining than instructive. Punishment by the Lord for cussin seemed a long ways away and vague to us children. In addition, church only lasted a couple hours each Sunday, and we could hear cussin from big brothers and sisters and get multilingual instructions from the hired men seven days a week.

Dillard H. Gates

When my two youngest sisters, Joyce and Iris, were about six and five years old respectively, they were playing with their dolls as little girls are wont to do. My older sister, Sis, who happened to be nearby was mildly startled where she overhead Iris scolding her doll. She appeared to be very disturbed with something the doll had done. She was "reading the riot act" to the doll using language that had obviously been acquired in the barnyard or from much older kids.

Upon hearing Iris's admonitions to the doll Joyce, as bigger sisters will, warned, "If you don"t stop swearing, you will not go to heaven."

Iris pondered the advice only briefly before responding with the convictions of a five-year old, "I guess I will not go to heaven then because I'm not gonna stop cussin."

SELLING ROTTEN EGGS

On our farm the chickens were not confined to the chicken pen except when they were young. They required little special feeding as they functioned as scavengers around the farmstead. The chickens had access to spilled grain, crop residues, and other choice morsels deposited around the barnyard by other animals. This also allowed the laying hens to make nests and lay eggs in many places other than the nest boxes in the chicken house. They built nests in the barn, in the hay mow, under the granary and in the weeds around the farmstead. It was a challenge to find the nests. When sent to gather eggs we did not go just to the chicken house but also made a circuit of the farmyard to get eggs from the scattered nests which we had discovered.

We were constantly on the look out for new nests. I don't know what an old hen is thinking about when she lays an egg; however, it seems that her natural instinct would be to make little chickens rather than omelettes. If a hen successfully hid her nest and accumulating a few eggs, she became broody and began setting on the nest. That signaled the beginning of the incubation period for the eggs in that nest.

Occasionally an old hen would hide a nest well enough that it was not found during our egg gathering excursions. We found out that the hen had been setting only when she showed up in the barnyard with a brood of chicks.

The Gates store was only a couple hundred yards east of our house. The store provided local farmers a market for cream and eggs which were sold for cash or exchanged for groceries. We didn't have many extra eggs, but on occasion we would accumulate a few dozen and took them to the store. Also, sometimes we kids secretly sneaked a few eggs a day until we had accumulated a dozen or so. We then took the eggs to the store and sold them for ten to fifteen cents a dozen and bought candy with the proceeds.

On one occasion Jack and I found a broody old hen sitting on a nest containing over a dozen eggs. Based upon the behavior of the hen and the appearance of the eggs, we suspected the eggs were well along in the incubation process.

Jack and I both thought it would be a good idea to take the eggs to the store, and exchange them for candy. However, we were apprehensive that Nora Swick, proprietor of Gates, store would candle the eggs and discover they were about ready to hatch. We decided to try to get my next older sister, Sissy, involved in our nefarious scheme. She had a higher level of credibility at the store than either Jack or I. We told Sissy we had saved eggs over the course of a few days and now had a dozen.

We would share with her if she would take them to the store and exchange them for candy.

All went as planned. Sis exchanged the eggs for the kinds of candy Jack and I had told her to get. Luckily the eggs were not candled at the time of exchange. However, the following day when Sis was at the store Nora questioned her about the eggs. Sis told Nora that Jack and I had gathered the eggs and had assured her they were all right. Nora informed Sissy that she had candled the eggs and found them to be about ready to hatch. She returned the eggs to Sis and instructed her to take them out to the field and break them. Nora accepted Sissy's explanation of the source of the eggs but admonished her to make certain it didn't happen again.

As could be expected, Sis was embarrassed and furious about the incident. Jack and I denied we knew the eggs were about to hatch but she didn't accept our story and threatened to beat the tar out of both of us. However, Sis was good natured and her anger soon subsided. All of us, including Sis, had relished the candy. Sis didn't forget the incident nor did she ever again take eggs to the store for Jack and me.

In the short-run at least Jack and I were rewarded for our deceit. Mom was deprived of the dozen chicks the broody hen would have hatched and brought to the barnyard. Sis was an unwitting pawn. And Nora, the proprietor, provided treats for a couple of boys who didn't deserve them.

THE PIES THAT DISAPPEARED

Quilting clubs provided a diversion from the daily grind as well as an opportunity for the farm women to make beautiful bed quilts. Mom belonged to such a club made up of farm wives in the Gates neighborhood. I don't know how she found enough time from her work to participate in the club, but she did. The work she did in preparation for the club, when it was held at our house, just added to the burdens she carried each day. But the club provided an opportunity to see friends and neighbors that she saw infrequently even though they lived in the community.

Most of the ladies had kids which they brought with them when they attended club. The little ones played in the house or crawled around on the floor under the women's feet as they gathered around the quilting frame. Those big enough played outside, in the barn or otherwise tried to stay out of sight of their mothers.

The ladies talked women talk, whatever that was, as they pieced together quilt blocks or stitched a quilt stretched on a quilting frame in the front room. At the end of the quilting session before leaving for home, the club ladies were always served refreshments. Sometimes a husband stopped by to pick up his wife and joined the ladies for pie and coffee. Though the men were reluctant to admit it most enjoyed a bit of gossip themselves.

Club day morning Mom was up earlier than usual because in addition to her regular household duties she had to bake pies for the club ladies. As always, she baked extra pies for the family. As the pies for the club ladies and some extras for the family came out of the oven, she set them in the pantry to cool.

One club day when I was around ten years old, Mom baked pies and as usual had placed them in the pantry off the kitchen. Four or five other boys about my age including Alan and Doug Dewey had accompanied their mothers to club. As we played around the barn, someone got the idea that what we all needed was a piece of Mom's pie. Well, I knew where the pies were, but I wasn't sure how to get at them.

After a planning session we came up with a strategy that with luck might work. If it didn't, about all that was likely to happen was we all would get a spat on the butt and told to, "scoot out of here." We decided it was worth the risk. We carefully removed the screen from the window of my bedroom which was on the east end of the house and opened into the kitchen. We planned to abscond with three pies. I opened the window and two of the boys climbed through after me. The others waited outside to receive the pies as they were passed out the window.

We crawled across my bed which sat beneath the window, across the bedroom floor and through the open door to the kitchen. With me in the lead, we squeezed behind the kitchen stove and the big wood box which sat at the east end of the kitchen between my bedroom door and the door to the pantry. The riskiest part of the operation lay before us.

The ladies were gathered in the front room at the west end of the house. However, there was a direct line of sight along which we could be spotted if one of the ladies happened to glance our way while we were slipping from behind the woodbox across an open space to the pantry. Doug stayed behind the woodbox as Alan and I crept undetected into the pantry. I picked up a pie and handed it to Alan. He waited for an opportune moment and handed the pie to Doug, who immediately scooted back behind the stove and headed for the window. I grabbed another pie, handed it to Alan and he followed his younger brother Doug. I seized the third pie, slid quietly across the exposed open space and stayed as close to Alan as I could.

We delivered the three pies to our co-conspirators waiting outside. With pies in hand they headed for the barn as Alan and I closed the window and replaced the screen. We sat in the haymow elated at our success as we devoured the poached pies and wondered what our mothers would do when they discovered what we had done.

We soon found out as we heard Mom calling from the doorway, "Dillaaard, where are you?"

Her call was soon joined by other mothers calling the names of their wayward sons. After listening to a few calls, we hid the remainder of the pies under the hay. Then trying our best to appear innocent we sauntered through the barn door in response to the insistent calls. Apparently our acting was not equal to our pie stealing skills. Mothers grabbed sons by the arms, ears, or shoulders, probably reflecting their method of chastisement at home. One or two Moms shook their sons so hard it appeared they were trying to dislodge the pie so recently devoured.

I stood before my Mom as she sobbed, "Dillard, how could you do this to me? I am so mortified I don't know what to do."

I was feeling pangs of remorse. I was sorry for what I had done. What had seemed like great sport a short time ago now appeared little short of disastrous. We guilty pie snatchers were set in the back yard to contemplate our fate as the club ladies took their refreshments of coffee and the pies Mom had prepared for the family.

I don't remember if or how the other boys were punished for the pie filching fiasco. As for me I realized what I had done had hurt and embarrassed Mom. That in itself was punishment but certainly less than I deserved.

When the incident was related to Dad that night at the supper table, he gave me a meaningful look and asked, "Dill, can't you find something better than that to do?"

The voice was soft but the meaning was clear. The Gates Community Ladies Quilting Club had no more problems with me.

DIGGING POTATOES WITH ALICE

Alice was seven years older than me. She ran away from home the summer she was fourteen. But while she was home she was a dynamo of energy and ideas and was always up to something.

One fall afternoon Mom sent Alice to the garden to dig potatoes for supper. Though I was probably only five or six years old, Alice asked me to come along and help. She got a bucket from the kitchen, then grabbed a hoe from the garden gate as we headed toward the potato patch.

Alice tried to make a game out of the chore as she set about digging the potatoes. She suggested that I pick up the little potatoes that were my size and she would pick up the big ones which were her size. This sounded like great fun to me.

As little potatoes were exposed I hollered, "That's mine." Alice interrupted her digging as I grabbed the little spuds and tossed them into the bucket.

As Alice was chopping vigorously with the hoe, I spied a little potato she had not noticed. "That's my size," I exclaimed as I dived in front of her to retrieve the tiny tater. I bent over and reached into the potato hill while Alice was still chopping and the sharp edge of the hoe came down across the bridge of my nose. The blood spurted from my nostrils and the cut across my nose. I let out a yell like a banshee and grasped my bloody nose with both hands.

Alice grabbed me in her arms and tried to move my hands so she could examine the damage. The sight of the blood on my hands brought even louder howls from me. She used the skirt of her dress to wipe away the blood, snot and tears. Alice tried to console me as the wound appeared less serious than my squalls indicated

She grabbed the partially filled potato bucket in one hand and me in the other and ran to the house. The bleeding stopped shortly and Mom cleaned the cut and applied turpentine, the primary treatment for wounds in the Gates household. The turpentine burned and I let out a few more yips but the worst was over. In a few days the cut across the bridge of my nose healed and I was none the worse for wear.

I still have a small scar and a slight bump on the bridge of my nose. As I rub my fingers across my nose to adjust my glasses or wipe

Dillard H. Gates

away perspiration I feel the little bump and am reminded of a lively older sister who was always full of fun.

THE PENNY GRAB

When I was a kid, a penny was the basic coin of the realm. With a penny I could buy an all-day sucker, or a piece of chocolate candy, or a licorice stick, or an eraser, or a pencil. For only five pennies I could get a bottle of strawberry pop. An extra penny could mean a trip to the Gates store where I could stand in front of the round-topped, glass candy counter and contemplate the wonderful choices displayed before me. Needless to say, all of us kids were anxious to get our grubby little hands on a penny whenever we could.

Sissy and I were excited one day when Alice asked us if we would like to have a penny grab. I was only about five years old, but I knew of penny grabs at Fourth of July celebrations. Handfuls of pennies were tossed into the air and children scrambled to pick up as many as possible. If one was small enough to be allowed in the penny grab but big enough, aggressive enough or lucky enough, it was possible to snatch several pennies.

Sissy and I contemplated such a penny grab and agreed to participate. We were a little apprehensive when Alice led us toward the corral behind the barn.

As she pointed toward an old dishpan, she told us this was going to be a different kind of a penny grab. She confidentially told us she had scattered handfuls of pennies on the ground under it. We were to squat as close as possible to the dishpan and at the count of three she would jerk it upward and we could grab as many pennies as possible. We could keep all that we grabbed.

Greed overcame uncertainty and I was determined to grab the fastest and get as many pennies as possible. I was on my knees hovering as close as possible to the dishpan my hands at the ready. Deliberately Alice began the slow count. Tension mounted. Muscles tensed. As the count reached three Alice jerked the overturned dishpan from the ground. I had no intention of coming in second in this contest. The pan cleared the ground, and with both hands extended I pounced forward, right into a pile of fresh cow manure. Sissy was a little slower and did not dive so deeply into the cow pie. If that cow pie had been pennies, she wouldn't have gotten many.

My greed turned to tears as I knelt there on my knees with my arms covered with cow manure up to my elbows. Alice jumped up, waving her arms and laughing at my predicament.

My slower sister with only her fingers covered with manure puckered to cry then saw my plight was much more serious than hers. She joined Alice in the laughter, pointed a dirty finger at me and exclaimed, "You got a lot more than I did, Dill."

I rose to my feet still howling so loud I could have been heard in the next county. Holding my manure dripping hands away from my sides, I ambled toward the house to tell Mom. Alice immediately realized the implications of Mom seeing me covered with cow crap. She beseeched me to stop, led me over to the stock tank nearby and helped me wash that which was not pennies from my hands and arms.

Like most pranks around our place, nothing came of the incident. Mom thought Alice should have know better than to pull such a trick on little kids. When Dad heard about the prank, he showed little concern. In his way of thinking, any problem you could wash off in the stock tank couldn't be too serious. However, as he pulled me onto his lap to display an element of sympathy he smiled and offered this advice, "Dill, next time you better look before you leap."

Dillard H. Gates

SMOKING

"A cigarette is a little white tube with a fire on one end and a fool on the other." That definition was an early exposure to the evils of smoking. I first heard the lament while listening to Uncle Josh on the old Edison phonograph in our front room. It must have made sense as it stuck with me.

Neither Dad nor Mom smoked, but it seems that most of the men in the community did. Most of the smokers rolled their own and Bull Durham was the standard brand of sack tobacco. Bull Durham was referred to by some as floor sweepings from either a tobacco shed or a horse barn. A manifestation of those who rolled their own was the string and tag hanging from a tobacco sack stuffed in the shirt pocket.

As a little guy I was fascinated by the apparent skill required to roll a cigarette especially if the wind was blowing and it usually was in Nebraska. It was amazing how a man could hold a little cigarette paper in one hand, shake tobacco from the sack onto the paper, roll the paper around the tobacco, lick along one side of the paper and form the tobacco and paper into a cigarette. The final step was to twist the end of the cigarette to prevent the tobacco from falling out. Then with cigarette between the lips, the smoker searched his pockets for a match. The match was lighted by a quick scratch of the thumbnail, struck on a pants leg, or other convenient abrasive surface. With hands cupped around the match flame the smoker lit the twisted end of the cigarette. The first drag on the cigarette followed immediately by clouds of smoke from the nose and mouth seemed to provide the smoker with a kind of satisfaction which I did not comprehend. The ritual of rolling and lighting a cigarette was a feat I dreamed of emulating even though I believed that smoking was a bad thing

Most smokers rolled their own. However, there were a few who could afford the cost or occasionally splurged and smoked tailor-mades. The cost of a sack of Bull Durham was a nickel, while the cost of a pack of Lucky Strikes or Camels was fifteen cents or more. Somewhat akin to watching someone roll a cigarette was the fascination of watching the ritual of opening a fresh pack of tailor-mades, extracting the first cigarette, grasping it between the lips and lighting up. This too was followed by the big drag, the clouds of smoke and the apparent immediate satisfaction.

I do not recall Dad telling me not to smoke. I do not even remember him telling me that it was a dirty, unhealthy habit. However, I always knew I was not supposed to smoke and that if Dad caught me smoking I would likely get my butt kicked. Maybe this bit of conventional wisdom was provided by my older siblings or primary grade teacher. Even so, there was a fascination about smoking and despite the risks I was curious and had to give it a try.

On a few occasions I asked a hired man for a cigarette. I do not recall one ever directly giving me a smoke. However, sometimes one would lay his tobacco sack and cigarette papers where I could reach them, then pretend he did not see me as I struggled to roll my own. I remember Henry Worth, our neighbor who always smoked Lucky Strikes, performing a similar subterfuge. On many occasions while I was with him in his car, he would take his cigarette pack from his shirt pocket, extract two cigarettes, place one between his lips, and lay the other on the dash in front of me. He was not directly offering me a smoke but was certainly making a cigarette available. I assume he thought that if Dad found out I was smoking he could rationalize that he had not given me a cigarette.

As a kid my fascination with smoking continued. My brother Jack, my sisters, and I used to make cigarettes out of whatever materials were available. We tried to smoke alfalfa leaves, red dock (a weed that grew on the farm), Indian tobacco, and even sawdust. We wrapped our counterfeit tobacco in everything from regular cigarette papers to sheets of paper from the Sears and Roebuck catalogue.

A cousin, Ival Ash, experimenting with us out behind the barn, even tried smoking dry horse manure. He thought it was pretty good and suggested I give it a try. My fascination with smoking had not quite reached that level of intensity, and I refused his offer to share his pungent smelling but plentiful supply of smoking material.

THE SMOKING BARREL

Aunt Blanche and Uncle Art Predmore and their son Kenneth, from Gandy, Nebraska came to our farm one Sunday for dinner. Kenneth had some tailor-made cigarettes he had snitched from his dad. We boys and a couple of my sisters decided to have a smoke. We all went over to the shack, a multi-purpose building used for everything from bunk house to storage facility. There were several open-topped fifty-five gallon barrels in the shack that had been used as standards to support wooden planks on which meat had been placed for salting and storage.

We were all smoking up a storm when someone noticed Mom and Aunt Blanche coming across the yard toward the shack. All but me quickly put out their cigarettes, threw the butts into the stove in the corner and fanned the air in an effort to disperse the smoke. But I was the cagey one and also a bit slow. With the cigarette in my mouth I jumped into an open-topped barrel and squatted down. Mom and Aunt Blanche stepped through the door and into what moments before had been our secret smoking parlor.

"What at are you kids doing?" Mom asked, as if what we had been doing was not self-evident.

"Nothing," the guilty faced culprits responded in unison.

"Were you smoking?" queried Aunt Blanche as she waved her hand back and forth in front of her face to clear the air.

"Noooo," was the rather meek but still unanimous response.

"Then what is that?" Mom questioned as she pointed toward the thin column of smoke wafting upward from the barrel.

The smoking barrel turned out to be the smoking gun. I was caught in a trap of my own making with the evidence in my hand. We were all chewed out royally, especially Kenneth for swiping his dad's cigarettes and providing them to the rest of us. The verbal scolding from Mom and Aunt Blanche didn't bother us much. However, we breathed a collective sigh of relief when given the admonishment that if we would behave (whatever that meant) they would not tell Dad what we had been doing. That promise from Mom and Aunt Blanche relieved our immediate concerns, and like the smoke from our illicit cigarettes the potential problems of getting caught smoking vanished into the air.

THE BULL DURHAM THAT DIDN'T BUY LOYALTY

When I was in the sixth grade I managed to accumulate five cents. I decided to share my wealth with a couple of my friends, Jimmy Schmidt and Alvin (Pussy) Myers. Jimmy was in my grade and Pussy a grade ahead of us. They both lived a couple miles west of Gates and rode horses to school.

Following due consideration we decided that a bag of Bull Durham would provide the three of us with much longer lasting satisfaction than would five all day suckers, five jaw-breakers, five tootsie rolls, or five pieces of bubble gum. It was not an easy decision, for none of us got candy as often as we liked, but in the end it was unanimous.

While the other two waited outside, I went into the store with the nickel virtually burning a hole in my pocket. I fished out the nickel and held it up to the proprietor and told him the hired man had asked me to get a bag of Bull Durham and a book of cigarette papers for him. The store keeper probably didn't give my request a second thought. Kids bought tobacco products for their parents or others all the time. In actuality he probably cared little who the tobacco was for. Kids were not supposed to smoke but as a general rule little effort was made to prevent it. With the Bull Durham and book of cigarette papers in hand, I joined my friends waiting around the corner.

They then rode their horses over to our barnyard and waited while I caught and bridled ole Wrangler. The three of us on horseback headed west up the sandy, dirt road about three-quarters of a mile to the big hill. A large cottonwood tree surrounded by low growing brush grew along the north side of the road at the top of the hill. This was the spot we had selected to conceal ourselves while we participated in what we knew was a forbidden activity. We tied our horses and scampered into the bushes, hoping we were hidden from view of any passers-by.

I reached into my pocket and withdrew that on which I had been willing to invest my last nickel, that on which I had splurged just to be able to share with my friends. I withdrew the sack of Bull Durham and the book of cigarette papers, then each of us in turn clumsily rolled a cigarette.

Amidst fits of coughing, spitting and choking, all the while muttering how good it was, we finally finished our cigarettes. We agreed that one smoke was enough for now and that if we rationed the tobacco carefully we could have several more pleasurable sessions under the cottonwood tree.

Following further serious discussion, we agreed that the remainder of the Bull Durham and cigarette papers should be hidden under the tree where it would be safe but readily accessible to us when we were once again ready to repeat this manly endeavor. Our plan was implemented as we dug a shallow hole in the soft sand and lined it with leaves and grass. The Bull Durham was carefully placed in this protective nest and covered with small sticks, leaves and grass. The treasure was hidden, and only we three knew where. We then got back on our horses. Jimmy and Pussy headed on west and I high-tailed it back home hoping that Mom or Dad would not have noticed my absence and ask were I had been. I also hoped the strong, pungent, smell of Bull Durham tobacco smoke on my clothes or breath would not give me away. I figured if I stayed close to the hired man at dinner time any residual smell of smoke on me would be masked by his ever-present odor of sweat and tobacco.

We three co-conspirators reveled in our secret for the next day or two at school. I finally decided I wanted another go at the Bull Durham. So on Saturday I bridled ole Wrangler and headed for the cache under the lone cottonwood tree. It was my treasure, I had paid for it and saw no problem in having a smoke without benefit of the company of either Jimmy or Pussy. With great anticipation, I crawled through the brush to the spot where the cache had been hidden. I was surprised and disappointed to find the grass and sticks which we had used to build the nest scattered in the sand. The fruit of my wealth, the prized Bull Durham, was gone without a trace.

I stared in disbelief at the spot where together we had secreted the tobacco and laid plans for future smoking sessions and began to wonder if I had been deceived by those with whom I had willingly shared. I was more hurt than angry as I crawled back on ole Wrangler and trotted home. The following Monday I reluctantly approached my friends and asked if they had taken the tobacco. Both vehemently, but not convincingly, denied any knowledge of the disappearance of the Bull Durham.

Despite their pleas of innocence, I remained convinced of their guilt. But despite the loss of most of what I had bought with my only nickel, I learned a couple of lessons. A secret shared is no longer a secret. And the one who pays should retain custody of that for which he has invested his wealth.

Maybe this was also the beginning of the realization that one cannot buy friends. I also realized that I had wasted my nickel on something that smelled and tasted bad and (so I had been told in school) would turn my lungs black. Even at that tender age I was beginning to comprehend that, fascinating as it might be, smoking was probably not a good idea.

NO SMOKING, A SHARED TRUST

Dreams of becoming great athletes when we reached high school afflicted a few of my friends and me when I was in the seventh grade. We had been taught in school that smoking was bad for the lungs and restricted physical stamina. In addition, in my case at least, I feared the immediate results of what Dad would do if he caught me smoking more than possible long term complications. The thoughts of a rap alongside the head or a good kick in the butt were more compelling than potential lung problems fifty years hence.

In our youthful zeal we concluded that smoking reflected a character flaw inconsistent with trust, honesty, faithfulness and bravery. To confirm our commitment to these tenants, we joined together in a secret club known only to us as the Cedarwood Club. Charter members (the club never expanded) were Alan and Douglas Dewey, Jimmy Schmidt, with whom I had shared the Bull Durham and Dillard Gates. In addition to being the leader of the club, Alan was the artist among us. He was also imagined to be the bravest as his father had been awarded the Silver Star for bravery under fire in World War I. He carved icons out of red cedarwood (Juniper) which were to be carried on our person at all times. "Scented cedarwood" was our password. The icons were the symbols of our vows, our comradeship and pledge not to smoke.

I suppose the combination of my commitment to the Cedarwood Club, the bad smell and horrible taste of cigarettes, a concern for my health, and a fear of the toe of Dad's foot on my behind, provided a synergistic reaction that resulted in my decision not to smoke. Dad died when I was sixteen, but by that time the reasons for not smoking had become fixed in my mind. As a teenager or adult I never developed a desire to smoke.

A SICK CAT REINCARNATED

Animals around the farm were first functional and then maybe pets. Cats were no exception. There were two rather loose categories of cats around the farmstead: barn cats and house cats. The barn cats stayed in the barn or environs. The house cats hung around the yard but were not generally allowed in the house.

Barn cats took care of themselves and survived mostly on the mice they were able to catch but occasionally at the whim of the person doing the milking, they were given some milk. Sometimes the milk was poured into a pan for the cats to lap up. However, it was more fun for the milker to squirt milk to the cat. If a cat came close enough while a cow was being milked, we would often point the teat toward it and squirt it with milk. At first the cat would run for a short distance then stop to clean itself by licking off the milk. This would happen a time or so before the cat learned that the way to get fresh milk was to get within squirting distance of the milker. After a few sessions getting milk squirted directly on it the cat learned to sit on its back legs, and let us squirt milk directly into its mouth. Squirting milk at the cats was a diversion from the chore of milking and the cats seemed to like the free supplement to the mouse diet. Talk about a handout, those cats were probably practicing to become democrats.

These barn cats weren't actually pets, but they tolerated us and we allowed them to live in the barn in exchange for their service as mousers. We kids usually found their nests when they had kittens. Sometimes if we disturbed the kittens, the mother cat would take them by the nape of the neck and move them to a new location.

The cats that hung around the house were just barn cats that had become a bit more tame. The house cats stayed on the porch or in the woodshed. I guess both Mom and Dad felt that we kids were all the animals they could tolerate in the house. They roamed the field nearby and caught mice, as did the barn cats, but hung around the house and feasted on table scraps if they could get to them ahead of the dogs, the goat or the pig.

Sometimes the house cats became actual pets and were given names. However, the kids didn't get too attached to the cats as their life span was short. It seemed they were around for a few months, at the most a year or so, then died or disappeared. Their places were soon taken by the seemingly endless supply from the barn or by a cat that just showed up and decided to stay. After all, these were the days of the hobos and the WPA. Or maybe the cats were reincarnated hobos or WPAers who choose to come back this trip as cats with the expectation they would be assured of better food and lodging than they had before.

When my brother, Jack, was around ten or eleven and my sister Lee was a couple years younger a young tom cat joined the house cat clutch. He appeared to do alright at first but soon became thin and scraggly. We kids were aware of the cat but paid little attention to him until he became extremely emaciated and scrawny. It was obvious that cat was sick and suffering and probably about ready to expend one of its alleged nine lives.

Jack and Lee became very concerned about the sick cat. They were aware that it was a common occurrence on the farm to kill and dispose of animals that were sick or seriously injured. They concluded the humane thing to do was to put the sick cat out of its misery. Since the cat was not really a pet and did not belong to anyone in particular, they resolved to take care of the problem themselves. Jack decided the best way to kill the cat was to knock it in the head. The method was quick if done correctly and quiet and was frequently used on the farm to dispose of sick or injured small animals.

Jack found a good, strong club and together they coaxed the miserable little beast to the farmyard near the area where tractor fuel and gasoline were stored in fifty-five gallon barrels. The area was sandy and in the shade of big locust trees. Jack took the club and, using all his strength, delivered a mighty blow to the head of the cat. The cat flopped over and thrashed about. Jack continued pounding on the poor cat until it stopped struggling and lay still. Following a cursory examination of the mauled now muted mouser, Jack and Lee declared it dead. They scratched out a hole in the sand, placed the remains of the feline in the shallow grave and covered them with sand.

That evening Jack was helping me with the chores. We suddenly heard a mournful sound that might have been described as a cross between a loud squall and a meow. The wail continued, and Jack and I cautiously moved toward the fuel storage area. As we approached the site of the earlier execution Jack turned to me and in a shaking voice said,"Dill, that sounds like the cat Lee and I killed this morning."

We followed the sound to behind the fuel barrels and into the area beneath the locust trees. There in the shadows, in a shallow hole, still partially covered with sand lay the source of the mournful cries. The sounds were emanating from the mouth of the most beat-up and bloodied cat I had ever seen.

Jack was disturbed and troubled by the sight as he knew that earlier in the day he and Lee had killed a sick cat and buried it in the sand. Now there it was again, more emaciated and from all appearances in much worse condition than it had been in the morning, and much noisier. As we stood there beneath the locust staring down at the cursed cat trying to shut the piteous sound from our ears, Jack, in a trembling voice haltingly queried, "Dill, that cat couldn't come back to life could it?"

I was sure Jack didn't know the meaning of reincarnation. That poor pile of pulp, lying partially covered with sand in the shallow grave had lived as a sick cat, died as a sick cat and been buried. Given a choice I was certain it would not have wanted to be reincarnated as a sick cat. But there it was.

"No, Jack," I assured him, "The cat didn't come back to life. You just didn't get the job done right this morning."

After some discussion and agonizing we agreed the best solution to the dilemma was to shoot the poor creature. Somehow it just didn't seem right to try to beat it any more. We got Dad's 22 Remington. I put the long suffering cat out of its misery, and we buried it again in a deeper grave, but still in the shade of the locust trees.

I don't know if that episode used up one or two of the cat's lives, but if it was ever reincarnated, I bet it chose not to return to our farmyard, in whatever form it may have reappeared.

COYOTE PUPS, FROM PET TO PULP

The howl of a coyote may strike a romantic chord in some, but to farmers with poultry or sheep the sound is a reason for concern. Coyotes were common in the area when I was a kid but were not looked upon as a desirable part of the environment. Farmers of the community had a low tolerance for livestock and poultry losses attributed to coyotes.

Generally when one was spotted an attempt was made to chase it down and destroy it.

Dad kept a loaded rifle above the door of the back porch so that it was readily available if a coyote or other marauding critter was spotted in the farmyard. We kids knew the gun was there, we knew it was loaded and we were admonished to leave it alone.

Once in the early-spring season there was evidence of coyotes in the area. Dead or partially eaten chickens were found in the barnyard in the mornings. In addition, at night we often heard coyotes howling in the pasture to the south-west of the house. Sometimes we kids would mimic the coyotes and the coyotes would respond to our howls. The kid and the coyote howls intermingled and echoed across the grassy hills of our pasture. Though it was fun to hear them howl, we knew we were harmonizing with a potential livestock killer and that it must soon end.

Dad decided it was time to put an end to the night-time raids on the chicken pen. Early one morning he and the hired man headed toward the pasture equipped with the twelve-gauge shotgun, a shovel, a gunny sack, and a small roll of barbed wire. Following a short search they located the coyote den in the side of a hill. They listened closely at the mouth of the hole but could not determine if the mother coyote was at home, however they concluded there were pups in the den.

Dad decided to first try the easy way to extract the coyote pups from the den. If that didn't work they would dig them out. They unrolled about twelve feet of the barbed wire, bent it back then unrolled and cut off another piece of equal length. They twisted the two strands together forming a heavily barbed, semi-stiff wire probe about twelve feet long. They poked the wire into the mouth of the den then twisted and forced it downward into the hole. They heard a faint yelp as the end of the twisting probe poked the pups. Following a few more twists, they began to slowly pull the wire from the hole. As expected a coyote pup, its hair entangled by the barbed wire, was pulled yelping and snarling from the den. They untangled the pup from wire probe and placed it in the gunny sack.

Another listen at the mouth of the hole indicated there was a pup remaining. The next wire probe yielded another coyote pup which was plunked into the gunny sack with its litter-mate. After satisfying themselves there were no more pups in the hole, Dad shouldered the sack and he and the hired man headed back to the farmstead. Apparently the mother coyote had returned to the den area while her pups were being captured. She was spotted following, but always well out of shotgun range, as the men returned home with her pups in the sack.

Dad brought the sack of coyote pups onto the back porch and dumped them out for us kids to see. We thought they were cute little rascals even though they smelled bad and snarled as we tried to pet them. Dad had planned to show them to us kids, then knock them in the head. After all, "the only good coyote is a dead coyote," was the prevailing attitude among the farmers of Custer County. Following a session of haranguing and begging by the kids, Dad consented to let the pups live for the time being. We agreed that if there was a problem with the pups he could dispose of them later.

We kids took it upon ourselves to gentle the pups and trained them to take milk from a bottle with a nipple. We fabricated a pen on the front porch, cared for them like puppies and watched them grow. Once they were cleaned and fattened up they were cute and playful.

In early June Dad began mowing the first cutting of alfalfa. As usual little bunny rabbits were flushed out by the cutter bar. In past years we kids had gone to the hay field and caught bunnies as they scampered away from the mower. We tried to raise them but they usually died within a few weeks. This time when Jack and I brought a couple of bunnies to the house I had a brilliant idea. The coyotes were now around two months old and growing rapidly. I wondered what the pups would do if the bunnies were placed in the pen with them.

It didn't take long to find out. As we set the bunnies in the pen the pups retreated to the back, watching carefully. The bunnies sat quietly for a few moments then began to hop around. The movement of the rabbits apparently triggered the attack mode in the coyote pups. The pups had never seen a rabbit, but apparently the wild instinct remained intact. They leaped forward and each pup grabbed a bunny by the neck. The bunnies squeaked in terror but it was soon evident the coyote pups had made their first kill. The pups retreated to the back of the pen and proceeded to chew on the tiny rabbit carcasses.

At the supper table that evening Jack and I related the experience to the family. We described the plight of the rabbits and the predatory response of the coyote pups. The girls and Dad thought it was amusing and typical behavior for a coyote. Mom thought it was cruel and thoughtless. She begged us not to do it again.

Despite Mom's concerns, the next day Jack and I headed back to the alfalfa field in search of more bunnies. We caught a couple and put them in our pockets until time to go to the house for dinner. We slipped around the house to avoid Mom's scrutiny and quickly dropped the bunnies into the pen with the coyote pups. This time the pups were ready and pounced on the bunnies the moment they hit the floor. Though we were trying to be quiet, Mom heard a commotion and came rushing out to the porch. By then each of the coyotes had a bunny by the neck and had retreated to the back of the pen.

Mom, spurred by the sight of the coyote carnage, immediately went into action. She picked up a stick and stepped into the pen. She reached down and grabbed the limp body of a rabbit as the coyote growled through its teeth. She whacked the pup with the stick and pulled on the mortally wounded bunny. For a moment there was a stand-off. The coyote was reluctant to release his prey, and Mom had no intention of stopping the beating until it did. I guess after receiving several blows the coyote realized (if coyotes realize) that if it was to survive to hunt another day it had better let go of the rabbit. Mom gently laid the bunny body on the floor outside the pen.

The second coyote had continued to clutch his prey as Mom struggled to rescue the bunny from his litter mate. She now proceeded to give the same treatment to the remaining coyote as it snarled through its teeth and held tightly to the rabbit. As if on que from its mate, the coyote, now under attack, released its prey as Mom continued to whap it with the stick.

Mom stepped out of the pen with the stick still in her hand, and Jack and I stepped back out of her reach. For a moment I thought she intended to give us what she had just given the coyote pups.

With tears in her eyes and the bodies of the bunnies in her hand, she repeated the charge given to us the day before."Do not ever do that again," she threatened. "Don't you think little rabbits have any feelings?" Now take them out of here and bury them where the dogs will not dig them up," she ordered as she handed me the two lifeless and mangled little bodies.

I felt kinda bad for having hurt Mom's feelings but thought she was unduly concerned about the fate of a couple of rabbits. After all, it was natural for coyotes to kill rabbits and rabbits were unwanted pests in the alfalfa field. But I did as I was told, and I did not catch any more bunnies to feed to the coyote pups.

For the next few weeks there was little apparent concern for the coyote pups. We kids tried to play with them, but they seemed not to have the same playful characteristics displayed by dog puppies. If one of the kids hollered loudly, the pups set up on their hind legs and howled. We enjoyed the noise despite Mom's objections.

One day a stranger drove into the yard and said he had heard we had a couple of coyote pups. He said he would like to have one of the pups to give to a zoo. Dad didn't believe his story, but the pups were becoming a bit of a nuisance. Dad finally agreed to let him take one of the pups but asked him to let us know the name of the zoo to which he gave the pup. When the stranger drove out of the yard that was the last we saw or heard of him or the coyote pup. One down and one to go.

The remaining pup was lonesome following the loss of its mate. He was nervous and tried continuously to get out of the pen. One day in mid-summer he was successful and disappeared. We searched around the farmstead hoping we would find him but believing we would not. We assumed the coyote had heard the "call of the wild." A day or so later one of my little sisters came rushing up to me insisting she had heard noises, that sounded like the coyote pup, coming from the toilet hole. I peered down through the big hole of the two-seater and sure enough she was right. There half buried in the contents of the toilet pit was the whining and struggling coyote pup.

Talk about a dilemma. What should be done about a worthless coyote pup, down in the toilet, covered with crap. My suggestion was to get the rifle and put it out of its misery, but now Mom took the side of the crappy coyote. Shooting the pup under those conditions was, to her, too cruel to contemplate. Dad was not home so we had to solve the problem the best we could. Mom insisted we rescue the pup from the terrible mess it was in.

I went to the barn and found a length of small rope. I fashioned a slip knot and loop at the end of the rope and lowered it down into the toilet hole toward the struggling pup. After a few tries I managed to get the loop over the pup's head. I gave the rope a jerk and successfully lassoed it around the neck. I pulled on the rope and cautiously lifted the struggling, crap-covered coyote out of the hole. Holding the stinking, squirming mess at arm's length, I half-dragged, half-carried it out of the toilet. While I had been preparing the rope and snaring the pup Mom and a couple of my sisters, filled several buckets with water from the stock tank. When I had the crap-covered coyote out in the yard, Mom doused it with buckets of water. For a while I thought the damn thing was in more danger of drowning from the torrents of water dumped on it than it had been in the toilet hole.

Several buckets of water later, combined with brushing with a long-handled broom, the near-dead critter was clean enough to be placed into a tub filled with warm water and homemade soap. By this time the creature was so waterlogged and beat up that it offered little resistance to our rehabilitation efforts. The poor thing was scrubbed and rinsed and scrubbed and rinsed until all visual signs of its recent trip to the toilet were obliterated. However, the remaining odor was mute evidence of its recent pit stop. We secured a leash around the coyote's neck and tied it to the lilac bush in the front yard. We were not sure it would recover, but by this time nobody really cared.

The coyote pup proved to be a survivor. The clump of lilac bushes was about five feet in diameter at ground level and six to eight feet tall. The bushes made a suitable home for the pup, and there he remained secured by a light chain ten or twelve feet long. We kids watered and fed the pup and cleaned the area around the lilac bush where it lived.

The coyote family from which this pup was spawned had first attracted our attention by its forays into our chicken yard. So I guess the taste for chicken came naturally to this now nearly half-grown predator. Chickens on our farm were not confined to a pen and had the run of the farmyard, including the front yard. The problem started when one of Mom's fryers strayed too close to the lilac bush and quickly became victim to the same primeval urge that sealed the fate of the bunny rabbits earlier in the spring. The remaining feathers and bones were all the evidence Mom needed to condemn the very creature she had insisted be spared from a grave in the outhouse.

As time passed the coyote became extremely proficient in his chicken catching activities. He learned the length of his leash and seemed to consider any chicken venturing within the constrains of the chain to be in his territory. He lay quietly near the base of the lilac bush and waited for a chicken to move clucking and scratching into his domain. Then with near perfect timing he would spring forward, the feathers would fly and another of Mom's fryers provided fun and food for the wily coyote. The pup seemed to enjoy the game. He caught and killed more chickens than he could consume and buried their remains in the lilac bushes.

Mom was really in a quandary. She worked hard to raise chickens to feed the family, not that pesky coyote. She came to despise the beast but hadn't developed a solution to her problem. With each discovery of fresh feathers and another hole in the bushes containing the partially eaten carcass of one of her prized birds, her fury increased.

Then the crafty canine made the fatal mistake of attacking one of Mom's chickens as she watched from the kitchen door. My usually calm and gentle mother, dashed through the door across the front porch and the yard. En route to where the coyote had retreated with the chicken grasped in its jaws, she grabbed a sturdy, shinny stick I had left leaning against the porch wall.

"This is the last chicken you'll ever kill," she screamed as she brought the stick down on the coyote's head. Mom had lost it. She continued to scream incoherently as she rained blows on the predator that would prey no more. As Sissy, Jack, a few other siblings and I watched, open-mouthed and astonished, Mom proceeded to beat on the battered body of that coyote until she was exhausted. Suddenly as if emerging from a trance she stopped pounding. By then there was not enough left of that coyote hide to make a fur muff for a cupie doll. She dropped the shinny stick, staggered over to the porch and sat down on the step. There she sat with head in hands sobbing until Sissy and I, in an effort to console her, placed our hands on her trembling shoulder.

"It's OK Mom, it's OK," we stammered.

Neither of us knew what to do to comfort the one who always comforted us. However, we both knew for certain that the pile of bloody pulp laying in the yard would not bother any more of Mom's chickens.

Mom soon regained her composure. Wiping her eyes and blowing her nose on her apron tail, she directed me to bury the remains of the coyote pup. She also directed me to clean up the partially eaten chicken carcasses buried in the lilac bushes. She wanted all evidence of that heinous, hen killing varmint removed from her sight.

The saga of the coyotes was over. Whenever I hear the howl of a coyote, I think of the pitiful pup Mom saved from a crypt in the crapper and how it subsequently succumbed to her blows from a shinny stick merely because it responded to the call of the wild.

THE THREE MUSKETEERS

Pigs, dogs, and goats are normally not soul mates, but things on our farm were a bit abnormal at times. In this case three animals, a pig, a dog and a goat were fast friends and seemed to live in a world in which only they were prime characters. They appeared to be oblivious of the fact that they were different. Maybe those denizens of the barnyard were the precursors of multi-culturism and diversity in our society. Certainly their association represented a salutary degree of political correctness long before it became the lingo of the liberals.

The goat, old Snowball, had been a member of the family since shortly after the birth of my little sister Joyce in 1934. Though acquired for her milk Snowball became a favorite of the family. She did, however, have a couple of short-comings. Snowball was not confined and had the run of the farmyard. She seemed to especially like the rose bushes which for years had grown in the front yard. They were soon reduced to scrawny stubs. She also liked to spend an inordinate amount of time on the front porch. In the summer it was shady and in the winter out of the wind. She was a clean goat, but she was not house-broke. Thus, sweeping goat pellets from the porch was an almost daily job.

The dog, ole Speed, was a newer member of the family. One Saturday night Dad came home from town with the strangest looking pup we kids had ever seen. Dad had been on the lookout for another stock dog as ole Rags was getting old and unable to do the work required around the farm. Dad's plan was to raise this pup and train it to replace ole Rags when he finally moved on to the happy rabbit hunting ground in the sky.

"The Buddy Patrol"

The pup was alleged to be a cross between a Russian stag hound and a German police dog. It was a brindle color with long legs, big feet, and floppy ears. This pup was so ugly it was cute. We considered its heritage and concluded it would be able to run like the wind so we named it Speed.

Any animal to survive in the Gates farmyard had to be tolerant of kids. Speed was no exception. He grew from an awkward pup through even more awkward stages before he reached maturity. He was gentle and accepted the antics of little kids. Kids pulled his ears, legs, and tail. They sat on him, they pulled themselves up on him, and learned to walk hanging onto him. By the time he was fully grown he could open his mouth wide enough to envelope a kid's head, but he didn't bite. If the kids got too rough he merely moved out of the way. As Speed approached maturity Dad began to train him to work the livestock.

When Snowball was a productive member of the farmyard family and Speed was a growing pup, Jack and I decided to raise another runt pig. Pigs complete their growth span in a much shorter period than do goats or dogs. The pig grew quickly and became fat and lazy but also sort of a pet. For the most part the pig too had the run of the farmyard.

As the pig grew it lay around the farmyard, seemingly always in the way, waiting for someone to feed him. If he was given a boot to get him out of the way, he squealed like he was the most abused animal on the farm. In fact that pig had privileged status. He was handfed and got his ears scratched and belly rubbed while issuing little grunts of pleasure. We didn't name him as it was understood he would go to the auction or be butchered when he reached the appropriate size. Dad did say, however, that the pig acted a lot like a New Deal Democrat. It just lay in the shade as much of the time as possible and squealed for someone to bring it something to eat.

The common thread that united these three animals the goat, the dog and the pig was unknown but they hung together like the Three Musketeers. Together they did a good job of cleaning up table scraps that were dumped in the yard. Snowball was at a bit of a disadvantage in the scavenging department. Her diet was more restrictive than the dog or the pig's, but she did pick up any vegetable or bread-like material dumped into the yard. All three of them relished pancakes.

We kids besieged Mom to make extra pancakes so we could feed them to the Three Musketeers. We would stand on the back step with a plate of extra pancakes, and the Three Musketeers would line up in front of us, each begging in its own way for the pancakes being distributed. Speed wagged his tail, opened his big mouth and danced around trying to get in a spot where he thought the pancakes would be tossed. The pig would stand before us and give out a grunt or low moan to try to remind us of his presence. Snowball would give a low pleading bleat and try to get in front of the pig and ole Speed.

Tossing a pancake to Speed was about like throwing it into the slop pail. When a pancake was tossed in his direction, he just opened his mouth wide and the pancake disappeared with barely a chomp. If Speed could be somehow distracted, the pig could also catch a tossed pancake but had to chomp it a few times to get it down. In order for Snowball to get a pancake, it had to be given directly to her. Compared to Speed and the pig, she was a dainty eater. Often she would lose part of a pancake to one of her sole mates as she just couldn't get rid of one as fast as they could.

Together the Three Musketeers kept most of the edible trash and garbage out of the yard. If the droppings left behind were discounted, they kept the farmyard reasonably clean.

The Three Musketeers did not limit their foraging activities to our farmyard. Ed and Tresa Russell, who lived just east of the Gates store said the three frequently visited their back yard and stole the food put out for their dog or begged until they were provided scraps of their own.

All things must come to an end, so was the case of the Three Musketeers. When pig was big enough to top the market, he went to the livestock auction in Broken Bow. Speed matured into an oversized hound. He turned out to be too aggressive to be a good stock dog, so Dad sold him to a guy who had a pack of coyote hounds. Snowball continued as a combination pet and milk goat until she too was consigned to the slaughter house.

Dillard H. Gates

JUST SOMETHING TO DO

Recreation was not a formalized activity on the farm. When we were small we played with one another, dug in the dirt, played with the few toys we had, deviled Mom, or just sort of existed. As we got big enough we found things we could do by ourselves that were entertaining, at least to us. We could idle away our time in the swing hanging from the big box elder tree. For lack of something better to do, sometimes we boys would have a contest of skill to see who could pee the highest on the back side of the barn. Sometimes our main challenge was to keep out of the sight of Mom and Dad so they would not put us to work.

FEEDING THE CHICKENS

A common and necessary job was feeding the chickens. Normally that activity would not be very high on the excitement scale, but with a little imagination even feeding the chickens could be livened up a bit.

Sometimes as a diversion we would tie the end of a long piece of thread around a kernel of corn. We would then scatter a little corn in the chicken feeding area. Among the feed was the kernel of corn with the thread around it. The other end of the thread was clutched firmly in the hand of one of the kids sitting quietly a few feet away. The chickens would rush to the area where feed had been scattered and frantically snatch up the corn. In their haste to get as much corn as fast a possible the chicken would unknowingly pick up and swallow the kernel of corn with thread attached. After a few seconds when it was assumed the kernel was down the gullet the holder of the string would give a quick jerk. We kids laughed at the sight when the old hen jumped, let out a squawk, and threw back her head as the kernel of corn attached to the thread was extracted. The process would be repeated until the corn was gone or the chickens departed in fright. Anyone who would not find this exciting would probably be bored watching grass grow.

HIKEY INDUCED ACTIVITY

Hikey (carbon di-sulfide) was a useful and versatile product on the farm. It was used to kill prairie dogs, to run-off stray dogs, to send the neighbor's scrub bull home, and sometimes just for entertainment.

It was fun to watch dogs run that had a little hikey poured on their backs, but we never gave the treatment to our old dog Rags. We had no particular connection to the barnyard cats so with nothing else to do we occasionally gave them the treatment. Cats generally reacted vigorously to an application of hikey. A cat with a couple spoonfuls of hikey down its back would meow, squall, roll on the ground, run in circles, go full blast up a tree, or with tail held high take off like it was being chased by all the dogs in Custer County. This was great fun and entertainment which was readily available and affordable.

However, the old red rooster gave the most interesting and entertaining performance when a little hikey was sprinkled on his back. The ole rooster would sort of jerk his head, stomp his feet, ruffle his feathers, stretch his neck, then head for the nearest hen. Like a sex crazed maniac, he would grab the hen by the top of the head with his beak, mount up, then quickly and frantically do what roosters are supposed to. But the activity did not stop there. Like shots from an automatic shotgun he would repeat the process, I guess until the magazine was empty, leaving behind a wake of hens smoothing their feathers in bewilderment.

From the standpoint of entertainment hikeying the old rooster was definitely a step up from feeding chickens corn on a string. I don't recall any adverse affects from the hikey treatment, but maybe if chickens dream, they dreamed of that exhilarating, if brief, phenomena in the barnyard and wondered when it would happen again.

DANCING

It would be incorrect to say that dancing was not allowed in our house. The truth was that Dad allowed dancing only in the house. He would not permit my sisters to go to the country dances that abounded in the area even though there were no dance halls in the Gates Community. I recall Dad saying that he had nothing against dancing as such. However, he did not approve of the environments where most dances were held, nor the axillary activities and behavior reputed to be a part of the dance hall scene.

I had heard several definitions of dancing before I was old enough to completely understand the connotations of the descriptions. The definition, "Old fashioned belly rub," was understandable just from observing the juxtaposition of the dancing couple. However, as a boy, when I overheard my older sister describe dancing as, "A naval engagement without loss of seamen," I was completely baffled. I remembered the definition, but years passed and many biological changes occurred before I understood its implications.

Though there was not a radio in our house (Dad said there was enough noise without one) there was lots of music. There was the Edison phonograph with many records, the player piano and all of my older sisters played the piano. In addition, several of the neighbor girls who often spend the night with one of my sisters, played the piano. Also my Dad was an excellent mouth-harp (harmonica) player. The neighbor girls taught my sisters the basic steps, and they danced together in our front room. (It was perfectly acceptable for girls to dance together back in those days). Harriett Overgarrd, a friend of Sissy's, was a frequent visitor to our house and one of the best musicians in the community. In fact, she and her parents formed a musical group and played for many of the dances in the area.

Dillard H. Gates

  Despite our curiosity about what went on at dances and the desire to go see for ourselves, I am not aware that any of my sisters ever attended a dance while living at home. Dances and dance halls remained outside our scope of recreational activities, but the curiosity and the desire to have a look continued.

  When I was about fourteen or fifteen we had a hired man by the name of Cap Ward. He was a good worker and an excellent hired man despite his small stature, funny looks and strange behavior. One Saturday afternoon, when Dad was in town, Cap told me he was going to the dance at New Helena (Dreamland) that night. He asked if I would like to go along. The fact that I would like to go to the dance was axiomatic. However, as my behavior was controlled almost entirely by what I thought Dad would do if he found out, I was reluctant to make a commitment to accompany him.

  We finished the chores about dark and I told Cap that I would like to go with him to the dance but I had better not. Dad returned from town around eight-thirty and went directly to bed. Cap and I sat out on the hay wagon and talked for another half hour or so. Cap reiterated his intent to go to the dance. My resolve was weakening. I really wanted to see what things were like on the other side of the fence. Throwing caution to the wind, I agreed to go with him. I thought that by now Dad would be asleep. I planned to slip quietly into the house, pull on a shirt, clean overalls and my good shoes. I would join Cap in the barnyard in a few minutes. I intended to sneak back into the house when we returned from Dreamland.

  I slipped quietly into the house and into the bedroom I shared with my younger brother Jack. I peeled out of my shoes and dirty clothes and was fumbling in the dark for the clean ones.

  I froze in place as Dad's voice echoed down the hall. "Dill, where are you going?"

  Even before he had finished the short query about my intentions, I had completely changed my mind. When I heard "Dill", (the beginning of his question) I was preparing to go to a dance, but by the time I heard "going?"(the end of the question) I knew I was going to bed.

  Without hesitation and in absolute candor I replied, "To bed." I was thankful to be able crawl into bed with no further explanation requested.

Hay, Hell, Kids and Cattle

My problems were not over. How was I to inform Cap that I was going to bed and not to the dance? I lay on the bed virtually paralyzed with fear that Cap would come into the house after me. If so, surely Dad would believe I had just lied to him. The consequences of lying to Dad were more than I wanted to contemplate. He might not accept as truth that I had instantaneously changed my mind in mid-sentence and not lied. Dad had not asked me where I had been planning to go.

As I lay there pondering my predicament I heard a scratching on the screen outside the open window. I moved quickly to the side of the bed toward the window with the intent of whispering to Cap that things had changed and for him to just go away.

It was then I heard Cap call softly through the open window. "Dill, I have changed my mind, I decided not to go to the dance." I prayed that Dad had not heard.

"Yes," I responded in a quivering, barely audible voice, "I have gone to bed."

If Dad was aware of the last exchange between Cap and me he never mentioned it. After all I was in bed where I was supposed to be and I was damned glad to be there.

METHODIST POKER, A CARD GAME FOR THE UNBLEMISHED

Rook was a card game played with vigor in the Gates community. It was the pastime of choice of adults at local parties and various get-togethers and was a popular winter pastime in our house. The Rook deck contained fourteen cards of each of four colors and a joker. The rules were somewhat like bridge, but since it was not played with a poker deck it was deemed to be acceptable.

Dad was an excellent Rook player and always played to win. Mom didn't play very well. She couldn't remember the cards and feared Dad's wrath when she made a mistake. She did, however, frequently play rook with us kids on long winter nights. Playing Rook with Mom was fun. We kids could often beat her but we didn't improve our Rook skills much.

Sometimes Dad would also play Rook with the kids. We didn't have a card table in the house. When playing with us kids Dad would sit in his big chair at the head of the dining room table. His partner, generally the youngest kid playing, would lie on the table facing Dad. The other two players, their opponents, sat on the benches on either side of the table. It may have been an unorthodox arrangement to play cards, but it worked. We were taught the rules of the game and how to play our cards. Dad tried to teach us the strategy of the game, how to evaluate our own hands, and to analyze the hands of the opponents based upon their bidding and how to remember which cards had been played.

He was a good teacher, but even as a teacher he taught us that the objective of the game was to win within the rules of the game. There was low tolerance for poor playing and zero tolerance for cheating. You played the hand you were dealt to the best of your ability. If things didn't work out right you analyzed the problem and prepared for another hand. The lessons learned around the dining room table were not limited to table manners but to lessons of life as well.

STEALING WATERMELONS AND A BARBED WIRE FENCE

Stealing was considered a serious crime in the Gates community. No one locked their homes or removed the keys from their cars. "If it doesn't belong to you, leave it alone," was a common admonishment from both Mom and Dad. To be labeled as having sticky fingers was a burden hard to bear and difficult to shake. "Once a thief, always a thief," was the conventional wisdom where I grew up.

This tribute to morality was true in all cases except where watermelons were concerned. Somehow stealing watermelons was in a completely different category. Most farmers would gladly give you a watermelon if asked. Like many other pursuits in life, it is the chase rather than the catch that is challenging. Some sort of frowned on the idea, but most people shrugged it off as adolescent pranks unless the watermelon stealers tore up the patch while absconding with the loot. Stealing watermelons was just not considered a crime by most folks in Custer County.

Some farmers in the neighborhood, known to have great watermelon patches, looked on the practice with less favor than others, but even so watermelon stealing was viewed more as a contest than a crime. Some tried to hide their watermelon patches in corn fields or attempted in other ways to match wits with the watermelon stealers. Most of the farmers tried to scare hell out of anyone caught in their patch.

One evening in the summer of 1931 when I was six, my sisters Anna and Alice, asked Dad if they could borrow the car. Even though they were only thirteen and fourteen years old, they were experienced drivers and could handle the 1930 Buick sedan very well. Dad asked them why they wanted the car, and Anna admitted they were planning to pick up a couple of neighbor girls and go watermelon stealing at Stanley Swick's place.

Since the target location was only a couple or three miles away, Dad said, "Alright, but be careful."

Anna and Alice piled into the car and headed out to pick up their intended partners for the planned activities of the night. Dad thought this would be an opportunity to have some fun and maybe contribute some to the educational development of his mischievous and high spirited daughters.

As they disappeared down the road Dad grabbed his shotgun, a hand full of shells and hurried over to Ed Russell's place adjacent to the Gates store. He suggested to Ed that they take his car and hurry to the home of the intended victim before the girls got there. They would conceal themselves in the corn field near the watermelon patch and wait for the girls. When the girls were in the patch and intent on the task of selecting and carrying off choice melons Dad would point the twelve gauge into the air and fire a few shots while Ed and Stanley hollered as loud as possible. From their hiding place the men would watch the reaction of the girls as they were interrupted in the watermelon patch.

Dad's plans went as intended. It was a half-moon and visibility was limited. The three men concealed themselves in the corn field away from the expected route of the would be watermelon stealers. Another field of corn separated the road from the watermelon patch, and both fields were enclosed by barbed wire fences.

As they waited the men heard a car come down the road and stop. They soon heard wires squeak as the girls crawled through the barbed wire fence along the road right-of-way. They heard voices as the girls talked to keep up their courage and keep in contact as they moved cautiously through the corn field toward the watermelon patch. Once again the pranksters heard the squeak of wire sliding through fence staples as the girls parted the barbed wires and moved through the last barrier between them and their target for the night.

Once in the patch the other girls scattered, trying to locate the biggest and best melons. They thumped melons and checked their sizes concentrating on making choice selections. Soon arms were loaded and it was time to exit the watermelon patch.

The moment for action arrived. Dad emptied the magazine of the twelve-gauge into the night sky while Ed and Stanley hollered, "Let's get'em."

Terrified the girls tried to run while retaining their selected loot. They soon discovered you can run or you can carry watermelons, but it is difficult if not impossible to do both simultaneously. They dropped the melons, screamed, scattered like a covey of quail and running at top speed disappeared into the corn field.

The men had accomplished their mission; they had their fun. They were satisfied this would be a night to remember for the would-be watermelon stealers. Stanley went back to his house and Dad and Ed returned home.

Dad had not been home long before he heard the car drive into the yard. He appeared to be concentrating on the *Omaha Bee News* as the girls rushed into the house. Alice was wide-eyed and excited, Anna was in tears, her dress in tatters, and her arms and legs covered with blood. The sight of his two daughters in this condition brought Dad to his feet.

Both talking at once they tried to explain what happened as Dad examined Anna's wounds. Dad already knew the essence of the story.

However, the girls version of the story varied considerably from what Dad knew to be the facts. They reported that all the girls were in the watermelon patch when the shooting started and they heard bullets whistling through the corn plants around them. Both were certain Stanley Swick was shooting to injure if not to kill.

Anna was terrified by the shotgun blast, took off on the run and while in full flight ran head-long into the barbed wire fence surrounding the corn field. She had hit the fence at an angle and carried by her momentum slid along the fence. The barbs on the wire shredded her dress, and scratched and gouged the flesh of her arms, legs and belly.

Dad helped remove her ruined clothes and examined the lacerations. Mom washed and cleaned the wounds, and Dad applied the usual treatment of turpentine while Anna wailed in pain. Dad decided the wounds were only superficial and no further treatment was necessary. His diagnosis proved to be right: the wounds healed and there were no permanent scars.

Another practical joke had gone awry. What had started in fun ended with Anna being injured, luckily not seriously. A few days later Dad admitted to the girls his part in the incident. I don't know if they ever forgave him for it but I do know they never forgot the night in Stanley Swick's watermelon patch. And I don't know if Anna and Alice ever went watermelon stealing again.

A NEAR TRAGEDY IN A WATERMELON PATCH

John Bishop wouldn't intentionally harm anyone, but he came close to shooting two boys one night. Watermelon stealing was still an accepted form of recreation in the summer of 1942. John Bishop, who lived about three quarters of a mile north of Gates, had a good melon patch. The patch was located across the barnyard in a garden area a couple hundred yards southeast of the farm house. In the daytime the patch was clearly visible from the house.

John's watermelon patch had been raided several times during the late summer and he was getting a bit perturbed, not because someone had filched a few watermelons but because when so doing they had damaged the patch. He was a generous and congenial man and would give watermelons to anyone who asked. However, for my younger brother Jack, who had just turned fifteen and his friend, Howard Swick, being handed a watermelon lacked excitement and challenge.

Mom had given Jack permission to take the car and go see Howard, who lived about a mile south of Gates. As night fell and with nothing else to do, the boys decided to steal watermelons from John Bishop. They parked the car along the road south of Bishops' house. There was an apple orchard and woodlot blocking the view south of the house so the boys were sure the car would not be spotted. In the darkness they moved through the orchard, circled through a corn field and climbed through the fence into the watermelon patch.

Crouching low they tried to locate watermelons, by sight and feel. As they concentrated on finding suitable melons, they were startled by a shout, "Who's out there? Come out or I'll shoot."

The boys hit the ground like a dropped rock, huddled on the ground hoping if they were quiet John would assume it was a false alarm. They lay silently, side by side, hardly daring to breathe.

They heard footsteps coming across the barnyard toward the garden and John called out again, "Come on out, I know you're in there. Come out or I'll shoot."

Pressed against the warm earth they heard Mary, John's wife, beseeching, "John, be careful, be careful John, you'll hurt somebody dear."

The footsteps grew louder as John stomped across the yard toward the melon patch, with Mary trotting a few steps behind. John continued his threats to shoot as Mary begged him to be careful. Jack and Howard pressed against the warm earth and tried their best to be invisible. They prayed the darkness would shield them from John's view. He was now virtually upon them, and they could smell the strong pipe John clenched between his teeth. The boys were now in a situation where even though terrified they were afraid to move for fear John would shoot before they could identify themselves.

Suddenly John exclaimed excitedly, "There they are." At the same time he fired the shotgun into the ground ahead of him.

The full blast from the twelve-gauge shotgun tore into the earth a few feet from where the boys lay. They were petrified with fear, but remained still and quiet.

John stopped with Mary still a few steps behind. "I must have been wrong," he lamented to Mary, "If there was anyone was out there that should have brought them out."

With that he turned and with Mary trotting behind, headed toward the house. As he crossed the barnyard uncertainty lingered in John's mind. He was sure he had heard the fence squeak. He still wondered if someone was out there, so instead of going to the house he headed out to the road to have a further look.

As he moved from his driveway onto the road he could see a car parked along the road a short distance to the south. Now he was sure he had not been wrong. He approached the car and was shocked when he realized it belonged to Mom.

It was John's turn to be frightened. He knew it was some of Mom's kids who were trying to get his melons and he suspected it was Jack. He was worried that maybe the blast from his shotgun had found a target. He was beside himself with fear of what he might have done.

He rushed back down the road and across the barnyard toward the watermelon patch. As he approached the garden he pleaded loudly, "Boys, if you are out there please let me know. Please come out. I don't want to hurt you. Please, I just want to know if you are all right."

Jack and Howard were still clinging to the ground when John returned. They had been waiting to make certain John had gone back inside the house before attempting an escape. When they heard his reassuring words they assumed it was time to reveal themselves.

Still lying on the ground Jack called out to John and identified himself. Then still trembling with fear, he and Howard struggled to their feet. John stumbled up to them in the darkness, threw his arms about them and exclaimed, Thank god you are alright. Thank god I didn't hit you."

All the while, from a few steps back, Mary continued to chirp, "John, I told you to be careful. John, I told you to be careful."

While continuing to express relief that the boys were unhurt, John and Mary hurried them into the house. Hustling around like a hen with chicks, Mary poured lemonade and gave them cookies. The Bishops were overjoyed no damage had been done. They were our neighbors. They were our friends. They had a son, Eddie John, in the same grade at school as Jack and Howard and who buddied with them. If they had decided to steal someone else's watermelons that night, Eddie John may well have been with them.

    The boys retrieved Mom's car, and Jack took Howard home . An evening that started in fun had ended well, but with some horrifying and near tragic moments sandwiched between.

HAY

Putting up hay was a part of raising cattle. A herd of cattle, like a demanding mistress, can bring pleasure but require an inordinate amount of time and energy and have an insatiable appetite. During the summer while cows grazed green pastures, then lay in the shade chewing their cuds, we dripped with sweat as we struggled to put up hay for their winter rations. In winter we froze our butts bringing hay to the cattle as they stood in their long-haired winter coats, bawling impatiently for us to provide them with their sustenance.

Dad grew alfalfa for hay, and most of it was utilized for livestock feed. Also alfalfa was an important crop in a rather loose crop rotation system. In some years there was more hay than was required by the livestock so the surplus was sold. On occasion, when weather conditions and alfalfa seed prices were right, Dad also set aside some of the alfalfa acreage for seed. Alfalfa seed generally brought a good price and was a welcome source of income where cash was always in short supply. The amount of land devoted to alfalfa production varied from around eighty to one hundred acres.

Hay yields from the alfalfa fields were highly dependent on the amount of moisture received and varied from virtually zero to around two tons per acre. During the drought years of the thirties rainfall was a variable and scarce commodity on the plains of Nebraska.

Putting up hay was a major undertaking consisting of several separate but coordinated jobs and required a hay crew of at least five people. The hay was mowed, allowed to dry, raked into windrows and allowed to dry some more. It was gathered from the windrow and brought to the haystacker by a sweep which pushed it onto the head of the haystacker. The hay was then lifted onto the stack by the haystacker. The hay was dumped onto the top of the stack where a man, the stacker, moved the hay into place and tramped it tight to form the hay stack. The stacker had the hardest, dirtiest and hottest job in the hayfield. It was also the job that demanded the highest wage. If the going wage was one dollar per day for regular work, the hay stacker would be paid two to three dollars for those days actually spent on the stack.

There were always kids in the hayfield, riding the machinery with the men, chasing butterflies, pulling the legs off grasshoppers, running errands, or just watching and learning while trying to stay out of the way. They were learning not only how to make hay but also about responsibility, and when the kids were big enough they were put to work. The first job was that of water boy (yes, there were more girls than boys, but we were all called water boys). By the time I was five years old, Dad would tie a couple water jugs (one gallon glass vinegar jugs wrapped in wet burlap) together, drape them across old Wrangler's neck and send me to fetch fresh water. It took a lot of water to quench the thirst of the hard working, sweating hay crew. It was considered a butt kicking offense if someone in the hay crew needed a drink and the water jugs were empty.

Dad didn't use tobacco, but most of the hired men did. They bought Bull Durham for a nickel a sack and rolled their own, used chewing tobacco or both. Due to the fire hazard most of them chewed when working in the hay field. Little thought was given to the sanitary implications of sharing water jugs, and it was common practice to take a drink of water and pass the jug around. However, the tobacco chewers left a terrible tobacco taste in the water of each jug they used.

Even as a little kid I hated the tobacco taste in the water, and sometimes I told the tobacco chewers that they made the water taste awful. I didn't spit water back into the water jug when I took a drink, but I wondered if they did. Chewing tobacco was a man's right and water a necessity, and since I was just a kid, no attention was paid to my concerns. When I got big enough to operate a piece of machinery away from the stacking site I tried to keep my own water jug. However, it seemed if I got near a tobacco chewer the first thing he would do was grab my jug, take a swig and contaminate my drinking water.

I always wondered why Dad didn't have separate water jugs for the tobacco chewers, but he didn't. Work in the hay field was hot and dirty and working men had the priority. When a man wanted a drink he reached for the first available jug. I didn't like it but had the choice of going thirsty or tolerating the taste of tobacco juice laced drinking water.

MOWING HAY

Mowing was the first of several operations carried out in sequence as a part of the haying operation. It was the only job in the hay field that I liked, or maybe it was just the job I disliked the least.

When I became old enough to mow, we were using both horse drawn and tractor mowers. When I was ten or eleven I was plunked down in the mower seat, given the reins and told to start mowing. Like a lot of other things, I soon learned that there is a big difference between watching someone else do a job and doing it yourself. However, the horses were gentle and knew pretty well where they were to walk along the unmowed hay and we got along quite well. I had to guide them around the corners of the standing hay and soon learned to accomplish the turns without leaving uncut alfalfa at the corners.

Dad had purchased a new F-20, rubber-tired Farmall tractor in 1935 when I was ten years old. It was the first rubber-tired tractor in the community and it was great for mowing hay. When there was mowing to be done we all wanted to drive the tractor rather than the horses. The Farmall was not bothered by flies, did not run or walk away when it was not supposed to, did not have to be harnessed and hitched up in the morning or unhitched, watered and unharnessed at the end of the day. Of course the tractor had to be filled with fuel and greased. When I first began to drive the tractor, I was too small to fill the fuel tank so Dad or one of the other big people did that for me. But it wasn't long before I could drain tractor fuel from the storage barrels, climb up onto the tractor and pour it into the fuel tank.

There were problems, however, with both the horse-drawn and tractor mowers. Sometimes the sickle bar got clogged or a cutter-bar section would break. In the beginning this required help from Dad or a hired man. However, it wasn't long until I learned to clear the sickle bar and replace broken sections.

Despite the problems, driving the tractor and mowing hay was sort of fun. I liked the smell of the new mown hay and it made me feel big to be a working member of the haying crew. I felt bad, however, when I mowed into a pheasant's nest hidden in the alfalfa. It was especially bad when I mowed into the nest and the hen pheasant flushed and flew away with a leg, or maybe both, hanging down as they had been slashed by the mower sickle. Sometimes, I was rewarded by the sight of a hen pheasant with a brood of newly hatched chicks scampering away through the alfalfa as they escaped the mower. Sometimes I would catch a bunny rabbit, put it in my pocket, take it to the house and put it in a cage which we had made for that purpose. In hindsight it was not a very good idea to cage them as they usually died or a cat got them after a few days.

RAKING HAY

Depending on the weather, the new mown hay lay on the ground to dry for a half day or so. When the hay was partially dry, but before it began to lose its leaves, it was raked into windrows.

The hay rake was fourteen feet wide and normally pulled by two horses. When I was small the job of raking hay was usually done by one of my older sisters. However, we all grew into the job, and when I became big enough to hold the reins, stay in the seat and reach the trip pedal, I was considered ready to rake hay.

On occasion when the hay raking got behind, Dad would hook the rake behind the car. He pulled the rake a lot faster than the horses did so we could rake a lot of hay in a short time. Even though this was a fast way to rake hay, it made it a tough job for me. The ground was bumpy and I had to trip the pedal at the correct time to drop the hay into windrows while hanging onto the seat with both hands to keep from falling off. However, like other jobs on the farm, if Dad told me to do it, I did, and in the long run I guess it didn't hurt me any.

I remember one time when I was fourteen or so I was raking hay with a young team. They were well broke but not as gentle as some of the older horses. We were moving along at a fast trot and I was doing my best to maintain my seat on the rake. Between bumps I was dreaming of the neighbor girl when a pheasant flushed right ahead of the team. The horses spooked, threw up their heads and took off on a run. At first I jerked on the reins and tried unsuccessfully to control them. The ride was so rough that I took a rein in each hand then held on to the seat with both hands. The rake bounced across the hay field, and I feared I would fall in front of the rake and be dragged. I let go of the reins and threw myself backwards off the rake onto the ground. The horses continued to run toward the farmyard about a half mile away. The team, with the rake bouncing behind, ran through two gates that were difficult to manipulate the rake through even at a slow walk.

Anticipating the worst I followed behind the horses as quickly as I could. I was expecting to find a wrecked hay rake and maybe even an injured horse and already was worrying about what Dad would say and do. Dad, working at the hay stack, saw the horses running, jumped in the car and soon caught up to me. He picked me up and we followed in the direction the horses had taken. He asked me what the problem was and why I had let the horses run away. I told him about the flushing pheasant but omitted any mention of the neighbor girl. He reiterated that had I been alert I could have controlled the horses and the problem would not have developed.

When we drove into the barnyard we found the team standing calmly in front of the barn, with the rake intact, apparently undamaged. One of my older sisters, Anna, who had temporarily returned home had seen the horses run into the barnyard. She was standing by the team sobbing,"Poor Dill" as she feared I had been hurt in the run-away.

Dad was now more concerned about the damage the run-away might have done to the horses than about me. He crawled onto the rake, told me to follow in the car, and returned to the field where the run-away had started. He continued to rake hay until he felt like the horses were settled down, then turned them back to me. I continued with the job with no further problems and remained alert, at least for a while.

THE HAY SWEEP

The hay sweep was a piece of machinery used to move hay from the windrow to the haystack. The sweep pushed the hay onto the head of the haystacker so that it could be lifted to the top of the stack. Most hay sweeps were powered by two horses. However, Dad liked to do things in a big way so we had a bigger four-horse sweep. This permitted him to accomplish practically twice as much as a man with a two-horse sweep. It also took more skill to handle the four-horse team than the two-horse team. Dad usually operated the big sweep until my older brother, Hap, was able to handle the job. Then sometimes he and Dad alternated the jobs of hay stacker and sweep operator.

The four-horse hay sweep was a good place to train green horses that were being broke to work. The four-horse hitch required two horses to be hitched to either side of the sweep immediately behind the sweep head. The main structure of the sweep separated the two teams. Thus, there was an inside and an outside horse on either side of the sweep. The inside horse was trapped between the center portion of the sweep and the outside horse. It was often difficult to get the green horse properly hitched in the inside position. However, once in place its options were limited by the outside horse on one side and the sweep mechanism on the other. The outside horses were always older, experienced, and well trained. The driver sat on a spring seat immediately behind the horses, at the rear of the sweep, and controlled them with four reins, one to each horse.

The hay sweeping operation entailed getting a sweep-load of hay from the windrow, pushing it onto the haystacker head then backing away leaving the sweep-load on the haystacker head. A green horse soon found itself not only leaning into the tugs and pulling but, also backing up as well. There were times when the green horse didn't want to stop backing as it was fighting the other horses and the sweep. In such cases Dad just sat on the seat with the reins firmly in hand and let the horses back up until the green horse tired. When it stopped backing, Dad would give it a snap on the rump with the end of a rein and off they would go after another load of hay. Pulling the hay sweep was hard work, and the horses were usually rotated to another job or rested after a half day on the sweep.

In the mid-thirties Dad decided to build a power sweep to lessen his dependence on horses and to speed up the haying operation. He modified an old International truck which he had bought from a bankrupt implement dealer in South Dakota. He cut and shortened the truck frame, reversed the differential (rear end) and reattached it to the frame. This enabled the modified truck, now the power sweep, to run backwards while maintaining all gears. He then reversed the steering wheel and seat. The result was a short-coupled, tractor-like power-unit with speed and power and rear-end steering which permitted a short turning radius.

Dad then designed and constructed a sweep head to hang on the power unit. The sweep head was of unique design that permitted the machine to cross ditches or go over big bumps without getting hung up as was the case with fixed-head power sweeps. The power sweep was rough riding but fast and powerful and would do the work of several horse-drawn units. Dad always operated the power sweep unless Hap was around, then he sometimes shared the job with him. When my father died in the spring of 1941, I inherited the privilege of power sweep operator along with a lot of other jobs and responsibilities.

THE HAYSTACKER

The haystacker lifted the hay that had been pushed onto its head by the sweep to the top of the stack that was being built. The haystacker consisted of the head onto which the hay was pushed, stacker arms made of heavy timbers, an A-frame, a series of pulleys and a stacker cable. When the cable was pulled, it drew the pulleys closer together which caused the arms with the head attached to be lifted. When the arms and head reached the vertical position, the hay slid off the haystacker head and fell onto the growing hay stack.

The haystacker was strong and heavily built but like all machines it was vulnerable. If the load was too heavy, or for some other reason the cable broke while the load of hay was being lifted, the whole shootin match came crashing back to the ground. Sometimes little damage was done to the haystacker but often the head was damaged or one or both of the stacker arms broken. Whatever the cause hay stacking came to a halt until the damage was repaired. Materials with which to repair the haystacker were sometimes available at the farm, but if the arms or the cable were broken it usually meant a trip to town to get the necessary repairs.

For years Dad talked about making an all-steel haystacker that would lift bigger loads and would not be so susceptible to breakage. In the mid-thirties after the power sweep was completed, he set about building the steel haystacker.

The undercarriage for the steel haystacker was fashioned from the framework of an old Galleon road grader Dad had bought years before to maintain roads in the township. The arms for the haystacker were made from heavy steel truck frames. The A-frame and all cross-bracing was made from old car frames or steel beams salvaged from other old machinery. The pulleys were all steel and rolled on ball bearings. The steel cable used to lift the stacker was of heavier gauge and stronger than the cable for the old stacker. Only the head of the new stacker was made of wood.

Dillard H. Gates

The new haystacker was a strong piece of machinery and considered virtually indestructible. People from all over Custer County, and beyond, interested in putting up hay, came to the farm to see the new stacker and the power sweep in action. Dad was proud of the machinery he had built, and rightly so. Both pieces of machinery incorporated unique design features that probably should have been patented but were not. I was proud of my Dad and of the machinery he had conceived and fabricated in the shop on the farm.

Another vital component of the hay stacking job was the stacker team and the person who operated it. The stacker team was ordinarily a team of horses controlled by a driver. However, in our haying operations, especially after Dad built the power sweep and the steel haystacker, a tractor or truck if one was available, was often utilized as the "stacker team."

There was more to driving the stacker team, whether it was a team of horses, tractor or truck, than merely pulling the cable until the haystacker was vertical and the hay slid off onto the stack. There was often wind to contend with or the man on the stack might want the upcoming load placed in a certain position on the stack. It was also necessary when utilizing a tractor or truck as a "stacker team" to stop promptly when the cable was fully extended to prevent jerking the haystacker or possibly breaking the cable.

During the summer haying season of 1940 my father was having health problems. Dad had made arrangements to go to the Mayo Brothers' Clinic after the hay was put up. Several neighbors, as neighbors did in those days, came over with their equipment to help put up the hay.

One neighbor, Charlie McGraw came over and volunteered to use his truck as a "stacker team." Charlie was sort of an eccentric old codger who frequently "pushed the line" in his relationships with neighbors. He was commonly referred to as old "Ho Ho By God" as that is how he generally prefaced his remarks. On several previous occasions he had come over to watch the steel haystacker in action. He displayed uncommon curiosity and asked Dad more than once what would happen to the steel haystacker if the cable broke.

On this particular day old Charlie McGraw and his truck were functioning as the stacker team. Dad noticed that sometimes when the cable was about extended Charlie would give the truck a bit of extra gas and give the cable a good jerk. Dad was concerned about what was going on and reminded Ho Ho By God about the potential problems of jerking the cable. The next few loads went up without incident. Then wham, the truck hit the end of the cable with hard jerk and the cable snapped. The haystacker dumped its load of hay, bounced back from the stack, remained vertical momentarily, then crashed to the ground. Everyone in the vicinity of the stacker rushed over to see how the steel monster had survived the crash. After a quick inspection Dad discovered that except for the broken cable and a bent brace or two there was little apparent damage.

Old Charlie came ambling over to the haystacker, squirted a mouthful of tobacco juice in the dust at his feet, uttered his trademark expression, "Ho Ho, Ho,Ho by God," then followed with this curious, prophetic comment, "I always wondered what would happen if the cable broke." Well, he had just found out.

Old Ho Ho was gracious, if not contrite, and offered to drive Dad to Broken Bow to buy a replacement cable. Dad considered the offer but decided he had seen about enough of Charlie for one day and refused. While Dad was away purchasing the new cable the rest of the crew removed, straightened and replaced the braces. After a half-day downtime, repairs were made and the neighborhood crew was ready to get back at the job of putting up hay. Old Ho Ho by God suddenly remembered he had other things to do. He crawled into his truck and headed west across the hay field toward his home. Another neighbor hitched his tractor to the new steel cable and the hay stacking operation continued. Dad was never certain if it was maliciousness or curiosity that caused old Charlie to break the stacker cable. But knowing Charlie McGraw I would bet on the former.

With the generous help from neighbors, the haying job was completed. Dad made the trip to the Mayo Clinic only to find that he had a serious heart problem, a condition from which he never recovered.

MEASURING AND SELLING SURPLUS HAY

At times there was a surplus of alfalfa hay which Dad sold to commercial hay buyers, neighbors or other stockmen in the area.

Our alfalfa was in fifteen to twenty-ton stacks in the hay field. Hay was sold by the ton so it was necessary to determine the weight in order to complete the sale. If the purchaser planned to move the hay through town, the loaded truck could be put across a set of scales there and the weight determined. However, if it was not convenient to weigh a truck, another method of determining the weight of the hay was available. The dimensions of the haystack were measured, and a universally accepted formula was used to compute the tons of hay in the stack. This was accomplished by throwing a long rope over the top of the stack at the highest point. One end of the rope was made to touch the ground on one side of the stack and a knot was tied in the rope where it touched the ground on the other side. The distance between the end of the rope and the knot was then measured. The circumference of the stack was measured at ground level and near the top just before the taper that formed the dome at the top of the stack. This information along with a factor for compaction, estimated by the age of the stack, provided the basic data required to compute the weight of the hay in the stack.

A neighbor, John Bishop, was considered the official hay measurer in the Gates community. How he acquired the position I don't know. It may have been because at one time he had a long tape measure (later replaced by the rope) and that somewhere he had learned the formula for converting the measurements to tons of hay in the stack. Maybe more importantly John was considered by all who knew him to be a man of integrity. People trusted his measurements and computations and accepted the results. If the hay sale was between neighbors, John did the job for free. It was just a neighborly act. If the hay was being bought by a commercial hay buyer, he might collect a small fee.

The negotiations to arrive at a selling price for the hay and then determine the tons of hay in the stack was one matter. Sometimes collecting the money for the hay sold was another. I remember several occasions when Dad had to go directly to a hay purchaser, sometimes repeatedly, to collect.

It was a wise seller who knew whether to collect at the time of sale or give the buyer some time before payment was due. Most people in the community had developed a reputation regarding how they handled their debts. All the farmers in Custer County during the drought and depression owed money to someone. It was how they handled their debts that reflected the character of the man. .

I clearly remember a time when Dad was negotiating with a farmer living northeast of us for the sale of a stack of alfalfa hay. This individual, though part of an old time family in the area, had the reputation of not paying his bills and worse, of accumulating machinery, livestock and other items for which there was no bill of sale in evidence. The first time I heard a neighbor say that this man could roll up a mile of wire fence at night quicker than anyone in Custer County, I didn't know what he meant. I also recall a rumor about a tractor that disappeared from a farm and was discovered under a straw stack on his farm. Even my Mom who seldom said anything unkind about anyone once remarked, "That guy is so crooked he will have to be screwed into the ground when he dies."

He and his family were a rough, tough lot. Dad did business with them but used discretion and caution in their dealings. After some period of negotiations Dad and the purchaser arrived at a price per ton and agreed that John Bishop would measure the stack and compute the tonnage.

There were other discussions regarding payment for the hay that I did not fully comprehend at the time. The farmer wanted to pay Dad for the hay after he had transported it to his farm. I remember Dad saying that, "No, the hay will just stay in the stack until I have the money."

After the discussions were over and the man who had bought the hay left, I was still a bit confused and asked Dad why he was so insistent that he receive payment before the hay was moved. Dad then reminded me of the purchaser's reputation and the difficulty of collecting after the hay had been removed. He then related to me that, "The only way to make sure I get the money from him is to have the cash in hand while the hay is still in the stack." At the time I thought Dad was being a little hard on the man but later realized that in the face of all the stories, he was only being prudent.

Dillard H. Gates

THE HIGH SCHOOL YEARS

MY FRESHMAN YEAR

The transition from intermediate to high school in the fall of 1938 was memorable but also frustrating. I moved from a situation where I was one of the big boys in the room to that of a freshman. I would no longer be designated to choose up sides or be one of the first selected when someone else did the choosing. Not only was I a freshman but also physically I was a scrawny freshman.

Gates High school had instituted a program of six-man football in the fall of 1936 and became a member of the Little Six Athletic Conference. The other schools in the conference were Milburn, Westerville, Dry Valley, Oconto and Berwyn. It was a mighty conference, and Gates High School was on the threshold of an anticipated football dynasty. At the time I was in the seventh grade and was profoundly impressed when I saw the high school boys put on their blue and gold uniforms and begin football practice. I was certain that in a couple of years I would become a part of a glorious tradition.

Like any red-blooded American boy I wanted to play football. The first day of high school I informed the coach, W. G. Hendrickson, that I was ready and willing to play. I was thirteen years old and according to the cream scales in the Gates store where we all went to weigh in I weighed a solid one hundred five pounds. I wasn't the smallest freshman waiting to become a "Gates High School Pirate." I out-weighed Alan Dewey by nearly ten pounds and stood two inches taller.

But there were considerations other than desire and size. The coach was willing to take me on as the number of boys going out for football was limited. I was certain that I could play enough to letter even though the first team would be made up of big and experienced upper-class men.

But Dad said, "No," emphatically, "No."

Dad expressed two reasons to support his firm stand against me playing football. I wasn't particularly impressed with the logic of either, but his "no" certainly carried more weight than my "yes." Dad wanted me home promptly after school to help feed the cattle and help with the

Hay, Hell, Kids and Cattle

ever present chores. He said that if it was exercise I wanted I could come home and pitch a load of hay or shuck a load of corn.

More importantly he was afraid I would get my knees hurt. For years Dad had suffered with a bum knee as a result of being butted by a buck sheep. He had further aggravated the injury climbing onto and jumping down from large farm machinery which he operated. He knew first hand the problems related to bad knees and didn't want me to suffer as had he. So the hundred and five pounds of fighting tiger meat that dreamed of becoming the terror of the Little Six conference watched from the sidelines or helped run the chains during home games. If a game extended much past four o'clock, I had to miss the ending and get home to help Dad.

The coach was also the school Superintendent and high school teacher. He and his family lived in a vacated farm house about three-quarters of a mile southeast of school. Officially he was Mr. Hendrickson; however, the previous year he had been nicknamed "Thistle" by Buck Swick, one of the seniors. The name was deemed fitting as Thistle drifted about the country side like a tumbleweed being blown by the wind and we students never knew where he was. It was not uncommon for him to leave the school house for hours at a time. Sometimes as we looked out the school house windows, we would see him driving down the dirt road toward his home. Other times he just crawled into his car and disappeared. He was what we students considered to be a middle aged man and had been married for years. However, the older and presumably more worldly boys wondered if he spent so much time at home because he was enjoying a second honeymoon in the country.

When he was at school, if he found the students unprepared, he would simply dismiss class and tell the students if they didn't want to come prepared he was not going to bother with them. This was an incentive for us not to be prepared for class. Thistle taught freshman algebra. As students we soon learned his method of operation so some were always unprepared. As a result we progressed only to page eighty-nine in our algebra text that year. The best I can say about Thistle is that he was a good coach, but as my mother said, he too "Was as worthless as a whip socket on an automobile."

Hendrickson shared high school teaching responsibilities with Miss Mildred Steinspring. Gates High school was her first teaching job. Her home room was the ninth and tenth grades, and Hendrickson's the eleventh and twelfth grades. They sometimes switched rooms depending on the particular class being taught.

She was a pretty young woman, full of vigor and ambition and ready to begin making her mark on the world. It was soon obvious she was not prepared to deal with what she found at Gates. There were about a half dozen boys in the eleventh and twelfth grades whom though younger, were bigger than Miss Steinspring. They were typical rural high school boys whose behavior may have been marginal at best. Those boys were at the age when muscles were expanding and they were beginning to feel the pulses of manhood. Her behavior was exemplary and her demeanor shy. However, the face and form of the new teacher did little to quiet the hormones surging through the veins of those students. All of the boys in high school thought she was a beautiful gal, but the big boys had an advantage over the puny ninth and tenth graders. We could not flex our muscles to get her to notice us, but we did other equally foolish things in an effort to attract her attention.

For the most part, the students were on their good behavior when Mr. Hendrickson was in the building, but when he disappeared from the class room and someone spied the dust trail heading toward his home, there was a noticeable change of atmosphere. The boys didn't do anything particularly bad or harmful to Miss Steinspring, they just didn't pay much attention to her instructions.

A couple of boys in the classroom might begin playing catch with blackboard erasers, a bottle of ink, or about anything loose that could be easily tossed. When she told them to stop, they would toss the object to another guy, or sometimes girl and the game of catch would then continue between new players. This could go on until the kids tired of aggravating her or until in exasperation, sometimes in tears, she would leave the room.

On one occasion when Duane Bates, a tenth grader, kept talking to some of the other kids, including me, when we were supposed to be studying, Miss Steinspring repeatedly told him to be quiet, but to no avail. She put up with this behavior as long as she could but eventually lost all semblance of self control. She rushed down the aisle to where Duane was sitting and began pounding him on the head with her fists and screaming, "Shut up, shut up." Duane covered his head with his arms in a mock attempt to shield himself from the blows rained upon him. Most of the kids began laughing at what we thought was a hilarious situation.

Hay, Hell, Kids and Cattle

Duane turned part way around in his seat and called to me, "Hey, Dillard, she is sure beating up on me, isn't she?" His call broke the spell and Miss Steinspring dropped her hands, burst into tears and rushed from the room.

Her dramatic departure brought a sudden quiet to the room. Instead of a room full of kids who thought what they had been doing a few moments before was funny, we were now a room full of kids who suddenly realized that what we had been doing was not funny at all. We were embarrassed and without exception regretted our behavior, all knew we had mistreated a nice person, a young teacher who was trying her best to do what she was hired to do.

Prior to this incident Miss Steinspring had kept her own council and had not reported our shenanigans to Mr. Hendrickson. But this time when he returned she reported what had just happened as well as some of the things that had taken place before. Hendrickson assembled all high school students into one room, laid down the law and made it clear whether he was present or not behavior such as she had reported would not be tolerated. If repeated, we would first answer to him then be taken directly home for a discussion with our parents.

Our behavior was modified, and no one blamed Miss Steinspring for reporting our misdeeds to Mr. Hendrickson. We continued to tease and jest with her, but there were no more manifestations of disrespect. She stayed at Gates only one year.

I saw Miss Steinspring (Cowdin) over fifty years later at a Gates Community get-together at the Gates School. She was still a beautiful and gracious lady. I hope she has forgiven us for our bad behavior.

Something else happened during my freshman year which left the freshman boys frustrated and at first bewildered. It was not long after the school year started when we noted that the girls who had been our friends and girl friends in the eighth grade now had little time for us. It soon became evident that the eleventh and twelfth grade boys made a definite distinction between boys and the girls of the freshman class. The freshmen boys were now viewed by the freshmen girls and upper class boys alike as awkward, pimply faced, insignificant beings, which may have been the case.

On the other hand, the freshman girls, becoming women, noted with satisfaction their reflections in the mirror. And with a heightened awareness of the bulges in their blouses gazed beyond their childhood friends to the boys in the upper grades who had now become young men.

One of the freshman boys, Jim Schmidt, figured out what was happening sooner than the rest of us. "They are just feeling their titties," he aptly explained. "We are still boys to them, and they are now beginning to look for men." I am certain the upper classmen would have agreed with Jim. For without doubt, they looked upon the incoming crop of freshman girls as a resource to be exploited.

When basketball season rolled around, I wasn't much bigger than I had been in the fall, but I wanted to go out for the team. Basketball was a year-around activity at Gates despite the fact that we had only an out-of-doors dirt court. In the winter we often had to scoop snow from the court before we could play. After rains we played in the mud or waited for it to dry. There was a couple of neighbors who had big hay mows in their barns. They gave permission for us to practice basketball in the barns if we promised there would be no smoking. Fire was always a potential hazard in a barn where hay was stored. During the years we even played a few Little Six Conference games in the hay mows. It was not the best place in the world to play basketball, but it was the best we had and we were used to making do.

Dad wasn't so concerned about me getting my knees hurt playing basketball. Boys going out for basketball were released from class earlier than the rest of the students on practice days. This permitted me to turn out for basketball if I then hurried home immediately after practice to help with the chores. I would have agreed to almost any terms set by Dad as I had a strong desire to play basketball. Dad allowed a lot of leeway in his enforcement of the rules and I was able to make practice most of the time and never had to miss a game at home or away.

There were four big senior boys, Dale Douglas, Weldon (Buck) Swick, Harry Cosner and George Ash who provided most of the talent for the team and even won quite a few conference games. I remember in a game against Westerville I suddenly found myself with the ball in the open under the basket. I was hesitant to shoot as I thought that privilege was reserved for the big boys. Dale Douglas hollered, "Shoot, Dill, shoot." I was excited but I shot and scored. That was the only basket I made in a regular game during my freshman year.

Even though I was small and scrawny, coach Hendrickson let me play enough to earn my letter. I was proud to wear the "Blue and Gold" of Gates High School.

In those days the Nebraska High School Athletic Association would not allow a school to award a letter to a student athlete. The athlete could earn the letter but had to pay for it himself if he wanted one to wear on a school sweater. Dad gave me the fifty cents to pay for the big gold letter "G". Though we had to purchase the letters ourselves, we had earned them. Along with other team members, I was proud to receive my letter when Mr. Hendricksen handed it to me during an awards ceremony.

THE NEIGHBOR'S NAG THAT KICKED THE BUCKET

Corn fields are not pastures nor are they meant to be a grazing haven for a neighbor's horse. During the summer when I was thirteen years old, Dad was replacing the boundary fence of one of the corn fields that bordered the road north of the Gates store. For a period of time there was no fence along the road as Dad installed new steel posts on which he would secure the hog mesh topped by two strands of barbed wire.

During this period a neighbor's old, decrepit nag of a saddle horse spent an inordinate amount of time in our corn fields despite Nebraska law that livestock were to be confined and controlled by their owners. The neighbor, Raymond (Ramey) Ash, lived a quarter of a mile east of the Gates store and farmed the land across the road east of our corn field.

His idea of what constituted a good fence was a far cry from that of my father. As a result, his stock spent a good share of their time on the wrong side of the fence. The old horse was just the most recent example. While our fence was being replaced, the old nag had only to step over the fence around Ramey's field and cross the road into our corn field. On several occasions Dad had directed me or one of the other kids to chase the ole nag out of our corn field or to catch and take him home.

One Saturday when Dad was in town, Jack and I spotted the skinny, decrepit old horse gleefully chomping and stomping our corn. We decided to try a tactic other than simply driving him from the field. We jumped on ole Wrangler, rode down to the field where the trespasser was filling his empty gut at our expense and trampling on the corn plants. We secured a rope around his neck and led him back to our barn.

In the past Jack and I had tin-canned a few stray dogs. We thought it was great fun to see them run with the cans tied to their tail and banging against their back legs and behind. Generally a dog that had been tin-canned did not return. We decided to see if the technique would be equally effective on a horse.

We took an empty five-gallon oil can from the shop and dropped in a bunch of old bolts and other small pieces of metal, anything to make it rattle. Using baling wire and binder twine we securely tied the can to the tail of the nag. It was strategically hung at a height so that it would strike the horse between the back knees and hocks. Jack led the horse from the barn as I followed behind carefully supporting the can and contents so they did not rattle or strike the back end of the horse.

Once out of the barn Jack slipped the rope from the neck of the ole plug, and I slammed the oil can down against its back legs. We both screamed like gut-shot panthers and waved our arms. That emaciated and here-to-fore poky pony took off like a scalded cat. That nag, which we thought was on its last legs, put on a performance that would have put the legendary "Ole Strawberry Roan" to shame. It jumped and snorted, then bucked and farted and with ears laid back streaked across the barnyard, around the granary, out onto the road and headed east.

Jack and I followed as fast as we could. By the time we reached the road where we could see, the speeding steed moving by instinct alone, with the rattling oil can alternately hitting him on the legs and the back was going through the intersection at the Gates store heading toward home at top speed. That nag was so intent on making the best possible time that it completely ignored the "School, Go Slow" signs posted along the road near the school intersection. We had no way to clock him, but odds are that crazed charger established a new road record for the one-half mile from out barn to his.

The oil can treatment must have worked. I don't know if Ramey Ash found the can on the horse's tail, figured out what happened then kept the plug confined or if the poor ole horse just stayed at home out of fear that another oil can might be lurking somewhere in a field of corn.

Many times later I mused that if I could find a legitimate way to make a horse that looked as bad as that nag run as fast as that one with a can on its tail, I could clean up at the Capetown races. Certainly nobody would place a bet on such a nag to win, place or, show.

THE LAST SCION

New babies appeared at our house frequently, if not on a regular schedule. By now I knew how babies happened, but I never knew when Mom was pregnant.

In the spring of 1939 when I was fourteen, my sixteen-year-old sister, Gee, and I were scooping a load of grain from a wagon into the granary. Gee related she would share a secret with me if I would not tell any of the littler kids. After I pledged my silence, she disclosed that Mom was going to have another baby. My youngest sister, Iris, was three and one-half years old and I thought she was probably the end of the line.

Gee went on to tell me that she was "put out" with Dad because he had gotten Mom pregnant. She expressed the opinion that Mom had enough kids and enough work without another one to care for. She stated rather emphatically that if Dad would just leave Mom alone this would not have happened. Though Gee was sixteen going on seventeen she may have lacked a full understanding of marital relationships or she may have been reminded of the aggressive back-seat behavior of some of the local boys she knew.

Mom continued her work around the house, and even though I was now aware she was pregnant, I noticed no particular change in her work habits or behavior. She tended to be a bit on the heavy side and always wore loose-fitting dresses so her condition was not apparent to me. However, early in July Mom began to slow down a bit. Even though it was not quite her time she and Dad decided it was time to go to town so she could receive care and be close to the doctor if complications set in.

A now-married older sister, Alice, and her family lived in Sargent. Arrangement had been made for Mom to stay there and for Alice to care for Mom her during her confinement. Gee and Sissy were now big enough to take care of the house and the little kids, so this time Dad did not have to be concerned with finding a hired lady.

Sissy and Gee handled the domestic chores OK, however, they soon learned the truth about the amount of work required to make the household function. They quickly realized that their contributions to the total work effort when Mom was around had been meager. Then one morning at the breakfast table Dad announced that we had a new baby brother, Larry Goodwin: Larry because Mom liked the name and Goodwin the name of a great-great-uncle who had been a railroad engineer.

Mom's confinement following Larry's birth was extended. Apparently her tough and resilient body was at last reacting to the years of hard work and child bearing. Mom required more care than Alice could provide so Dad moved her to a nursing home in Sargent. In a few weeks she was on the road to recovery.

Even though there were lots of kids around the house, the new baby boy was welcomed into the family. We needed another boy to help provide a balance to a family that was heavily skewed toward girls. As was always the case, the new addition quickly became our idol and learned to manipulate the family and to get his own way.

When Larry was just a year old toddler, he found he could get his own way by holding his breath. Sometimes when disturbed he would hold his breath until he turned blue, frightening the wits out of Mom and us kids. Unless there was someone close enough to catch him, he would fall to the floor. Mom was afraid he would hurt himself. Dad told us to ignore him and let him fall. Once he bumped his head a time or two and found he was not getting the attention he wanted, he would give up the performance.

The cure for the breath-holding escapades came suddenly when Larry pulled his breath-holding trick in Dad's presence. As the toddler held his breath and began to turn blue Dad told us to leave him alone. When finally Larry toppled to the floor Dad quickly grabbed him up and dunked him head-first into the water bucket setting on the washstand. The cold water caused Larry to catch his breath, and he quickly changed color from a blue to a red-faced screaming baby. The treatment was specific, precise and effective. On occasion Larry threw temper tantrums as children are wont to do, but never again did he use breath holding as a means to get attention.

Baby brother Larry remained the pride and joy of the family. He was a year and one-half old when Dad died in the spring of 1941.

THE SKIRT THAT RODE UP HIGH, A MYSTERY NOT REVEALED

As years passed my curiosity about all aspects of sex, including my own sexuality, was heightened concurrent with the biological changes occurring in my developing mind and body. The topic became a frequent subject of conversation among my siblings and me and with friends and schoolmates. I suppose it would be safe to say that as I matured I learned what little I knew about sex from observations made in the barnyard, from the hired men, my peers at school and, oh yes, *Webster's Dict*ionary and the *Book of Knowledge*, the set of encyclopedias at school. I would not recommend that educational process to anyone, but that's what was available to me and I imagine most of the other boys in the community. At home the subject was just not discussed with my mother or father.

Neither of my parents ever uttered one word of clarification or explanation on the subject. Without being told so directly, I developed the belief that somehow this natural phenomena was not nice at best and even dirty or vulgar. This did little to help me understand the changes taking place within me and those I observed taking place in my older sisters. Nor did it explain or help me understand the reasons for or ramifications of the new babies which regularly joined our family.

Hired ladies were a normal and accepted part of my childhood. Dad frequently hired women to care for the family while Mom was absent giving birth to another baby or when she was sick and required extra help with the kids and the household. For the most part these hired ladies were surrogate mothers to me as they, partially at least, filled the void left by Mom when she was away. However, as I matured a bit there was an inkling of change developing in my scrawny body and inhibited mind.

By the time I was twelve or maybe thirteen, biological changes within me tended to make me more aware of differences between girls and boys and to arouse my curiosity about those differences. About that time we had a hired lady, Opal Albright. She and the family from which she came were long-time acquaintances of Mom and Dad. She was a rather plain looking young woman with a young son, whom I had been told, she had acquired without benefit of marriage. She got along well with the kids, was a hard worker, and was happy to help outside of the house if need be. She frequently joined in playful scuffles with my older sisters an me and seemed to especially enjoy it if the scuffling involved body contact with me. I thought she was always pretty nice to me, but that may have been just my imagination.

One afternoon I climbed astride ole Wrangler to bring in the milk cows. Opal indicated she would like to go with me, just for the ride. I was riding bareback and scooted back on ole Wrangler, she crawled up in front of me and we took off down the road toward the pasture.

When riding a horse double and bareback, the natural tendency is for the person sitting behind to slide forward and press against the one riding in front. As ole Wrangler trotted down the road, I slid forward against Opal's back and she suggested that I put my arms around her to steady her as she was not an experienced bareback rider. Opal was wearing a dress, not the most suitable attire for riding.

By the time we had gotten over a couple hills in the pasture Opal's dress had worked up above her hips, exposing her long slender legs. She entreated me to hold her tight as she didn't want to fall off as Wrangler went up and down the hills. For a while we rode in silence. After a bit she asked me if it bothered me to see her legs exposed to the extent they were. "Shucks, no," I responded. Why should I be bothered, I had lots of sisters and had seen lots of bare legs before, but I was not being completely candid with her as for some reason seeing her exposed legs was not the same as seeing my sisters'. I didn't really know why but somehow the feelings, the thoughts, the biology all seemed to be mixed up with that forbidden subject, sex.

My imagination shifted into full gear as her dress slipped higher and gathered almost at her waist. Curious little thoughts began to flicker through my mind as I held her tightly around the waist to steady her on the horse. I began to wonder if maybe this was the beginning of the solution to the mysteries which haunted me. Were these observations precursors to a peak behind that heretofore barricaded door. I may have tightened my grip around her waist, and even scooted a bit closer, subconsciously hoping that these actions might hasten the revelations.

Then without warning an image of the stern and disapproving face of my Dad flashed into mind. Even faster than a cold shower, that image erased any lascivious thoughts that may have been developing in my immature and muddled brain. The door, which had appeared on the verge of opening, slammed shut. The young and scrawny arms, that only moments before encircled the warm and yielding waist, now dangled by my sides. The view of the long, slender, legs which had just stimulated the strange curiosity within me now paled. The potential revelations remained forbidden mysteries.

Sensing the abrupt change in me Opal asked if I was alright. She didn't know what had caused the sudden change in me, but she had not seen the image of my Dad. I assured her I was OK as I tried to focus my attention on other things.

    I soon discovered she could ride bareback quite well without my support. Though her dress remained high on her hips, I began to think that maybe her legs were about like my sisters' after all. Once again she became just the hired girl who was going with me to bring in the cows. Whether real or imagined, the incident remained fixed in my mind. No further overtures were made, that is, unless I was too naive to interpret the signals.

THE SOPHOMORE AND JUNIOR YEARS

The fall of 1939 brought a big change to Gates High School. We had two new high school teachers, Superintendent, Richard B. Mease, and his wife Flora. They were a young couple and with their baby girl, lived with the Perry Myers, a farm family about one and one-half miles west of Gates. Mr Mease had grown up on a farm in central Nebraska and was accustomed to country life. His wife had grown up as a city gal, so the facilities, customs and mores of rural Custer County were a bit shocking if not disconcerting to her.

In part I imagine due to their age, the new teachers developed a reasonably good rapport with the students. We boys did not give the Superintendent's wife the static we had given Miss Steinspring, or maybe because the four big boys had graduated and we lacked leadership.

The new teachers remained at Gates for two years, and their style was in sharp contrast to that of Hendrickson. The Superintendent was a large man bordering on the obese. His wife was a slender, attractive woman and considered herself to be quite sophisticated, not uppity, just sophisticated and she displayed the manners, the dress and the style in an attempt to make the point. She was also incredibly naive. She often wore her hair in a tight, french-braid which she would leave untouched for days if not weeks. She had big brown eyes, a nice smile, was pleasant and generally liked by students and parents. She tended to wear two-piece tailored suits with tight skirts.

Rumor had it that the Superintendent's wife was admired by a few of the post-high school young men of the community. Some may have confirmed personality characteristics that we high school boys only imagined. I remember my Aunt Dora commenting that she would not blame her for being attracted to any one of several young men of the neighborhood, considering the fat slob to whom she was married. However, as far as I know none of the fantasies, if they actually existed, became reality.

Mr. Mease was a much better teacher than his predecessor if for no reason other than he met his classes regularly and expected us to do the work assigned. He was no great shakes as a coach, but he didn't know it. He was a good math teacher and taught the freshmen students more algebra in six weeks than the present sophomores had learned the entire previous year. The entire sophomore class should have repeated algebra, but of course we didn't. He was able to teach us a bit of geometry, but as far as I know no budding mathematicians emerged from Gates High school as a result of his tenure.

THE SUPERINTENDENT'S WIFE

Mrs. Mease taught social studies, English and typing. I have no recollection of a thing she taught me in English or social studies, but I do remember her demeanor in the class room. There were usually empty desks in the room. When holding class she would frequently sit on one of the empty desks toward the front of the room with her feet in the seat, facing the class. Often times she would sit on a desk immediately in front of me. If she would have sat there with her tight skirt pulled up a bit for the sake of comfort, and her knees primly together, it would have been only slightly distracting.

However, this was not the case. She sat directly in front of me with her knees immodestly parted. It was clearly evident that she did not wear flour sack bloomers like those of my sisters. It was also quickly evident that the scene presented resulted in mixed reactions, even in a dumb, naive country boy like me. The first problem was what to do with my eyes. If I stared straight ahead I was gazing at what I considered to be forbidden territory. If I looked at her face and dropped my eyes to my notebook, or raised my eyes from my notebook to her face, the view included if momentarily, a glimpse of something which, even I knew, should have been reserved for the Superintendent.

I could turn my head to one side or the other in an admittedly feeble attempt to avoid the tantalizing view. Even so this motion had to be accomplished with head lowered in an attempt to avoid the silent but visual siren's song that seemed to draw my attention back to the scene lurking before me. My eyes were like the hand of a compass. Regardless of how the compass is moved, when steadied, the hand always returns to magnetic north. Despite the stress, despite the fear of being caught staring into the land of the unknown, for my eyes, magnetic north was straight ahead.

Reactions during these class periods with Mrs. Mease posed on the desk before me were not limited to eye movement alone. On these occasions the subject matter being presented by the teacher was nullified by the view thrust before me. At fifteen years of age I was still more boy than man, but there were times when manifestations of manliness in my scrawny, boyish body would have been embarrassingly evident had I been called upon to stand for recitation.

Mrs. Mease also taught typing. I have no doubt she was a good typist and a good teacher. My older sister, Sissy, took typing from her and could type over seventy words a minute before she graduated. Other students acquired varying degrees of typing skills; however I was more interested in playing, or maybe fantasizing about observations made during English or social studies classes, than learning to type. After all, why did I need to type? I was going to be a farmer.

The teacher presented typing instruction in segments. Each segment consisted of typing exercises that had to be completed letter perfect. No strike-overs, erasures, or spelling errors were permitted. I made little attempt to do the assigned work properly, but she would give me a big smile. In retrospect maybe she too was thinking about the other classes. She would mark my paper with a grade "B" and return it to me. I thought it was great to get by with a minimum of effort. Though she may have been sweet to me, she cheated me by not demanding that I perform properly. She moved on to teach other students and I moved on as well, with severe deficiencies in my typing skills but with the vision of the forbidden valley fixed indelibly in my mind.

Dillard H. Gates

In 1996 Mrs Mease sent me a Christmas card containing her picture, in a modest pose. She was still a beautiful woman. I cannot help but wonder if she was aware of the emotions she aroused while perched on a desk in front of the class during English and social studies.

THE SUPERINTENDENT

In addition to his academic, disciplinary and administrative duties, the Superintendent was responsible for care of the school grounds and buildings. Discipline was normally not much of a problem, but there were exceptions.

The sun shown bright on Gates High school the morning following Halloween in the fall of 1939. The results of Halloween night activities were clearly evident. The school outhouses lay on their sides, there was a wagon on top of the school barn, and the schoolhouse windows, that could be reached from ground level were covered with soap.

After 9:00 o'clock when all students had gathered in their rooms, Mr. Mease called for all students to assemble on the south side of the school building. He announced that all high school and seventh and eighth grade boys would get to work and clean up the mess that had been made the night before. He didn't ask if any of us had participated in making the mess around school. It was just as well he didn't as no one would have admitted it and the mess had to be cleaned up anyway.

The younger boys were assigned the job of cleaning the lower windows. The big boys had the responsibility for straightening up the out-houses. We all joined in the work in good spirits. It was a nice day, we were not in the classroom and we were actually having fun. It was sort of an extension of Halloween night activities. When we had the out-houses back in an upright position and over the holes, we were told to get busy and help finish cleaning the windows.

It was soon evident that one of the problems limiting the window cleaning job was a shortage of window cleaning materials. Rags were needed to wash and dry the windows, and the supply available at school was limited.

My younger brother Jack was included in the first window cleaning detail. I had overheard Mease ask him a couple of times if we had extra rags at our house. Jack had told him, "No," or that he didn't know. Mom was temporally in a nursing home in town suffering from latent complications connected with childbirth.

I had acquired a rag from somewhere and was haphazardly rubbing around on one of the windows. The Superintendent approached me and asked, "Do you have any rags at your house."

Having overheard him make the same request to Jack and maybe still a little invigorated by the Halloween spirit, I responded, "What's the matter with you? Don't you believe my brother?"

His anger flared, his face flushed and he repeated in a louder voice, "Do you have any rags at your place?"

Depending on how you would define rags, we probably had more rags at our place than anything else. Virtually all the clothing we wore as well as our bedding and towels were patched or badly worn. By many accounts much of it would have been classed as rags, but it was what we had, it was what we used and it served the purpose.

My retort was quick and purposefully disrespectful, "No, and I wouldn't give them to you if we did have!"

There we stood, toe to toe, staring at each other: a scrawny but defiant, one hundred twenty five pound sophomore and an incensed, two hundred twenty-five pound Superintendent. The stare-down was brief. Then he hissed between clenched teeth, "Get back to work, wash those windows!"

Still staring at him and with a rag in my right hand, I reached out and without looking began smearing the rag around on the window.

"Wash that window properly," he instructed in a menacing tone.

I knew I was on thin ice but somehow could not back down. As my school friends and teachers watched in disbelief at what was happening, I responded in as cocky a tone as I could muster, "If I'm not doing it right, maybe you should show me how."

My retort apparently triggered emotions in Mr. Mease that were beyond his immediate control. He sputtered an incoherent response, spattering me with spittle. Red faced and with eyes bulging he grabbed me around the neck with both his big, meaty hands.

I realized immediately I was in a precarious situation. Compared with me he was a big man. My first thoughts were that he would throttle the voice out of me so that I could not give him any more lip, then let me go. These thoughts soon changed to alarm as he continued to squeeze and I began to run short of air. The school kids stood around, transfixed, witnessing but not responding to what to me at least was becoming a critical situation.

Reason must have overcome rage and he released me from his grip. I slumped against the side of the school house gasping for breath. As he turned from me he ordered, "Get up to the locker room and wait for me!"

Reluctantly I went inside the schoolhouse and up the stairs. En route I resolved that he would not get his hands around my neck again if I could prevent it. I realized the odds against me, but if it came to a fight I was determined to knock off a few chips while he was whittling me down to size.

I waited apprehensively in the locker room dreading what I was sure to come. After a few suspenseful minutes I heard heavy footsteps on the stairs. The locker room door opened, the Superintendent entered, and closed the door. As the door slammed I realized I was alone in a small room with a big man who had only recently displayed very hostile intentions toward me. I recalled a quote from a Western novel I had read some years before, "Hope for the best but prepare for the worst."

By now Mease appeared to have regained his composure. Once again our gazes met and in a low, threatening voice he said to me, "Dillard, you know I could just beat the hell out of you."

There was no doubt in my mind about that, but I was still determined. If worse came to worse and I had to stand and fight, I would do my best to convince him that this trip to the locker room was not a walk in the park. I continued to look squarely at him, braced myself and replied, "You probably can; whenever you are ready just get at it and we'll see."

Without doubt he could have beat the hell out of me, and some might argue that he should have. But better judgement prevailed. Certainly he realized the consequences of beating up on one of his students, regardless of the provocation. His job at Gates would have been over and it may well have meant the end of the teaching career for which he had trained.

He raised his hands, palms up, as if in supplication and in a conciliatory tone of voice stated, "Dillard, we have to work this out." He continued, "Let's see if we can talk about it."

So we talked. He had not realized that I felt he had insulted my brother when after getting a negative response from him he asked the same question of me. He did not know my mother was ill and away from home. He acknowledged he had overreacted to my admittedly disrespectful behavior toward him. He was sorry he had grabbed me by the neck and concerned about student reaction to the incident. We agreed that I would rejoin the work party and continue to clean soapy windows. He would try to find more cleaning materials so that the work could be finished as soon as possible and we could all get back into the class rooms where we belonged.

The Halloween cleanup was finished and school again returned to normal. Since the wagon on top of the school barn was of no particular trouble to anyone, it remained in place for several weeks until the farmer to whom it belonged dismantled and removed it from the barn roof.

Mr. Mease and I entered into an undeclared and fragile truce. We got along OK and for the most part each did what was expected. He was the Superintendent, the teacher and the coach. He was also the husband of the English and social studies teacher that had expanded my vision. I was a sophomore and junior during his tenure, a teenager struggling with the changes taking place in and around me as I tried to establish my identity. I was moving slowly from boyhood to manhood. I did not fully understand what was happening and was frustrated by the change.

The incident was over but the memory remained. We did not have another conflict of interests until the early spring of 1940.

INTRA-SCHOOL FACTIONS

It seems axiomatic that wherever there are groups of people factions develop. So it was at Gates High School. In this case the factions tended to be rather loose. Most members except the top echelon tended to drift between factions displaying little allegiance to either. Some students completely ignored the factions and considered them irrelevant at best and probably stupid. After all, the entire high school body at Gates would have numbered no more than thirty-five.

My big sister Gee, a senior, was the nucleus of one of the factions. The other formed around our cousin Rachael Robertson who was in my class. The basis of the friction between the two girls was Jim Chrisman, a junior who had previously dated Gee, lost interest and took up with Rachael. Jim was a handsome and personable young man who had entered Gates after having dropped out of another school a couple years earlier. Thus, Jim was two or three years older than others in his grade. He was past twenty when he graduated the following year. He was smaller than average for his age, but he was mature. At Gates High he was a man among boys, and this fact contributed to his attractiveness to the girls. Despite the age and maturity factor, he was accepted and well liked. If a vote had been taken he most certainly would been elected as the most popular man in high school.

As a result of the friction between Rachael and Gee, the kids tended to take sides, depending on whose stories they believed, and migrated into loose groups. As Gee's brother I found myself involved in a controversy that really didn't mean much to me, except I had to stick up for my sister. However, rumors flew, stories fabricated, then exaggerated and polarization became more pronounced within the student body.

Spring came early to Gates in 1940 with its usual components, the birds, the bees, the flowers and the hormones. Rumors were flying, but I cannot recall their specific essence, only that somehow Jim, Rachael and Gee were involved. Rachael was angry so Jim had to be angry. Gee was angry so, as her brother, I was supposed to be angry. I wasn't, but I was confused and wanted to stand up for my sister.

I was heading home from school one afternoon. When I reached the Gates intersection Jim called to wait-up as he wanted to talk to me. As he approached, followed by several of his faction, I could see that he was angry. As he came up to me, he was talking a bit incoherently, I thought, about my spreading lies and that I better stop and tell the truth. The truth was that I did not know what he was talking about and I told him so. By then quite a group of students from both factions had gathered around us as we stood in the road. I suggested that we move on across the intersection onto the adjacent land. The group trailed along, and the invectives continued as we moved from the sandy road, across the ditch to the field on the other side.

The die was cast when Jim challenged,"If you weren't so yellow you would take back what you have said."

I didn't even know what I was being told to recant, but according to how I was brought up those were fighting words. I didn't want to fight Jim as he was almost five years older and bigger than me. I threatened that if he did not take back those words he would have to whip me. That suited him fine and he reached out and struck me along side of the head.

Hay, Hell, Kids and Cattle

We sparred and thrashed around for awhile, neither doing much damage to the other. We finally closed, he wrestled me to the ground, put his knees in my guts, his hands on my shoulders and held me down.

I was in that position when the Superintendent rushed up to us. He asked what was going on, and Jim retorted that he was teaching me a lesson for telling lies. Mr. Mease then angrily told me to get out of there and go home.

From my position at the bottom of a two-man pile I replied, "I'm not in much of a position to go anywhere and besides I'm already home. It is all of the rest of you that are not home. This is my Dad's land."

That remark seemed to infuriate the teacher and may have reminded him of the past Halloween clean-up detail. He literally screamed at Jim, "If you are half the man I think you are, you will let him up and knock him down again!"

Jim proceeded to do just that. After he had repeated the process a couple more times, supported by the cheers of the Superintendent and his other supporters I decided I was fighting a losing battle. My friends kept urging me on and hollering that if I just kept going I would win. That may have been so; we'll never know. What I did know was that they were not getting the crap knocked out of them and I was.

With my shoulders pinned to the ground but without apology, I admitted defeat. I was beaten but unbowed.

Surrounded by his supporters and with the Superintendent's arm around his shoulder Jim left the battle field in triumph. I shrugged off the condolences of my support group and Gee as I trudged across the barnyard to the house. I had suffered no real damage but was lonely and dejected. Coming in second in a fist fight is a lot different than crossing the finish line behind the leader in a two-man foot race.

My father was in poor health, suffering from what turned out to be a terminal heart condition. Though I was sore in a few spots, the fight had left no visible marks on my face. I did not plan to tell Dad about the scrap or to confide in him about the problem. I was still not angry at Jim, but I was still puzzled. However, I was pretty damn put out with the Superintendent. His behavior was petty and biased. Despite his personal feeling about me, he had not conducted himself like a Superintendent or a gentleman. He had exhibited a complete lack of leadership.

Despite my intentions not to tell Dad, my sisters felt otherwise. We had hardly settled around the dinner table that evening until they blurted out to Dad their versions of the incident. After listening to their stories Dad asked, "Dill, is that right?"

I responded, "Yes, but I still do not understand what it was all about."

"Are you alright"? he continued.

" I'm a little sore in spots, but I'm alright," I replied stoically.

"If you are alright, then don't worry about it", advised Dad. "When you grow up you will be able to whip three like Jim Chrisman, and don't be concerned about that teacher. He seems to have neither the sense nor the physical attributes to worry anyone, but, just keep your eyes open," he further admonished.

The remainder of the tenure of this Superintendent and his wife was relatively serene, at least from the standpoint of my relationships with them. My Dad continued to refuse me permission to play football. I was allowed to play basketball as long as it did not interfere unduly with the farm work. Even though I was not very big, I played hard and was proud to be elected Captain of the basketball team in my Junior year.

MARY ALICE BELL, THE SCHOOL BUS INCIDENT

Beginning in about 1937 the Gates School District provided transportation for those students living more than one mile from school. The transportation was provided not by school buses as we now know them, but by modified stock trucks, pick-up, or utility vans. The buses were driven by one of the parents of the community or by a high school student old enough to get a driver's license and considered mature enough to shoulder the responsibility.

In the spring of 1940 the school bus that served the students living west of Gates was a converted Model-A Ford stock truck. Plywood had been secured to the insides of the stock rack and a roof attached. Wooden benches were fastened to the plywood around the inside perimeter. The spare tire was placed on the floor and scooted to the front of the bus where it was partially covered by the front bench. Some of the kids sitting on the front bench had to rest their feet on the spare tire which forced their knees above the normal seated position.

The bus was owned by Mr. Chrisman and driven by his son Jim. Chrisman's lived near the edge of the area which the bus had to service so it was convenient for them to establish a bus route The students were picked up in the morning. The bus remained at school all day, then delivered the kids home at the end of the day.

At that time of my life I was madly in love with Mary Alice Bell, a lovely, brown eyed, dark-haired girl one year behind me in school. She lived about one and one-half miles west of Gates with her two older brothers, Boyd and Gene and a younger sister Dorothy. Their parents had both died of cancer in recent years. Since Mary Alice and Dorothy were among the last to get on the bus, they had to sit on whatever bench space was available.

Some of the high school boys decided to force them, especially Mary Alice, to sit on the front bench with her feet on the spare tire and her knees elevated. This was not a lady-like position, but Mary Alice accepted their horseplay, let them have their fun and did her best to keep her dress pulled down over her knees. This game went on for a few days without Mary Alice or any of the other kids saying anything to me about it. I guess the little game became boring, so Walter Mannel, a kid in my class, decided to raise the level of excitement.

One morning Mary Alice boarded the bus and found her usual seat on the front bench with her feet on the spare tire. Walter pulled a couple of ping pong balls from his jacket pocket and attempted to throw them up under Mary Alice's dress. He and several of the other boys on the bus thought this was pretty funny. Mary Alice failed to see the humor in the situation and besieged him to stop. Walter was apparently enjoying the game so much that he did not stop until the bus pulled into the school yard.

On that particular morning I was at school before the bus arrived. The kids tumbled from the bus, stood around in small groups, headed for the school house, or across the road to the Gates store as there were still a few minutes to kill before classes began. Finally, Mary Alice, with tears in her eyes stepped through the bus door and slowly descended the steps.

Seeing her plight, I asked if there was a problem. She shook her head and replied, "No."

I knew better than that. Mary Alice was a generally happy and outgoing girl. Certainly she was not crying without reason.

I urged her to please let me know what was bothering her. Finally she related her story of the seating arrangements on the bus and the ping pong ball tossing game that had stopped only a few minutes before. I was enraged that anyone would treat Mary Alice in such a vulgar manner.

Walter was standing near the school house with a couple of his friends and co-conspirators, waiting to see what was going to happen. I rushed over to him, grabbed him by the shoulder, turned him around and exclaimed, "You damned, dirty dutchman! Mary Alice just told me what you have been up to. If you or any of your cronies ever touch Mary Alice or bother her again, I will beat the crap out of you."

Walter sort of smirked and retorted, "There are three of us, maybe we will just beat the crap out of you."

"OK," I responded, "The three of you probably can, so if you want to have at it. But before you begin just think about this. If you do, I will whip every one of you every time I see you alone. You are either going to have to run in a pack for a long time or leave Mary Alice alone."

I walked back to comfort Mary Alice and assured her she should have no more problems on the bus. But just in case, I extracted a promise from her to let me know if she was bothered again. I thought the incident was over, but no such luck.

MRS. MANNEL

Walter's older sister, Francis, and my older sister, Gee, were the best of friends, an she and Gee often stayed overnight with each other. Francis was a friendly, outgoing gal who was always welcome in our house. The two of them made up the entire Gates High School graduating class in 1940.

Mrs. Frank Mannel was a hard working, outspoken, immigrant woman who was reputed to have a red hot temper if provoked. She spoke with a German accent that seemed to become more acute when excited. She liked to read, and we had loaned her books on several occasions. Frank and Mrs. Mannel were neighbors, but lived at the margin of the Gates community. Our families had become acquainted when Francis came to Gates as a freshman and Walter followed a couple years later.

One Saturday, a few days following the ping pong ball incident with Mary Alice, I was in the shop with Dad repairing machinery for the coming spring season. The shop set just north of the driveway, which extended from the road through the barnyard then up a slight raise to the house. We both looked up and saw Mrs. Mannel, carrying several books in her arms, prancing up the driveway toward the house. Neither Dad nor I thought anything about it and continued with our work.

A few minutes passed and Dad remembered he had left his pliers in the house and asked me to go get them for him. With nothing in mind except getting the pliers for Dad, I went up to the house, through the entry hall, opened the door and stepped into the kitchen. There stood Mrs. Mannel in the middle of the room. Her face was red, as she waved her arms and shouted at Mom and Gladys Jacobsen, who was visiting Mom that afternoon.

As I stepped into the kitchen, Mrs. Mannel turned and accosted me in her now heavy German accent, "Vhy for you call my Valter damn dirty dutchman?" she challenged.

I was taken aback by the sudden onslaught, but the incident with Walter was still fresh in my mind. "Because that's just what he is," I retorted.

Moving toward me she continued with emphasis, "My Valter is a goot boy! Vhy you call him damn dirty dutchman?" (Later Gladys told me she thought Mrs. Mannel was going to hit me)

"He's a damn dirty dutchman because of what he did to Mary Alice Bell," I replied.

"Vhat you say my Valter do to zhat girl," she demanded.

She stood with red face and labored breath, listening while I told her of the behavior of Walter and the other boys on the bus. I also related to her what I would do to Walter if he ever bothered Mary Alice again.

"I don't believe you, my Valter not do anyteng like dat," she responded as she rushed out of the house, slamming the door behind her.

She did not walk back down the driveway past the shop but went around the house to the road, where Mr. Mannel was waiting in the car.

I returned to the shop with the pliers, and with no comment about Mrs. Mannel we continued to work until chore time. After supper that evening the family was gathered in the dining room recounting the activities of the day.

"What did Mrs. Mannel want?" Dad asked.

"She wanted to know why Dillard called Walter a damn dirty dutchman," Sissy answered.

Dad glanced over at me and said, "Dill, you better lay off Walter."

Dillard H. Gates

I jumped to my feet, rushed over to where Dad was sitting and without thinking blurted out, "If Walter ever does anything to Mary Alice again, I'll beat the hell out of him and I don't care what you say!"

Those were strong words from a fifteen year old who had never talked back to his Dad. However, I thought I had done the right thing by standing up for Mary Alice and that the action of Walter and his friends was vulgar and insulting.

Dad was taken aback by my uncharacteristic outburst. He had no knowledge of my fuss with Walter nor did he realize I felt so strongly about Mary Alice. "Well, what did Walter do that was so bad?" queried my father.

"I can take care of the problem myself," I responded, barely able to restrain the tears, "but since you insist I'll tell you".

The flood gates were open and the story of Walter and friends treatment of Mary Alice came pouring out. When I finished Dad looked over at my sisters and asked, "Is that right?" Both Sis and Gee nodded in agreement.

Dad reached out and laid his hand on my shoulder and quietly said, "That's alright, Dill. You probably handled the situation alright under the circumstances. But unless they do something again, why don't you just leave them alone?"

Mrs. Mannel never did forget my treatment of Walter even though I suspect that Francis verified what had happened. For a couple of years when we chanced to meet at a school function or in town, she would look the other way to avoid acknowledging me. In those cases I would always politely greet her with,"Hello, Mrs. Mannel," even though my motive was neither sincere nor polite.

Walter and I were classmates, and both were in the 1942 Gates High School graduating class. Mary Alice continued to be my girl until her brothers left the farm to work in defense plants after the beginning of World War II. Another high school romance was terminated, but we remained friends until her untimely death in the mid-seventies.

INHERITING BOOTS THAT I COULDN'T FILL

My Dad was a giant in my eyes. He was a big, husky man who worked hard and always shouldered more than his share of the load. Many times I heard neighbors say, "You can always count on Howe Gates to pick up the heavy end of the log." But he was more then strong. He was wise. He was gruff. He was tough. He was tender. He was a disciplinarian. He was humorous. He was autocratic. He was caring. He was wise and a man of vision. He was human. He was my Dad.

However, in the summer of 1940 he began to slow down. His stamina was decreased, he had gained weight and was often short of breath. He pushed as hard as he could but he knew all was not well. He was concerned for his own health and for the ultimate welfare of his family. There were still eight kids at home. Gee had graduated in the spring and now worked as a hired girl for Dick Roberts, a farm family that lived a few miles west of home.

During her senior year in school Gee had been dating Eddie (Fritz) Christian a young farmer who lived with his family six or seven miles west of us, outside the Gates community. Gee had met Fritz through her association with Francis Mannel, her friend and senior classmate. The fact that Fritz was a Catholic was a problem with Dad. He knew the Christian family as good, hardworking, honest people but he was not ready to have a Catholic son-in-law.

By the time Gee graduated from high school her romance with Fritz had passed the casual stage. She had sworn me to silence and confided that she and Fritz were planning to get married after she turned eighteen in August.

Her new job placed her in close proximity to the Christian farm. I suspect Dad knew what was in the wind but said nothing to me about the situation. I imagine the memory of the day in the hay field in 1932, when three of his kids left home, still haunted him. He had always been close to Gee and I am sure dreaded the thought of losing her.

As a result of his health problem Dad was trying to get the farm work in a position so that he could go to Mayo Clinic. He saw little of Gee and she continued to date Fritz. The summer slipped by and recognizing Dad's health problems I felt guilty not telling him of Gee's plan to marry Fritz. True to her word, after she reached eighteen, the age of consent, she and Fritz went to Kansas and were married, but not in a Catholic ceremony.

As we worked together around the farm or when we were alone, Dad talked to me about his condition. For the first time he asked me if I thought I could run things if he was gone. This was scary stuff for a fifteen year old who had always thought of his Dad as invincible. He talked to me about the mortgage on the farm held by the Federal Land Bank and about his shortterm debt to the Security State Bank in Broken Bow. He took me into his confidence and tried to prepare me as well as he could in case I did have to take over.

Dad gave me the combination to the big, steel safe that sat in the corner of our dining room and when no one else was around, showed me how to open it. There were papers in the safe that he explained to me and told me what I should do with them should the need arise. He did not talk to Mom about his problems, the papers, or the financial situation pertaining to the farm. I don't know why he didn't talk to Mom about his concerns. In fact I do not recall Dad ever having an extended discussion with Mom about anything.

Dad had made arrangements to go to the Mayo Brothers' Clinic in Rochester, Minnesota, when the corn was laid by and the hay put up. When those jobs were completed, Dad and a neighbor crawled into the old V-8 Ford and headed for Rochester.

Dad was put through the Clinic, and it was determined that he had a severe heart condition. The increase in his weight was primarily the result of water accumulating in his body.

I did not know then and still do not know the medical diagnosis of his condition. In those days it was called heart trouble. Maybe today it would be called congestive heart failure, a non-specific medical term that may include many conditions.

He was confined to the Mayo Brothers' hospital and given treatment to remove excess water from his system. He was also put on a strict diet of primarily fruits and vegetables with only an occasional small piece of very lean beef. This was mighty hard on a man whose main diet for the previous fifty years had consisted of fried meat, the fatter the better, milk gravy, bread and potatoes.

In retrospect I believe his lifelong diet, high in animal fats, contributed to development of his heart problem.

He remained at Mayo Brothers' for six weeks. During that period he lost sixty-five pounds. A lot of the weight loss was water, but a lot of it was a part of the Dad I had always known. When he was finally able to come home, he was extremely weak, thin and hardly recognizable.

Mom prepared his special meals and he stuck with his restrictive diet. Due to his weakened condition, for a few weeks his activities were limited to moving about the house and short walks to the barn to look at the livestock. He spent a lot of time reading and of course there were always little ones to entertain and help care for. My youngest brother, Larry, was just over one year old, and Joyce and Iris were not yet in school.

Though I was only fifteen, I became Dad's driver. Driving was not a problem for me as I had been operating the car since I was nine years old. I drove Dad round the farm allowing him to see how things were going. As he regained some of his strength, I drove him to Broken Bow and Sargent so he could attend the livestock auctions and visit with friends. I remember several occasions when people who had known Dad all his life did not recognize him on the street as he had lost so much weight.

During one of these trips Dad related to me his disappointment that Gee and Fritz had married without his being informed. He admitted he had been opposed to the marriage because Fritz was Catholic, but now that they were married he accepted it and realized he would have to make the best of it. He reiterated that he wanted to help them if he could. If they wanted to get started farming on their own, he would like the opportunity to give them some of the extra machinery around our place. He requested that if I saw Gee or Fritz to let them know that he would like to talk with them, but he asked me not to mention his desire and intent to offer assistance.

During a subsequent trip to Broken Bow a short time later, Dad and I were walking along on the north side of the square. We spotted Gee ahead of us window-shopping at one of the stores and called to her. She turned toward us. Her face expressed first shock, then fear and determination as she saw Dad. It was the first time she had seen him since her marriage and his return from Mayo's Clinic. Compared to when she had last seen him, he was now a walking skeleton.

Gee was obviously stressed and immediately on the defensive. As we approached, Dad reached out and said to her, "Gee, I would like to have a little talk with you."

Dad merely intended to wish her well, invite her and Fritz home and make her the offer he had discussed with me. Apparently Gee, always headstrong and impulsive, thought Dad was going to jump down her throat for marrying Fritz.

Without waiting to hear what Dad had to say, she lashed out, "I don't want to listen to you. I don't care what you have to say. Fritz and I are married and there is nothing you can do about it." With that she turned on her heal, stuck her nose in the air and pranced away.

I called to her as she moved away from us but received no response. Without Dad having said a word of anger or censure another of his children had stormed out of his life. Gee had just made a Grand Canyon out of a plough furrow and would live to regret it. Dad and I stood in startled silence as she disappeared in the Saturday afternoon crowd. He never had another opportunity to discuss the matter with her.

Under Dad's direction and with help from a neighbor, John Jacobsen, we managed to get the fall work done. When it was corn picking time, neighbors pulled out of their own corn fields and into our yard with their teams and picking wagons. In a few short days the corn was out of the field and in the granary.

In those days when a farmer had a serious problem, the neighbors pitched in and helped. They did it because it was the right thing to do. It was an accepted part of what it meant to grow up and live in Custer County. Helping a neighbor in time of need was a part of our being. I don't know if we learned it at our father's knee or assimilated it as we grew up in a community where the sense of neighborhood prevailed.

Maybe after being away for fifty-five years that is why I still think of Custer County, Nebraska and, the Gates community as home.

With the help of my brother, Jack, and the direction and encouragement of Dad I managed to get the cattle fed, the chores done, stay in school and play basketball. During this time when we were by ourselves, Dad continued to talk to me about taking care of things. He helped me understand what had to be done and why. He was shifting the burden of family responsibility from his once strong, but now weakened shoulders, to the weaker but maturing shoulders of his oldest son still at home.

Hay, Hell, Kids and Cattle

In January of 1941 I became sixteen. Shortly thereafter Dad accompanied me to Broken Bow to get my driver's license. Even though I had been driving for years, a drivers license gave me a new sense of freedom. It represented one of the rights of passage from boyhood to becoming a man. Dad had permitted me to take the car to school functions during the school year even though I did not have that magic card. Now I could drive to town without fear that I would be stopped by the Highway Patrol. Now I could take Mary Alice to the movies.

As winter loosened its grip on the wind-swept plains of central Nebraska, Dad began to make plans for the spring. He was feeling better and had regained a bit of strength. However, he was but a shadow of the man I had known only a few short months before.

The previous fall we had driven our cattle home from summer pasture on Hap's ranch southwest of Dunning. During the drive home, with their consent, we crossed pasture and rangeland belonging to several farmers and ranchers. During the winter we had been notified that the cattle of one of the ranchers whose land we had crossed were infected with lice. There was a federal lice control program in effect which mandated that all cattle with lice had to be dipped. Since our cattle had passed over land where infected cattle grazed, they were considered to have been exposed to lice and would have to be treated.

We had an old livestock dipping vat on the farm. However, it had not been used for years and was in a bad state of repair. Dad thought it would cost more to repair the vat than to transport the cattle to another dipping facility. He made plans to visit one of the ranchers whose land we had crossed and who had a dipping vat to make arrangements to treat our cattle at the same time he treated his.

March 31, 1941, was a bright and sunny day in Custer County, but as usual a bit windy. When Jack and I arrived home from school, Dad informed us that he was going up northwest of Anselmo a few miles to confer with the rancher who had the dipping facilities. He told Jack to come with him and if need be he could drive. I was instructed to move some of the cattle from where they were grazing into another field where they could forage on the remaining crop aftermath and then do the evening chores.

I was very unhappy about the job Dad had given me despite the fact that I could do the work much easier than my little brother. I thought I should have been selected to drive for Dad and be involved in any arrangement made to treat the cattle. Dad and Jack got in the old 32 Ford and headed west toward Anselmo. Unknowingly, he was driving out of my life for that was the last time I saw my Dad alive.

Grumbling, I saddled ole Wrangler and proceeded with the job of rounding up the cattle and pushing them through the gate into another field. It was less than a hour later that I saw Ed Russell's Terraplane bumping across the field toward me. He drove up to where I was sitting on Wrangler, and I noted that he was accompanied by C.B. Phillips, another neighbor who often helped Ed in his auto repair shop.

Ed looked at me and said quietly, "Dillard, you better put your horse in the barn and come with us; something has happened to your Dad."

I kicked ole Wrangler in the ribs and rode back to the barn as quickly as possible. As I jumped into the car with them I questioned, "Should I tell Mom?"

"No, you better not," Ed responded.

As we drove rapidly out of the yard and headed up the road, I saw Mom standing in the yard with a puzzled look on her face, wondering where Ed and C.B. were taking me so fast.

We rode in silence for a few minutes. I was bewildered about what was happening and had not yet grasped the significance of the situation.

"Where is Dad and what is the matter with him?" I inquired cautiously.

"He is in Anselmo and it may be worse than you think, Dillard," C.B. responded.

"Do you mean that Dad is dead?" I questioned.

"Yes," He replied

For the remainder of the trip to Anselmo I sat alone in the back seat crushed by what had just been related to me. I had known of Dad's condition for the past several months. I knew he had been preparing me for this moment and had thought I was growing into the job, but I suddenly realized I wasn't ready. There was still so much he had not told me about running the farm, caring for the family and being a man. I didn't want to "pull on his boots" or become the head of the house. I wasn't through being a boy. I just wanted my Dad.

As we drove into Anselmo we saw a small crowd of people had gathered near the open door of a service station. As we got out of the car

Glenn Fox, the County Sheriff, hurried over to us. He put his arm around my shoulder and said, "I'm sorry, Dillard," and led me through the crowd.

Dad's body lay on a make-shift table that had been hastily constructed by placing a couple of doors on saw-horses. My brother Jack, not yet fourteen, with tears in his eyes was standing by Dad. I took a deep breath, gritted my teeth and tried to behave like the man I thought Dad had been training me to be.

After a few minutes I asked Jack what had happened. He told me that he and Dad had been driving five or six miles north of Anselmo on the road toward Dunning. This was a grassland area and was the southern extremity of the Nebraska Sandhills. The Burlington Railroad paralleled the State Highway. Jack noticed a small fire burning in the grass fifty yards or so east of the railroad tracks and called it to Dad's attention. Dad then told Jack that the fire had probably been started by sparks from a railroad locomotive that had passed by only minutes before. He immediately stopped the car and told Jack they would have to quickly extinguish the small blaze to prevent what could become a dangerous and destructive prairie fire.

Dad always had a short-handled shovel attached to the back of the car between the spare tire mounting and the car body. He hurriedly unstrapped the shovel and they climbed over the fence and headed for the small fire burning in the prairie grass. Jack said they had moved as quickly as possible considering Dad's condition.

When they reached the fire Dad readily put it out with a few shovels full of sand directed at the base of the flames. Dad threw a few more shovels full of sand on the hot perimeter then checked to be sure no sparks remained. They then headed back toward the car with Jack a few steps behind Dad.

After a few steps Dad turned to Jack, waved his arm in a southeasterly direction and said, "If we hadn't put out that fire it would have gone over there." With those words his arm dropped to his side and he slumped to the ground, onto the grasslands which moments before he had been trying to protect. Jack said he called to Dad as he rolled him onto his back. Getting no response he lifted Dad's eyelid. The pupil was dilated. It did not contract. He knew that Dad was dead.

Jack ran back to the highway and flagged down the first car that came along. There were two men in the car that we later learned were acquaintances of Dad. Jack told them what had happened. They rushed across the grassland to were Dad's body was lying to verify the story that Jack had just related to them. While one of the men waited at the site Jack and the other man hurried back to the car and drove to Anselmo to notify authorities. Someone called the Sheriff in Broken Bow. Jack asked them to also call Ed Russell at Gates, have him locate me and bring me to Anselmo as soon as possible. He told me later that he did not want them to tell Mom because he didn't know what she would do.

I asked the Sheriff, a longtime friend of Dad's, to call the Schneringer and Johnson Funeral Home in Broken Bow to pick up Dad's body. I also requested that he remove Dad's watch and wallet and give them to me. There was little more I could do so the Sheriff suggested that Jack and I go home with Ed and C.B. and tell Mom what had happened.

The John Jacobsen family lived just over a mile west of our house. Ed suggested we stop there, tell them of Dad's death and have them accompany us to give the message to Mom. When we arrived at their house, we found they had already received word and had gone to be with Mom. It was with heavy heart that I found my sobbing Mother sitting in our living room, surrounded by several of my sisters and neighbors providing comfort to her in those first moments of grief.

Hay, Hell, Kids and Cattle

The following morning Mom and the kids gathered in the dining room to talk about final arrangements for Dad. Among other things she was concerned about funeral and burial costs. It was then I revealed to her that Dad had put four hundred dollars in the safe to be used for that purpose. Dad had shown the money to me a few months earlier and asked me not to say anything about it until the need arose.

Funeral services were held for my Dad in the old Gates church on April 3, 1941. The church building had served the Gates community for a wide variety of functions since it was built in 1903. As far as I can recall, Dad's was the last funeral to be held in the Gates church.

It was a cold and blustery day with wet snow falling when Dad was laid to rest in the Gates Cemetery in a plot purchased by his father many years before. There he joined his father and grandfather, for whom the Gates community was named, two infant sons, his first wife, two brothers and many other relatives who were buried there. Land for the cemetery had been provided years before by his father Herbert P. Gates and grandfather, Stillman Gates. It was located on the same section of land on which my father was born on March 31, 1886.

Life on the farm was different from that moment on. The rock on which our family was based was shattered. Mom remained with a big family of kids, the youngest only eighteen months old, a big mortgage on a dryland farm and spring planting time just around the corner. Her role had changed she was no longer just a subservient wife and mother with virtually no experience or understanding of the business side of running the farm. She was still cook, housekeeper, seamstress, nose wiper, healer of hurts and all of the other things she had always been. In addition she was now expected to be the primary decision maker. She faced the future with fear and misgivings. With concern and trepidation she related to me, "Oh, son, I just don't know what I'm going to do."

To make matters worse, even before Dad was buried, one of my older half-sisters confided to a neighbor and family friend that she and her husband, looked forward to getting their share of Dad's estate. They were not going to turn it all over to Ethel, my mother. They apparently had misguided and exaggerated ideas about Dad's financial status and mistakenly believed he had a cash reserve stashed somewhere and that they had a right to their share. That which my half-sister confided to a neighbor soon reached the ear of my mother.

Years before, Dad had been a moderately wealthy farmer. However, medical bills, the drought and depression had reduced his asset to little more than the heavily mortgaged farm. He had no cash reserve, except the money he had put in the safe to cover burial expenses. Earlier in the spring Dad had reluctantly made arrangements for a Federal Feed and Seed loan to provide funds for spring planting. It had troubled him deeply to have to ask the Federal Government for help, even in the form of a loan.

On the night of Dad's death, John Jacobsen talked to me about the responsibilities I would now have to shoulder. He entreated me not to consider quitting school and assured me he would help with the farming whenever necessary. So we stayed on the farm for another season. Cash flow was a real problem. After I had planted our corn a couple of the neighbors hired me and our Farmall tractor to plant corn for them. They had adequate time and machinery to do the job themselves but it was a way for them to help us with our money problems.

Though I was only sixteen I struggled to fill the role for which Dad had tried to prepare me. Even though he had entrusted me with information and given me instructions about what to do in the event of his death, I was ill-prepared to step into the boots that had been dropped before me. Mom provided help and encouragement. I was certainly not the head of the household, but I was the oldest boy at home and she relied upon me to run the farm. Discipline was never one of Mom's strong suits, but expectedly my sisters and brothers resented it when I tried to take over that role. In retrospect, I was probably a bit harsh and overbearing sometimes as I flexed my muscles and tried to do the job which I thought Dad had passed on to me.

Sis graduated from high school in June of 1941. She had taken her typing teacher seriously, though she had not faced some of the same distractions I had, and was an excellent typist. She soon landed a job in the Triple A (Agriculture Adjustment Act) office in Broken Bow. In spite of Dad's concerns, one of his daughters had now taken a job with the government

We somehow made it through the summer. The work and the struggle convinced Mom that she did not want to stay on the farm. Her concerns were compounded by the fact that now two of my half-sisters were making noises about getting their share of Dad's estate. Mom decided she did not want to stay on the farm, try to meet mortgage payments, then have to turn part of the farm over to them at a later date. A. Paul Johnson, an attorney in Broken Bow who had been a friend of Dad's, assured her there were legal ways to get around the estate problems, but Mom had enough. She was tired of the dirt, the drudgery, and the work and had no desire to fuss with her step-kids. She wanted off the farm and was giving serious thought to selling what we had and moving to town.

By the time the fall harvest was over, Mom had definitely made up her mind. Money was still short, the work appeared endless and the future bleak. She decided to have a dispersal sale, then try to buy a house in town with her share of the proceeds. All we had to do was survive the winter.

FUSSIN ABOUT FODDER, A MATTER OF MONEY OR PRIDE

Now that Dad was gone, I had the responsibility for helping Mom run the farm and provide for my siblings. We were faced with the ever-present reality that cash was in short supply.

We had grown fodder sorghum in the summer of 1941. Following harvest Mom decided to sell the fodder, which was considered excess to the winter forage needs of our cattle. She anticipated that returns from the fodder sale would help alleviate the money problems. An older half-sister and her husband said they were short of feed and would buy a load at the going price.

One day shortly thereafter he came to the farm with his team and hayrack. We went to the field and I helped him load the fodder. Mom looked forward to receiving the money from the sale but wasn't as prudent about collecting for the forage as Dad had been when selling alfalfa hay to the farmer north of us. Days and then weeks passed and Mom did not receive payment for the fodder.

Mom and I were in Broken Bow one Saturday afternoon a few weeks later, and by chance I happened to encounter my brother-in-law on the street. I may have been feeling my oats, overplaying my role of Mom's protector and reveling in my position, real or imagined, of responsibility for Mom's welfare. I knew we were short of funds. I knew he had bought the fodder, and I could not help but recall the attitude he and my sister had expressed about getting their share of Dad's estate.

We chatted for a few minutes but he said nothing about payment for the fodder. I finally decided that I had to take the initiative. I took a deep breath and challenged, "When are you going to pay Mom for the fodder you bought?"

Taken aback by my abrupt approach, he responded, "I'll pay you for the fodder."

"That's what you said when you hauled it away," I retorted adamantly, "but Mom needs the money now."

Red faced and angry he pulled a check book from his pocket and spat the words at me, "OK, I'll pay now if that's the way you feel."

"That is exactly how I feel," I assured him, displaying more confidence than I felt as I watched him write out a check to Mom. As I recall the check was for fifteen dollars.

When I met Mom later in the afternoon, I related my experience and handed her the check. She scolded me for having the encounter. Despite our need for money Mom would have rather not been paid for the fodder than to make a fuss about payment for it. It was easy for anyone to take advantage of Mom. If someone did her wrong, she would generally pass it off with the remark that revealed so much of her personal character, "Just forget about it. They know they have done wrong and they have to live with it. I don't."

Later that evening Mom and I were at home with the rest of the family. There was a knock on the door and my sister walked into the house. She demanded, "Dillard, come outside I want to talk to you."

I was somewhat astonished but followed her out to the yard. As we walked toward her car she informed me that her husband was in the car and that he had things to discuss with me. She also told me that En route to our house they had picked up the neighbor, John Jacobsen, and that he was also in the car. I guess they felt that before the planned discussion was over John might serve as an arbitrator, advisor, referee, judge or witness.

As we approached the car, my sister said to me, "Dillard, you had no right to jump on him the way you did in town this afternoon. You and Ethel should have been glad that we were willing to take some of the fodder off your hands. You owe him an apology."

"I don't owe him an apology," I returned, "When he got the fodder he said he would pay for it. Weeks passed and Mom heard nothing from you. If I had not hit him up for the money, I doubt she would have ever been paid."

The exchange continued for a few minutes. Neither my sister or her spouse had received the satisfaction they expected from me. Completely exasperated she finally threatened,"You know, Dillard, my husband could get out of the car and beat the crap out of you."

"I don't think that would solve the problem," I replied more calmly than I felt, "but if that's what he wants to do, then he should just get out of the car and do it."

I don't know if the presence of John prevented that from happening or if he had second thoughts about the advisability of a full grown man beating the hell out of a sixteen year old kid in his own front yard. Or there may have been was some concern that the scrap might not be as one-sided as he had first visualized. To my great relief he stayed in the car. I was of the opinion if he got out of the car he could probably do as my big sister had threatened, but I was determined that if he tried, before he had accomplished his mission he would realize that he had not been on a Sunday picnic

Apparently, in this heated, verbal exchange we exhausted our vocabulary of invectives and ran out of anything more to say. I stood unrepentant knowing that Mom had cashed the check and had the cash in her pocket. My big sister may have grown tired of haranguing her little brother and just gave up. They finally started the car and drove out of the yard. They had not achieved what they had set out to accomplish, but they may have left with a different opinion and better understanding of me than they had when they charged into the yard earlier in the evening.

A CAR OF MY OWN

During the summer I had begun to test my wings and express my desire for more independence. After lots of coaxing I was able to convince Mom, or at least get her to concede, that the old 1932 Ford was just not adequate to take care of my transportation needs and those of the rest of the family. After all, I had a girl friend and in the fall I would be a senior. She reluctantly agreed that if I could figure out where the money would come from I could buy a car.

I suggested that after threshing I could sell enough grain to cover the cost of a Model-A Ford. Model-A's were older than our V-8 but were reliable, used little gas and were easy to maintain. After harvest we sold a load of barley to Jim Tarleton, a farmer friend of the family who lived near Walworth about five miles east of us.

Now with money in hand I could hardly wait to start looking for my new car. I had made up my mind that I was going to buy a coupe because Gladys Jacobsen, mother of my best friend Harry, sometimes insisted on accompanying Harry and me on dates. A coupe could accommodate only four. With three in the seat and one on a lap there would be no room for a tag-along mother.

I poured through the classified adds in the Custer County Chief and searched the used car lots in surrounding towns. We finally found a 1929 Model-A coupe for sale by the Ecker Brothers who operated an auto repair business in Broken Bow. The car was reputed to have been completely overhauled and in top condition. I had hoped to be able to find a 1930 Model-A as they were slightly larger and with smoother lines than the 1929s. From my standpoint the deal was just too good to pass up. I handed Ecker fifty-five dollars and became the instant and proud owner of my first car, a 1929 Model-A Ford coupe.

I spent hours huddled with my new possession, polishing and adding sporty lights and extra accessories. The Model-A provided me with reliable and low cost transportation and an extra measure of freedom. And I was right. Harry and I could now take out our girls, unchaperoned.

TRESPASSER FROM THE WEST

Sunday was a day of rest for some in the Gates community, but it was also a day for recreation. An occasional ball game was about the most exciting thing to break the calmness of a Sunday afternoon at Gates. The ball, games while not spontaneous, were at best poorly organized. Pick-up teams from neighboring communities would get together at the schoolyard for an afternoon game. Spectators sat on the ground or watched the contests from cars parked along the baselines. Horns blared to signal approval of a move by the favorite team or to protest the call of the umpire.

The Gates community portrayed a rather puritanical aura. Playing ball on Sunday afternoons was acceptable, but even on the hottest days liquid refreshments were limited to cold water, lemonade, or soda pop from the store across the road.

Anselmo, a small town thirteen miles to the west, was considered by some in the Gates community to be virtually a den of iniquity. It was a commonly accepted fact that kids in the Anselmo school drank beer, drove their cars too fast, and were generally up to no good. It was even rumored that Anselmo girls were fast. The behavior of the kids from Anselmo was not surprising to the self-proclaimed moralist of Gates. It was to be expected from those raised in a Catholic community.

The tranquility of one Sunday afternoon was shattered when a couple of cars raced onto the school yard and parked haphazardly near the spectators watching the ball game. The doors flew open and teenaged girls and boys literally tumbled from the cars. It was evident that their inherent boisterousness was enhanced by the contents of the beer bottles clutched in the hands of some of the boys.

There were also a few boys from the western fringes of the Gates community who had ridden their horses to the Sunday afternoon ball game. These boys were friends and acquaintances of the Anselmo trespassers as they went to the same church and had also attended the same school prior to transferring to Gates.

The Anselmo boys were behaving in a most inappropriate manner, probably exaggerating the affects of the beer they had been drinking. The girls in the group, while obviously tainted by their association with the drunken ruffians, were not imbibing but were talking with their acquaintances on horseback. I noted that one of the girls with long brown hair and brown eyes asked Hop Spanel, who now attended Gates, if she could ride his horse. At first he refused but later offered to trade a horseback ride for a bottle of beer. After some negotiations the little gal succeeded in extracting a bottle from one of the beer drinkers and effectuated the trade. This was considered near brazen behavior as judged by the lofty standards expressed by the staid citizens of the Gates community.

The Gates community elders, the keepers of the morals, the protectors of the virtues of the youth, were concerned about the conduct of the Anselmo adolescents as their demeanor changed from boisterous to rowdy. A disagreement, undoubtedly brought on by the beer, erupted between two of the Anselmo boys, Jim McGinn and Edward Holley. This shouting match soon escalated into a fight, and the combatants threw ineffective punches, staggered, and cursed. Each was urged on by his respective suds guzzling supporters. Certainly this was not acceptable conduct for the eyes and ears of those who had gathered to enjoy a Sunday afternoon ballgame at Gates.

When the invectives reached an intolerable crescendo, a couple elders of the community stepped in to restore peace and tranquility. The Anselmo gang was told to clean up their act or to leave immediately. The bleary eyed and belligerent boys rounded up their charges, loaded into the cars and kicked dust, gravel and sandburs into the air as they raced across the school yard, onto the dirt road, and headed west toward Anselmo.

The good citizens of Gates breathed sighs of relief mixed with mutterings of "Good riddance of bad rubbish" as they watched the two cars speed westward. I expressed alarm when I noted the second of the two cars veer sharply and turn into the driveway to our farmstead which was about two-hundred yards west of the Gates store.

Since the death of my father in the spring, I had assumed the self-appointed role of eldest male and household protector. I took off toward home on the run, concerned about what the drunken louts from Anselmo might do. There was machinery in the farmyard and tools in the shop. The unsavory reputation of those encroachers from Anselmo preceded them into our yard. I was certain they were up to no good.

I rushed around the granary and up to the car which had stopped near the stock tank. "What are you doing here?" I demanded in my most aggressive tone as I leaned over and peered through the open car window.

"The car stopped," responded the beer-sotted driver.

"I don't believe you and you can't stay here," I retorted angrily. "There's no telling what the likes of you might be up to."

"The car won't run," the driver slurred as his passengers stared at me in disgust. They appeared to be taken aback by this vitriolic attack by a son of the soil of Gates.

"Then I will pull you out onto the road away from our place so you can't bother anything," I rebutted emphatically.

I stomped over to the Farmall parked in the farmyard firm in my self-righteous resolve to rid our farm of this drunken rubble. I grabbed the crank of the tractor, gave it a tug, and started the motor. I drove over to the shop, selected a big log chain, then pulled the tractor up in front of the stalled car. I hooked the chain onto the drawbar of the tractor and the bumper of the Ford full of what I considered to be Anselmo hoodlums. The Farmall moved forward, tightened the chain, and I jerked the car out of the farmyard and about fifty yards down the road to the west. The driver managed to get the car started as I was dragging it down the sandy road. I unhitched the chain from the car bumper and it roared away, leaving me in the dust beside the tractor.

I was satisfied that I had been able to remove the potentially damaging drunks from the environs of my home. I was disgusted with the antics of the Anselmo boys, but there was a tingle of concern in my mind for the safety of the girls riding in the car, especially the little brown-eyed one who had traded the beer for a ride on Hop's horse.

Dillard H. Gates

THE SENIOR YEAR

With the coming of fall, 1941, I began my senior year at Gates High School. It was the beginning of my twelfth year at Gates. I was sixteen. I had my own car, though little money to run it. I had been burdened with new responsibilities since the passing of my father, but as a result of my changed status had also acquired more authority in the family and more freedom. I recognized Mom's dependence on me and tried to be responsive to her desires.

I loved my mother and my brothers and sisters, but I was slipping the leash and looking toward the time I could be on my own. I even decided to change my attire for my senior year. I hung the bib overalls on a nail in the closet. They had been my standard dress for as long as I could remember. I bought a couple pair of half-pants (jeans) which I considered more appropriate to my imagined and self-appointed status.

We had new teachers for my senior year. Mr. and Mrs. Grant Sterner, who had been teaching in Broken Bow opted for the country life, (I don't know why) and came to Gates. Mr. Sterner was the Superintendent, coach and teacher. Mrs. Sterner was the other high school teacher. The Sterners, especially Mrs. Sterner were strict, no-nonsense teachers. A look from her would instantly purge any thoughts of devilment or mischief from the mind of any student, freshman or senior. But they were good teachers and may have been a bit ahead of their time for Gates school. They expected us to learn, to behave, and to be respectful. They expanded our horizons and inspired some of the students to the realization there just might be life beyond Custer County and a livelihood other than farming.

Mr. Sterner explained simply and logically that the use of profanity was an open admission of the limitations of one's vocabulary. As I recall profane language was not a major problem at Gates but most certainly it was there. His words and his example helped to prevent the use of language considered by some an expression of manhood from becoming a problem. I remember more than one occasion, usually during sports practice, when someone would slip and a word not generally accepted in mixed company would pop out. Sterner on hearing the explicative would quietly inquire of the culprit, "You can find a better way than that to express yourself, can't you?"

Throughout the school year Mr. Sterner also taught us, especially the boys, that while anger was a normal part of the human psychic, like other emotions, it must be controlled. To lose your temper was a manifestation of loss of control. He was working with boys becoming men trying to understand themselves and to establish their position among their peers and others within their social environs.

Anger, like other emotions, lingers near the surface of most teenagers. It probably is often expressed suddenly as a result of a combination of hormones, ego, self-righteousness, self-pity or imagined grievances. We boys were no different from others in that regard. As for myself, I had a quick temper that would often surface with little provocation at home or at school. Before the death of my father I had generally been able to keep it in check if he was around. Without Dad to provide the damper, my temper tended to express its self more frequently.

When Mr. Sterner observed manifestations of a surfacing temper in any of us boys, he would pull us up sharply with the firm rejoinder, "Don't you think you better try to get yourself under control?"

I don't know the affects of his quiet admonitions on others. For me they were significant, maybe pivotal. A quick temper is a devil I struggled with throughout my life. Mr. Sterner did not cure my temper problem, but without doubt he contributed greatly to helping me get control of this emotion which impairs judgement and blinds the senses to concern for self or others.

FOOTBALL

With Dad gone there was no longer anyone to forbid me to play football. Mom would have preferred that I not play as she didn't want me to get hurt. I brushed her concerns aside and joined the Gates High School Class D, six-man football team. I was no longer the puny, one hundred and five pound kid who had wanted to play football as a freshman. I now weighed one hundred forty pounds dripping wet and still longed to be the most ferocious Pirate to ever sail the gridiron seas of Gates High or the Little Six Conference.

Size-wise I was about average for the team. We were all farm boys who worked hard and I suppose were pretty tough, meaning we could take a lot of punishment. But as a football team we were not very big, very mean or very good. A lasting lesson we learned during the football season was that being tough did not translate directly to winning football games.

The quality of the football team was reflected in the quality of our football field. About one-half of the field was covered by beat-out grass, consisting mostly of sandburs. The remainder of the field was bare dirt or covered with gravel, the residue from building the new school house in 1937. Anyone getting tackled or knocked down on our gridiron was doubly punished: first when hit by the opposing player and next when he hit the ground. Football players at Gates spent an inordinate amount of time soothing skin abrasions and picking out sandburs.

Despite the coaching skills of Mr. Sterner and the fact that we played hard, we did not win many games. We were embarrassed when Dry Valley beat us. Even some men teachers were going to war and they had a woman coach.

One crisp Friday afternoon we played Berwyn on their home turf, a cow pasture with white lines designating the field. We took the field undaunted by the fact the Berwyn team was big, good and reputedly mean. The coach assured us that, like us, they could put only six men on the field at a time.

"Now go get em," Sterner urged us as we left the pre-game huddle and charged onto the field.

By the end of the first half we had yet to make a first down. On the other hand, Berwyn had scored every time they had possession of the ball. By the end of the game Arnie Duschnec had a broken leg, Hop Spanel had a broken nose and the rest of the team looked and felt like they had spent the afternoon inside a revolving cement mixer. Berwyn may have had only six men on the field, but at times it seemed to the outgunned Pirates they may have had a dozen. Regardless of the number of men on the field, when the game was over, as I recall, they had scored eighty-six points. Though we labored mightily for four quarters, when the final whistle sounded we remained scoreless.

My football career at Gates was less than spectacular. The number of athletic scholarship offers I received matched our football score against Berwyn. Yes, we were iron men in those days, we played both offense and defense but we just couldn't win any games. I played halfback on offense and lineman on defense. I did manage to score a few touchdowns during the season, but the only play I remember distinctly from my illustrative career was a defensive play against Oconto.

Oconto had the ball. I was playing defensive lineman. Their quarterback faded back to pass. I suddenly found myself through the offensive line, charging through their backfield toward the quarterback. He put out his arm to protect himself from my charge. Instead of attempting to avoid the stiff arm, I grabbed the quarterback by the wrist, dug in my heels and whirled him in a circle. After two or three revolutions with me at the center and him on the perimeter of the circle, he was still on his feet but struggling to maintain his balance. As we continued to spin around, I let go of his wrist and he tumbled headfirst to the ground.

Pleased that I had prevented the pass I stood watching as he angrily scrambled to his feet. With head down he came at me like an enraged bull. Before we collided the referee stepped between us grasped the infuriated quarterback by the shoulder pad and exclaimed, "Hey, young man, what's the matter with you?"

"That stupid idiot doesn't know how to play football. He doesn't know how to play football," he screamed angrily at the referee.

"Take it easy," the referee warned "The tackle may have been a little unusual but there was nothing wrong with it."

I was pleased with my accomplishment, even though it probably looked a little silly, and the encouragement from my teammates. I returned to my defensive line position, ready to continue to raise havoc in the backfield of Oconto. I have not seen reference to that play in the annals of high school football, but, in an athletic career of few wins and many defeats even a small victory remains memorable.

The highlight of the football season was when Mr. Sterner escorted the team to Lincoln to see the University of Nebraska play the Pittsburgh University. He offered to take five of us to see the game if we would pay for the gas. Sterner had a new 1941 Studebaker Champion. The car got good gas milage and gasoline was less than a quarter a gallon. Five of us boys dug up the money and agreed to go with him. Lincoln is about one hundred seventyfive miles from Gates, and we planned to make the round trip in one day.

We left Gates early one November morning. Mr. Sterner wanted to arrive in Lincoln early enough that he could show us around the University of Nebraska campus before the game started. We also made

Dillard H. Gates

a quick tour of the Nebraska State Capitol building with the golden Sower on top. In 1941 it was one of the tallest buildings in the Midwest and was unique in at least two ways. The people of Nebraska had raised sufficient funds so the Capitol building was paid for by the time construction was completed. It housed the State of Nebraska Unicameral Legislature, the only one-house legislature in the nation.

This was the first trip to Lincoln for any of us. It was the farthest I had been away from home. We were awed by the splendor of the city and the majesty and the mystery of the University of Nebraska.

We poor country bumpkins were overwhelmed by the crowds and marveled at the size of the stadium. I clearly remember our seats were on the east side of the stadium toward the north end. It was a colorful and impressive experience for kids who thought football games in the Little Six Conference were about as exciting as it could get. Before we were exposed to the festivities associated with the University of Nebraska football game, we had thought the parades and hoopla of the Custer County fair were the epitome of ceremony and ritual.

The presence of losers like the Gates High Pirates must have been a bad omen for the Cornhuskers as they lost the game to Pitt. We arrived back at Gates late that night, weary but thrilled with the experiences of seeing our capitol city and the University of Nebraska.

At the time it would have been incomprehensible for me to dream that within the next ten years I would become the first graduate of Gates High School to be awarded the Bachelor of Science from that notable institution. Or that eighteen months later I would rack up another first when I was presented with the Master of Science degree.

The remainder of the school year was passed exerting just enough effort to meet the Sterners' demands but not their expectations. Apparently they saw a dormant potential in some of their students of which we were totally ignorant. They did provide encouragement, but at that time the vision of most of us did not extend beyond the low hills of central Nebraska.

Our basketball team was about on a par with our football team. I believe Mr. Sterner was a good basketball coach. He taught us there was more to the game than shooting at the basket. There was a strategy that included both offense and defense and hard work and sportsmanship were involved. But the combination of poor practice facilities and limited basketball talent sorely taxed his coaching abilities. We continued to practice basketball on the dirt court or in nearby farmers' hay mows. We played hard and may even have won a game or two.

The coming of spring ushered in the beginning of track season. I went out for track, but my talents in that regard were limited. Dad had commented years before that I ran too long in one place to win any races, and I jumped like I was grown to the ground. And I was just not horse enough to excel in the events that depended upon strength. I attained the climax of my track and field career when I won third place in the shot-put at the Custer County Class D track tournament. This was no great victory, even for me, as first place was won by a kid from Dry Valley High who was even smaller than me.

THE BIG BROWN EYES THAT BRIGHTENED MY LIFE

March is a windy and blustery month on the plains of Nebraska, but sometimes the sun does shine. Such was the case in the spring of 1942 when a new ray of sunshine came into my life. The Charles Mohatt family, formerly of the Anselmo community, moved onto the Frank Spanel farm located on the western fringe of what was generally considered the Gates Community. One morning in mid-March I walked into the classroom late and the other students were already seated. There she sat no bigger than a minute with big brown eyes, long brown hair and a shy smile. That first demure smile hinted at the existence of underlying mysteries. *Some of which I have yet to solve even after fifty-five years.* And with that smile my derogatory opinion of at least some of the things associated with Anselmo began to waver.

Anastasia Mohatt was a quiet, friendly and welcome addition to the sophomore class of Gates High School where outsiders were few. As it turned out, she was also the little brown-haired gal who had traded Hop Spanel a bottle of beer for a ride on his horse at the ballgame the previous summer. She had been in the car which I had unceremoniously dragged out of our farmyard. Unbeknown to me she already had an opinion of the hot-head from the farm just west of Gates.

My social skills were limited. I was attracted to the little buxom, brown-eyed beauty but lacked the confidence to ask her for a date. After all, she was new in school, I didn't know her family, I didn't know if she shared my feelings, and she was Catholic. Yes, I knew some Catholic girls, but I had never gone out with one. And the stories I had heard about Catholic girls made the challenge more mysterious and intriguing.

Gates High was putting on a school play in the spring of 1942. Since Anastasia had arrived too late to have a part in the play, she was assigned the job of raising and lowering the roll-down stage curtain. She came to the play that evening with her mother and father and two little sisters. I wanted to take her home after the play but could not work up enough courage to ask her. After agonizing for a while I came up with an idea that would allow me to be in close proximity to her if not actually her date.

Harry Jacobsen, my closest friend, had known the Mohatt family several years before when they lived on neighboring farms in Eureka Valley fifteen or so miles southwest of Gates. In addition to having known her before, he was also blessed with a better gift of gab than was I. I suggested to Harry that he ask Anastasia if he could take her home. The kicker in the plan for me was that Harry did not have a car and would have to rely on me for transportation. My car was a Model-A coupe. She might be Harry's date, but she would have to sit tucked snugly between us on the ride to her home. It was not a satisfactory solution but held the promise of being better than nothing.

I guess the plan worked satisfactorily. Charlie Mohatt reluctantly gave permission to let Harry take his daughter home. He was a bit concerned that she would be in the company of two boys, one of which he did not know. Anastasia(Ann) was Harry's date, but during the three mile drive to her home I was acutely aware of her presence beside me.

Things must have worked out alright, and we delivered her to her home without incident. She got out of the car and waved goodnight as Harry walked to her door with her. I vowed the next time I drove into that farmyard Ann would be with me and Harry would not be along.

I did work up enough courage to ask Ann to go with me to a few school functions before the end of the school year. We seemed to get along OK, we enjoyed each other's company, but nothing earth-shaking occurred. Faye Douglas a Junior, was my date for the last-day-of-school picnic and party. *I learned later to the disappointment of Ann.* But we remained friends. I continued to think that little body and the brown hair and big brown eyes were awfully cute.

Fifty-six years later I revel each day in the light of those big brown eyes.

HIGH SCHOOL GRADUATION, PRE-DRAFT INTERIM PERIOD

It was ironic. The class of 1942, the last to graduate from Gates High School, was also the largest. Two members of the class, Alan Dewey and I, had attended Gates School for all twelve years. When I was handed my diploma I was the last member of the Gates family to graduate from Gates High School. Other members of the class of 1942 were: Verlene (Sandy) Cosner, Verna Dressen, Arthur Dye, Delvin Harrold, Walter Mannel, Jim Schmidt, Albert (Hop) Spanel, and Eula Swick. Racheal Robertson had been a member of the class throughout high school but transferred from Gates to Broken Bow in the spring of 1942 so technically was not a member of our graduating class.

Beginning with the fall of 1942, kids desiring to continue with high school were forced to attend school in one of the surrounding towns. Most went to Broken Bow, but a few went to Sargent or Anselmo. Gates school continued with grades one through eight.

As of this time, 1997, Gates School is still going strong with two teachers teaching eight grades. The school remains the focal point for the Gates Community.

The cowardly Japanese attack on Pearl Harbor on December 7, 1941, had cast a dark pall across the nation. It altered family make-up as young men volunteered for military service or responded to the draft.

Dillard H. Gates

The outlook for the future changed for each of us as we approached graduation. We boys realized, some with hope, some with trepidation, that we too could soon be called to active duty. As for me, I looked forward to joining the service as a means of breaking the bonds with boyhood and finally being recognized as a man. Like most of my friends, I looked forward to the service as an adventure rather than the serious undertaking that it was.

I was seventeen when I graduated from high school. My friend, Harry Jacobsen, who was a year behind me in school, and I had decided to have a last fling before entering military service. We made plans to head west for Wyoming as soon as school was out. We had heard jobs were plentiful out there, wages better and more importantly it was away from home.

SLIPPING THE LOOP

I was finished with high school. Mom had the farm rented out so I was "on my own" for the few months remaining until I entered the military service.

The night of our last-day-of-school party, Harry and I packed our suitcases in the boot of my Model-A coupe and without going to bed headed west, up Highway 2, at thirty-five miles an hour. We wanted to get some distance from home so planned to drive as far as western Nebraska or eastern Wyoming before making job inquiries. We hoped to find jobs where we could remain together.

In western Nebraska we stopped at a big cattle feedlot and asked about work. Yes, they had work to be done, shoveling manure out of the feedlot. The pay offered was fifty dollars a month with board and a bunk in the bunkhouse. The feedlot was enormous, the manure deep and odoriferous. There was a future in the job alright as the task of cleaning the feedlot appeared endless. We were told we could begin work the next day. Somehow the idea of seeking adventure in the west was just not compatible with spending the summer in a stinking feedlot on the business end of a manure shovel. We had sufficient money in our pockets to last a few days so decided to keep driving.

Hay, Hell, Kids and Cattle

THE BIG SHEEP OUTFIT

We spent a day with some of Mom's relatives in Torrington, Wyoming, then headed on west to Wheatland. We got word that the Swan Land and Livestock Company was looking for ranch hands at the Slater headquarters, so we headed south from Wheatland. We checked with the ranch foreman in Slater and were offered jobs. We were surprised but elated when they offered us sixty dollars a month plus board and a bed in the bunkhouse when the work kept us near the headquarters ranch at Slater. However, we could expect to be out on the range a good share of the time taking our meals at a chuck wagon and sleeping on the ground. There would be tents available if it rained but we would need a bedroll. This sounded like the real West to us so we signed on.

The Swan Land and Livestock Company was a big outfit with land holdings extending from western Nebraska to Laramie, Wyoming. The unit we were hired into ran over one hundred twenty-five thousand head of sheep. The company headquarters were located in Chugwater, Wyoming, a few miles south of Slater.

It wasn't until the summer of 1997 that I learned that the Swan Land and Livestock Company was the model used by James A. Michener for the huge land and livestock enterprise in his book, Centennial.

The foreman, Johnny Kurtz, told us we could begin work the next day. He said if we needed to we could go to the company store in Chugwater and purchase, on credit, bed rolls and any other supplies we might need. The cost for the gear would be deducted from our paycheck at the end of the month.

He then showed us the mess hall and the bunkhouse. The bunkhouse was like a small barracks as the company hired dozens of men. It was a substantial building, clean and well kept. It contained rows of metal beds on which we could pitch our bedrolls when we got them, a few tables for writing or playing cards and a few chairs. It also had electric lights and inside toilets and showers. Those were niceties that neither Harry or I had in the homes we left in Custer County, Nebraska.

The mess hall was a separate building adjacent to the bunkhouse. There was a single large table extending the length of the room with benches along either side. The mess hall was clean and neat. It was run by a woman from the Slater community assisted by two teenage girls whose parents lived on ranches in the neighborhood. The girls were the personification of stories about the farmer's daughter. They were pretty, vivacious, full of life and the focus of attention whenever they were in sight.

Meals, breakfast, dinner and supper, were served family style, and all hands were expected to take their meals at specified times. However, for those who had to work or were late for most any reason, there was always food. There was always a pot of coffee on the stove for those who wanted it, day or night. We soon found that the ranch provided high quality food and the cook did an excellent job of preparing the meals. As it turned out she was sort of a mother figure for all of us.

As the foreman was showing us around headquarters, it became obvious that the vast majority of the ranch hands were Mexicans. The foreman told us that Mexicans made up about three-fourths of the ranch crew. He said they were generally good workers and had experience with sheep. He asked us if it would be a problem for us to work with them. Neither Harry nor I had experience with anyone except inhabitants of Custer County, and they were ninety-nine percent white. We assured Johnny that we had no concerns working with anyone. We expected to do the work assigned and would willingly work with any of the ranch hands to accomplish our assignments.

When we hired on, the foreman was getting organized for one of the many big jobs associated with a sheep ranch. The job was cutting (castrating) and docking (cutting off the tails) of the spring-born lambs. The sheep were managed in herds of about six hundred ewes with their lambs. Each herd was controlled by a sheepherder and his dogs. The herds were strategically dispersed across the rangeland to assure proper utilization of the rangeland forage.

Most of the sheepherders had a herder's wagon which was their "home on the range." However, a few preferred tents. The herder wagons contained a bed, stove, food and all the other gear necessary for the herder to stay out on the range and care for the sheep. The wagon was covered with a large canvas top, not unlike the covered wagons that had crossed the prairies decades before. The herder's wagon was moved periodically by a camp tender as the herd of sheep was moved to new grazing land. The camp tender moved from herd to herd in a supply wagon pulled by a team of horses and brought required provisions to the sheep herders.

In preparation for the cutting and docking job, the ranch crew, of which Harry and I were a part, prepared equipment and loaded wagons with necessary supplies. The ranch crew with its caravan of supply and equipment wagons and the chuck wagon then headed for the field. The camp tender would have notified the herders in a given vicinity that the ranch crew would be in the area at a given time to take care of the lambs in their herds. We went to designated areas and set up temporary corrals made from snow fence and large enough to contain a herd of sheep. Several herds of sheep would then be brought into the area so they could all be worked from a single corral set up. Great care was taken not to co-mingle the herds.

Once the corrals were set up, a herder with the help of his dogs moved a herd into the corral. The sheep were then run through a cutting gate and lambs separated from the ewes. This accomplished, the lambs were pushed into a smaller pen. Designated members of the ranch crew caught the lambs by hand and carried them to the cutting and docking table.

Each lamb was held upside down with its head toward the holder, and a front and back leg grasped firmly in each hand. The lamb was set on the narrow table with its genitals exposed and tail extended. The table was long enough that several lambs could be presented at one time.

While the lambs were being separated and penned, the cutting and docking crews were preparing for their jobs. A fire was started to heat the docking irons. The docking irons resembled a chisel made from one-inch steel stock, flattened on one end to form the cutting edge and with a wooden handle on the other. The docking irons were heated to near red hot in the fire then used to cut the tails from the lambs. The hot iron would cauterize the wound, prevent bleeding and reduce the likelihood of infection. About all the cutting crew had to do in preparation for their job was to sharpen their knives.

As the lambs were placed on the table, one of the docking crew with a hot iron in hand grasped the tail and pulled it over a cutting block on the table. He then brought the cutting edge of the hot docking iron down on the tail about an inch from the rump of the lamb. The lamb struggled and bleat as the acrid odor of burning flesh and wool blended with the pungent smells of sheep manure and sagebrush. All lambs, males and females alike, were docked.

The cutting job on the male lambs was only slightly more complex than docking but to the uninitiated more crude and distasteful. The lamb remained in position following docking with its back legs pulled apart and its bag (scrotum) exposed. The cutter grasped the end of the bag with the fingers of his left hand (assuming he was right handed) and stretched it upwards. The end of the bag was then removed with a horizontal stroke of his sharp knife. Normally the nuts (testicles) were positioned in the now lower portion of the truncated bag near the belly of the lamb. To expose the nuts the cutter then grasped the base of the bag with the thumb and forefinger of both hands squeezing slightly beneath the nuts forcing them upward through the truncated bag. Both hands were required to hold the nuts in place and prevent them from slipping back into the base of the bag. The cutter then leaned over the lamb, clamped the nuts between his teeth, and raised his head with the nuts firmly in his grasp. He either spit the nuts on the ground or placed them in a bucket if someone had talked the cook into having a mountain oyster fry that night.

As the work was completed on each lamb, it was dropped back into the pen with the ewes. The lamb immediately began the process of finding its mother. When all lambs had been treated and returned to the pen with the ewes, they were left together for an hour or so to allow them to "mother up" before the herd was pushed back out to the rangeland.

The cutting job was actually not as distasteful and messy as it at first appeared. Most of the ranch crew learned to carry out both the cutting and docking jobs. It was just part of what was expected if you were going to work on a sheep ranch.

Over thirty years later while serving as Professor and Director of the Rangelands Resources Program at Oregon State University I surprised some of my faculty and graduate students when I used the technique to castrate the male lambs being used in a research project.

When the cutting and docking was finished preparations were made for another major job, shearing. The main shearing facilities for eastern Wyoming were at the Slater headquarters. Instead of the crews going to the field to shear, all the sheep in the region were trailed to Slater. It created logistical problems to assure the herds were at the shearing facilities at the correct time while preventing the herds from intermingling.

The shearing was done by a commercial crew. Shearing was a hard dirty job, but a good shearer could take the wool from a sheep in a minute or two. The shearers were paid by the head, so they moved fast and woe to the ranch hand that did not keep the shearer pens full so the next sheep was always available.

In addition to helping handle the sheep the ranch hands filled the big, wool sacks, loaded them onto trucks, hauled them to the railroad siding nearby and loaded them into boxcars. That too was a hot stinky job, as were most of the jobs associated with handling sheep.

FROM SHEEP HERDER TO GANDY DANCER

After a couple weeks or so, the shearing season at Slater was drawing to a close. The ranch crew was to be transferred west to another shearing facility near Laramie. A few days before transfer time I was approached by Andy Day, the Section Boss of the Colorado and Southern Railroad section in Slater. He said they were in need of a couple or three section hands. I was offered an astounding rate of pay, fifty cents an hour with time and one-half for over forty hours and double pay if called out between regular quitting time and starting time in the morning. The railroad would also provide a bunkhouse at no charge. However, I would be responsible for my own meals. The offer sounded to me like my ship was coming in early. The catch was that I had to be eighteen to work for the railroad. All I had to do was immediately age six months, so I lied about my age.

I accepted the job and asked if there was room for a couple of my friends working for the ranch. They too were under the age of eighteen but solved the problem as I had. The three of us drew our pay from the Swan Land and Livestock Company. The next Monday morning, eager but under-aged, we began work as "gandy dancers" for the Colorado and Southern Railroad at Slater, Wyoming. We were issued Social Security cards based upon our stated age.

Bob Day, the son of the boss, also worked on the section. We three new hands made arrangements with his wife Verta to provide our meals and pack a lunch for us on work days for one dollar a day. If we missed some meals on week ends she would prorate the meal charges. She also agreed to do our laundry for a small extra charge.

Andy Day was a great section boss. He expected a lot out of us but was a good teacher and always more than fair. He taught us how to align track, tamp ties, drive spikes and other jobs related to railroad maintenance. He was a boss that was definitely on the side of the men. He followed company rules, but when there were questions he tried to slant solutions in favor of the section hands rather than the company. Off the job he and his family treated us like a part of the family.

The Congress had passed a law, effective sometime during the summer, requiring all young men to register for the draft upon reaching the age of eighteen. The railroad had forwarded orders to Andy to take any eighteen year olds working for him to Chugwater so they could register. As registration day approached we three had to confess to Andy that we had lied about our age. He had suspected as much but had been willing to give us a try anyway. When the Supervisor came by in the afternoon of registration day he asked Andy if all of the eighteen year olds working for him were registered. Andy assured him that all his crew was properly registered. He simply omitted the fact that he had no eighteen year olds on his crew.

When we left Gates in the spring Harry had intended to do as I was planning, work until he was eighteen and then volunteer for the military. However, as the summer waned he began to think about returning home and finishing high school. He contacted his dad, John Jacobsen, about his desires. His dad informed him that he had not told him to leave in the spring and was not asking him to return home now. However, if he wanted to come back home and finish high school, that was fine with him. He was his son and he was always welcome.

We reluctantly told Andy Day of our plans and turned in our time. Our railroad days were over. We loaded our gear into my Model-A and headed back east to Custer County, Nebraska.

It had been a good summer. I had learned a lot about sheep ranching and about working on the railroad. I learned that I could work alongside of experienced, mature men and hold my own. I had also learned it was sometimes necessary to "stand my ground" or get shoved aside, or run over by others who liked to flex their muscle or otherwise attempt to intimidate. On a few occasions I had to recall what Dad had related to me as he was attempting to prepare me make it on my own. "If you don't run, nobody can chase you." I stood my ground a couple of times in disputes with belligerent and insulting ranch hands who thought a green farm boy from Nebraska should be easy pickin's. There were moments when I wondered if Dad's advice remained prudent, but it always did.

Dillard H. Gates

MY LAST STAND IN CUSTER COUNTY

Following my escapade in Wyoming, I returned to Broken Bow and decided to stay in the area until time to enter the military service. At the time, Mom was still living on the farm but was looking for a suitable house in town.

THE GRAVEL PUMPING OUTFIT

My oldest sister, Ruey Poland, owned and operated a gravel pumping outfit which had been left to her by her husband who drowned in an accident at a gravel pumping site. With the war on, there was lots of construction underway that required gravel. The gravel business was going well, and she was in need of additional help. She offered me a job helping with the gravel pumping rig and driving a gravel truck. The pay was sixty cents an hour and she would provide my room and board.

When I began working for Ruey, her gravel pumping rig was set up in a slough off the Calamus River. She had a contract with the State of Nebraska to provide gravel for roads between Taylor and Sargent and south of Sargent on the road toward Westerville. The pumping operation went on twenty-four hours a day.

On my first job as a gravel truck driver, I had the night shift: 6:00 p.m. through 6:00 a.m. That made for a long and tiring night, and to help fight sleepiness I tried smoking cigars. They were vile tasting things: they made me about half-sick and the smoke hurt my eyes. But the combination of bad taste, nausea and smoke in my eyes kept me awake. My relationship with cigars terminated when the all night driving job ended.

Other than the problem of keeping awake all night, the job was relatively easy. I backed the gravel truck under a large overhead gravel hopper into which the gravel had been pumped. I activated a lever to open a trap door that allowed the gravel to flow into the truck box. The box was filled to capacity to meet contract requirements. All drivers, including me, were stopped occasionally by gravel inspectors who checked the loads for compliance. The gravel was then hauled to the proper road location. State engineers had surveyed the road areas being graveled and had driven stakes along the edge to designate where the gravel was to be placed. I lined up the truck between two stakes and dumped the gravel. Back and forth from gravel pit to the dump site was the scope of the job for the entire twelve-hour shift.

The night shift was drudgery, but when I worked all night and slept all day there was little time to spend money or do anything else.

When the road graveling contract ended Ruey got a government contract pumping gravel for the Army Air Force Base being constructed near Ainsworth, Nebraska. This meant moving the gravel pumping rig to a site on the Elkhorn River near Atkinson. Once Ruey accepted the contract she was under constant pressure from the Army to move the gravel pumping outfit and begin providing gravel.

Moving and setting up a gravel pumping rig was a hard and laborious process. Complex machinery and large equipment had to be dismantled, loaded on trucks, transported to the new site, unloaded and reassembled.

The pumping machinery sat on a raft in the river or pond. The raft was supported by fifty-five gallon oil drums. An eight-inch pipe extended from the gravel pump to the large gravel accumulation hopper on the bank. The hopper was located in a position providing access to gravel trucks which transported the gravel away from the pumping site. In this case the gravel was hauled to a railroad siding, loaded on open railroad cars then shipped to the airport construction site fifty miles to the west.

Ruey had a good crew, of which I was the junior member. They knew their jobs, worked hard and tried to meet work schedule targets. Like most gravel or other construction crews, they tended to be a somewhat coarse and rugged lot. While all worked hard on the job, some drank hard when the work day was over. It was not uncommon for some members of the crew to come to work feeling a bit "worse for the wear" following a long night in a local saloon. It was often clear they felt a lot worse at the beginning of the work day than when work ended the previous day. They squinted through bloodshot eyes and stroked their aching heads, but they worked and they got their jobs done.

I was still young and unsullied. It was hard for me to understand what pleasure some of the crew got from drinking so much at night then suffering with a hangover the next day. However, they treated me well. They taught me a lot about the work, and they kidded me a lot about many aspects of life I was yet to experience. I was energetic, strong, naive, and curious. I was the boss's little brother but did my share of the work and we got along fine.

THE SHINY CAPTAIN AND THE MESSY MAJOR

We worked hard to get the gravel rig assembled. We were all aware of the war and the need for gravel for the airbase. In the process of setting up the gravel pumping rig, the crew was being constantly harassed by a young Army officer who had been assigned the job of contract manager. He was constantly looking over our shoulders, but from a sufficient distance that he did not soil his freshly starched and pressed uniform, telling us what to do and urging us to work harder and faster. The fact that he had never seen a gravel pumping rig before apparently meant nothing to him. His Captain's bars were shiny and new, he was full of himself, he was an officer, a gentleman and a leader of men.

One day the crew was on the raft in the gravel pond. We were dirty, greasy, working hard, anxious to get the gravel flowing and trying to meet contract expectations. The young captain suddenly appeared on the raft, freshly shaven, with clean and uncalloused hands and in an immaculate uniform. Judging from his appearance he could have been ready for a general's inspection, but that gravel barge was a long ways from an army base and the motley crew not subject to military protocol. As usual he began to harass us about not working hard enough and being too slow. The crew foreman responded, "We are doing our best and things are coming along fine."

The foreman's response went unheard by the captain as he stepped gingerly around the greasy machinery on the raft, careful not to soil the spotless uniform. He continued to harass, cajole, then to threaten us about what would happen if we did not heed his warnings.

Even though I was the youngest and least experienced member of the crew, I knew, or thought I knew, when I had enough. Maybe Dad's adage, "If you don't run, they can't chase you," came to mind. In my mind this pompous ass was way out of line. He would have liked to panic us into a work frenzy whenever he appeared. I stood up from where I was working on the gravel pump, stepped toward the army brass that spouted orders like a drill sergeant, held up my hand and ordered,

"Stop, that's enough. Shut up and get your ass off this raft or I am going to kick it into the water."

That apparently got his attention. His face flushed and he turned on the heel of his polished shoes and headed over the catwalk to the bank. "You will hear about this," he shouted back once he was safely ashore. He jumped into his vehicle and kicked up two rooster tails of dust as he sped across the field and back toward the highway.

The crew had a good laugh about the incident and agreed the guy had it coming. However, we wondered what repercussions would result from the incident and if my sister, Ruey, would be penalized for the behavior of her crew.

Later in the day, still assembling machinery down on the barge, we heard a car pull up on the bank next to the gravel pit. We looked up and there stood another Army officer, this time a major. This guy certainly was not cast from the same military mold as the captain. He was short and fat, and his uniform looked like it had not seen a press in days. He had his service cap pulled down on his forehead and a big black cigar clamped between his teeth. He looked tough and hard-nosed, but hardly military. He stood on the bank awhile, with hands on his hips, gazing down at us. We all thought, "Now we are going to find out what the captain meant."

After viewing the scene below where we were working, the major shouted down to us, "How are you boys doing?"

"Fine," was the apprehensive response.

"Are you all getting enough to eat?" the major questioned. Again our reply was in the affirmative.

"Are you getting enough to drink?" he questioned further. He received a mixed response from the crew. Some of them would never get enough to drink.

"Well, are you getting enough lovin?" was his final question. The response from the crew was loud but again not unanimous.

"Now that you have all of those things taken care of we would appreciate it if you would get this rig going as soon as possible. We sure do need that gravel," he called back to us.

With that he crawled back in his car and drove away. There was no more harassment and no more shiny captain. The major checked in with us occasionally and continued to be the contract manager.

Dillard H. Gates

I drove a gravel truck for my sister Ruey for a couple of months. I saved enough money to trade my old Ford for what in my eyes was about the fanciest car I had ever seen, a 1937 Terraplane coupe. It was maroon in color and ran like a top. I had decided that I might as well travel in style the last few months before I offered myself to my country as cannon fodder. I could scoot over the hills from Atkinson to Gates or Broken Bow in short order.

BIDING MY TIME

Since I planned to enlist just before I reached eighteen in January, I decided I would like to work closer to home so that I could spend more time with Mom and the family. I quit my job driving the truck and working on the gravel rig and moved back home. I worked for farmers in the community to keep myself in pocket money.

In September my friend Harry Jacobsen had enrolled at Broken Bow High School for his senior year. This greatly expanded his circle of friends and acquaintances, and mine as a result of our association.

It was through Harry and his new circle of friends that I met another little gal that was to occupy a lot of my time until I left for the service the following April. Oma Hawk was a little blue-eyed, blond freshman at Broken Bow High. Despite the fact that she loved to dance and I could not dance a step, we hit it off pretty well and I spent as much time as I could with her. I was also accepted in good stead by her mother and stepfather, Sherm Parkinson. She also had a big sister, Nona, who was the main squeeze for Marvin Booth, the star athlete of the Broken Bow High School.

Pool was a popular pastime for the boys in Broken Bow High. I also liked to play but was not very good at the game. The combination beer joint and pool hall in the Bow was a popular but rather unsavory place. It was frequented by beer drinkers, who were often about three sheets in the wind, recreational pool players, watchers, and on occasion a pool shark. It was dirty and the air blue with smoke and profanity. There were frequently missed spittoons along the tobacco-juice splattered walls, and the floor was covered with cigarette butts and sawdust. I did not smoke and was years from having my first drink. I didn't like the surroundings but it was the only place to shoot pool and a good place to socialize.

THE BULLIES OF BROKEN BOW

MY FIRST ENCOUNTER

One evening late in the fall of 1942, Harry Jacobsen and I were quietly shooting a game of eight-ball. It was a rather busy night, and the pool hall was filled with beer drinkers, pool players and kibitzers. Harry finished a shot, and out of nowhere a young man stepped up to our table and began to put his cue in place for a shot. I didn't know the guy but recognized him as an employee of Luther's Construction Company in Custer County.

The construction company consisted of an extended family involved in the gravel pumping business, trucking and construction. The Luther family exerted a lot of power around Custer County because of its financial status, connections and alleged ruthlessness. The principals and their employees were looked upon by many people in Custer County as a bunch of bullies at best or in some cases outright thugs. It was alleged that they were prone to pick fights with people they were certain they could whip, or if the odds appeared to be against them, to double up on the adversary or use a tire iron or jack handle as an equalizer.

I was reluctant to have a run-in with anyone from the outfit but at the same time did not want a stranger butting into our pool game. I reached out with my pool cue, placed the end of it under the tip of his cue and flipped it up and away from the table and said to the intruder, "No, it's Harry's turn."

He stepped back and nodded.

When Harry finished, the guy quickly moved into place, put his cue on the table and again prepared to take a shot. Once more I reached over with my cue and flipped his cue away from the table. This time I retorted, "No, now it is my turn."

"When's it gonna be my turn?" He exclaimed angrily.

"You don't have a turn," I replied, "My friend and I are playing pool and you are not a part of this game."

We bantered back an forth, "Yes, I am."

"No, you're not."

Dillard H. Gates

By now I was getting quite concerned and hoped I would be able to cool the situation without having trouble with a surrogate of the construction outfit. It was obvious he had been drinking, and I imagined he was a rough and tough street fighter. My hopes were dashed when he lashed out with the challenge, "You son-of-a-bitch come outside and I'll show you whether I can play pool or not."

That was a challenge I could not ignore. From my point of reference a man could deflect most any curse except the one just leveled at me. Scared as I was, I could see no alternative but to accept his challenge. The honor of my mother must be defended regardless of circumstances.

"OK, let's go," I responded, trying my best to portray a bravado I did not feel.

He headed out the back door of the pool hall with me close behind, followed by kibitzers, spectators, his supporters and my friends. As I trailed behind the guy I remembered words of advice Dad had given me years before. "The best defense is a good offense," and "If you are forced into a fight, try to get in the first lick."

We walked out into the alley, with the crowd from the pool hall behind. No one had made a move to stop us. In those days a good fist fight was considered an acceptable spectator sport. The ruffian came to a stop with me a step behind him. As he turned to face me I gathered my courage and my strength and driven by fear slugged him squarely in the face. He hit the ground with blood streaming from his nose. He rolled over on his belly and began to pull his legs under himself. I knew immediately that I didn't want the bruiser to get up. I was sure if he did he would maul me to a pulp. As he struggled to regain his feet I jumped astraddle of his back, grabbed his hair in both hands and proceeded to pound his face into the pavement of the alley. There was no question in my mind but that I was fighting for my life.

Shortly I felt a hand on my arm and heard someone say, "OK, Dillard, that's enough, he's whipped." I looked over my shoulder to see one of my new-found friends, Kenny Bendowsky, exhorting me to stop. Still shaking from the adrenalin charge that had prepared me for fight I stood over the scum, still on the ground, and warned him to never bother me again.

As he lay there on the ground he muttered through the blood pouring from his nose and swollen lips, "You just wait, my boss will take care of you."

The fight was over. I had won, but now I was faced with an even greater challenge. What would the Luther gang do, when, where, whom, and how many were likely to accost me?

For the next couple of weeks whenever I was in Broken Bow I watched my back and the people around me. Rumor had it that some of the Luther family were on the look out for me and the defeat of their employee would not go unavenged. I was still a rather scrawny kid who weighed less than one hundred fifty pounds. I didn't look like a fighter. I didn't feel like a fighter and I was scared of what I feared was to come. I even considered enlisting early to escape the threat that hung over my head. But if I did that it would be paramount to letting them chase me. Again I remembered Dad's admonishment, "If you don't run they can't chase you." I decided to stick it out.

MY SECOND ENCOUNTER

The Lewis Café on the west side of the Square was a popular hang-out for Broken Bow High School kids. There was a large room in the back where they congregated to drink coke, snack, do a bit of light petting and dance to the nickelodeon.

Two or three weeks after the pool hall incident I was in the back of the Lewis café, participating in the fun and enjoying the companionship of my friends and the other kids gathered there. Suddenly there appeared in the doorway the mostly healed, wantabe pool player and the son of Chuck Luther, his boss, who was reputed to be the meanest roughest and toughest member of the clan. The son, Boyd, was around twenty years old and weighed over two hundred pounds. He glanced around the room until he spotted me, then nodded my way, turned and walked out.

This was it. High noon had arrived in the early evening. There was a back door leading from the café to the alley. Some of my friends suggested I leave that way and head home. Despite my suddenly aroused fear, pride prevented me from taking that course of action. A confrontation was inevitable; it might as well be now. At least I had friends with me that I hoped would step in if necessary and rescue me from slaughter.

Word came back to me that the Luther, his previously beaten employee and a couple other members of the gang were waiting for me in front of the café. I asked some friends in the crowd, including Marvin Booth and Kenny Bendowsky, to watch my back so that nobody could get me from behind.

What had been a fun-loving crowd a few minutes before turned quiet and serious. With my back protected, followed by the rest of the kids from the back room I walked slowly through the café and out to the sidewalk, prepared to take whatever waited for me.

A crowd milled about in front of the café waiting to see what was going to happen. After a short period the son of the clan leader separated himself from his cronies and strutted up the sidewalk challenging, "I guess I can whip any son-of-a-bitch here."

He repeated the challenge as he stopped in front of me and put his face close to mine. He looked big and mean and tough. Once more I was seized with fear but determined to stand and fight if that is what I had to do.

Trying to appear braver than I felt I returned his stare and replied, "I am not a son-of-a-bitch, but I guess it's me you are looking for."

"That's right," he spat back at me, "and I'm going to beat the hell out of you for what you did to my friend."

I suggested that if that was what he intended to do we should get off the sidewalk. With him ahead of me and followed by the crowd, we moved to a vacant lot just south of the Lewis café. As we moved toward the back of the lot, I was thinking only about how I could best defend myself against the man who was so much bigger and undoubtedly stronger than me. I also felt certain that as a part of the Luther clan he was an experienced street fighter. I decided my only chance, slim as it might be, was for me to prevent him from getting his hands on me. I would try to get in close, hit him a lick, then get back before he could counterpunch or grab me.

We faced off. I was still hoping that a bolt of lightning would strike or something else would happen to stop the fight before it started. As we stood there toe to toe he mocked, "Go ahead and hit me, you can't hurt me."

A cornered animal, regardless of size, in fear of its life can be dangerous. I felt both cornered and afraid.

In desperation, I took a deep breath and hit him as hard as I could flush on the jaw. Surprised he let out a grunt and staggered backwards. I moved in quickly hit him again and stepped back out of his reach. This went on for several exchanges. I kept moving around staying out of his reach and getting in a blow when I could. He was big, but he was also overweight and soon began to tire. Between breaths he requested that we stop to rest. It was then I began to feel that maybe I had a chance. I now had the brute on the run. If I could just keep up what I was doing and not allow him to rest, maybe I could survive or even beat him.

Urged on by the cheers of my friends, I continued to fight. Though big and strong he eventually was so tired he could hardly hold up his hands. The battle continued until he was so exhausted that he was unable to defend himself. I kept hitting him virtually at will but couldn't knock him down, so the fight went on. After what seemed an eternity to me he slumped to the ground following a blow to his jaw.

He was down, now what? I was afraid that if he ever got up he would still have the strength to overpower me if he could somehow get his hands on me. As he lay on his back I approached him and asked if he had enough. For an answer he drew his knees up to his chest then lashed out at me with both feet. I stepped back from the kick and grabbed his foot, a heel in one hand and toe in the other. I twisted the foot vigorously forcing him to roll over. As he rolled in the direction I was twisting I quickly reversed the thrust on his foot and rolled him in the opposite direction.

After rolling back and forth three or four times, he screamed in pain and hollered, "Enough."

As he lay there moaning, he repeated the threat his pool player crony had made a few weeks before. "You'll not get away with this," he blubbered through blood and snot, "You've not seen the end of this yet."

His friends helped him to his feet and half-carried, half-dragged him out to the street and to their car. We later learned his friends took him directly to the Caruthers hospital were he was found to have a broken bone in his ankle, a fractured jaw and several loose molars.

Now there were two down but the remainder of the clan to go. Rumors of threats against me were rampant in the town. On several occasions I was warned that out of town members were waiting to catch me alone. I saw the father of the beaten clan member on the streets of Broken Bow on several occasions during the next few weeks. I expected a challenge from him but none was forthcoming. From that point forward until I left for the service in April 1943, I took extreme caution around Broken Bow, especially at night. The rumors abounded but there were no further problems.

A few days after arriving home subsequent to my discharge from the Coast Guard in November 1945 I again encountered Chuck Luther, the father of the clan, on the street in Broken Bow. I was still wearing my Coast Guard uniform. As we met he smirked at me and snarled, "Do you still think you're tough?" I dreaded to think this was a continuance of the old feud. I had just returned from one and one-half years in the Pacific theater. The War was over. I certainly was not looking for more trouble with the Luther outfit. At the same time I thought I was in a much better position to defend myself, if need be, than when I was a skinny kid three years before. I stepped in front of the patriarch of the clan, looked him straight in the eye and calmly but firmly replied, "Don't mess with me and you will live a longer and happier life." Apparently that ended our war as I was never again bothered by the clan, though I always tried to keep a close watch if I was some place where some of them were present.

Aside from the imagined or real threats from the construction gang, my final weeks before enlisting were uneventful.

MOM'S MOVE TO TOWN

Mom finally located what she considered to be a satisfactory house and during the winter of 1942-43 moved to Broken Bow. Tragically, her equity in the farm following twenty years of blood, sweat and tears was barely sufficient to cover the cost of a minimum house. It was a small three-bedroom house with an outside toilet. It did have city water and an iron sink that drained through a pipe onto the ground outside the house. It was heated by a kerosene burning space heater which was located in the dining room during the winter and moved out to the porch during the summer. I guess Mom thought what had been good enough out on the farm was good enough in town.

There was also a small two-roomed building on the property which was to serve as the bedroom for the boys. We called it "the shack," which was an apt description considering the appearance and condition of the building. The house sat on a half block of land in the northern part of town. Access was by a dirt road that extended to the property from the pavement a block away.

I continued working for farmers in the area and sometimes stayed at the farms. Otherwise I made my temporary home with Mom. I spent as much time as possible with my new girl, Oma. For the most part that was limited to the week ends. She liked my fancy Terraplane, and I was proud to drive around town and show off both my gal and my car.

DON'T GO TO TOWN TONIGHT, SON

One Friday night in late December, 1942, it was cold and it looked like a storm was brewing. Two of my sisters, Sis and Lee, my brother Jack and I decided we would go to Broken Bow to a movie. Mom tried to talk us out of going because of the weather. It was nineteen miles to town and she didn't think it was very smart to drive that far to see a movie on a night like this. We brushed aside her concerns, piled into my car and took off. The Terraplane was a coupe, so to accommodate the four of us my little sister, Lee, had to sit on Jack's lap.

After the movie we stopped by Uncle Boyd and Aunt Mary Crables' house for a visit before heading home. Uncle Boyd was a dentist in Broken Bow and Aunt Mary was Dad's sister. Though Dad and Aunt Mary had not had much to do with one another for years, she was very good to us kids and we enjoyed stopping at her home whenever we could.

When we were ready to head home around 10:30 p.m. we piled back into the car. It was very cold, around ten degrees below zero. There was about an inch of snow on the ground and the windshield was covered with snow and ice. I scratched the ice from a small area on the outside of the windshield and frost from a similar spot on the inside. I couldn't see very well through the small hole and a light snow was falling, but I knew the defroster and wipers would clear the windshield before we got very far out of town.

The problem was we didn't even get out of town. The Burlington railroad running east and west divided Broken Bow into the north and the south side. It crossed the road to Gates a few blocks north of Uncle Boyd's place.

With my eyes as close to the windshield as possible, I headed slowly out of town waiting for visibility to improve. There were no warning signal lights at the railroad crossing. I heard or saw nothing ahead until a split second before the car reached the tracks. Then to my dismay I spotted a locomotive entering the crossing. My reflexes caused me to jerk the steering wheel hard to the right. The train crashed into the left side of my car, whirled the car around to the right then hit it again in the rear end. It was a moment of terror. I could not see out as all the windows were covered with frost. I could not see the train. I didn't know if we were still on the tracks or if the train was going to hit us again. As I braced for another impact, which I feared was coming, a picture of us being ground beneath the wheels of the train flashed through my mind.

A few seconds, which seemed like an eternity, passed and there was no further crash. I looked toward my sisters and brother still in the seat beside me and asked if everyone was alright. Lee replied, "Dill, my knee hurts."

My door was caved in and could not be opened. Still not knowing where we were in relation to the train. I emphatically stated, "Let's get the hell out of the car."

Jack and my sisters jumped from the car before me. As I crawled out I noted that we were off the tracks and the train had stopped beside us. Lee was standing near the car grasping her knee. Holding back the tears she repeated, "My knee hurts." As I rushed up to her I was shocked to see blood spurting from the side of her head. I knew immediately that an artery had been cut and was aware of the potential danger.

I called to Jack and Sis and told them to run back and get Uncle Boyd so I could get Lee to the hospital. I removed my coat, wrapped it around Lee and climbed back into the car to escape the cold. With Lee on my lap I tried to find a pressure point on her neck in an attempt to stop the bleeding.

In just a minute or so the car door was jerked open and a voice demanded, "Who the hell was driving this car?"

"Who the hell are you," I responded in a voice to match.

"The conductor of this train," he flung back at me as if he were God himself.

"Why the hell didn't you blow your whistle?" I questioned. "Shut the door, I have to take care of my sister now. I will talk to you later," I continued.

About that time another car pulled up to the railroad crossing now blocked by the train. A man climbed out of the car and hurried over to us, offering help as he approached. I left the train crew standing in the cold and carried Lee to the car. Still holding her in my lap, I kept trying to arrest the flow of blood.

It was but a short drive to the hospital. The good Samaritan rushed up the hospital steps ahead of me and called for the doctor, whose residence was in the hospital building.

I sat in the waiting room with Lee in my arms until Dr. Caruthers arrived. He instructed me to lay her on a table and in a reassuring voice stated, "Alright son, I will take car of her now. Will you please wait in the other room?"

Until that moment I had retained self-control. I was clear-headed and concerned only for the welfare of my sister. As I passed responsibility for Lee over to the doctor, the tension broke. I thought I was going to faint. I staggered from the doctor's office through the waiting room and out the front door. I slumped to the steps of the hospital and lowered my head between my knees. There I sat, in ten below zero temperature, too weak to stand.

That is where Uncle Boyd, Sis and Jack found me a few minutes later. They had gone to the scene of the accident and the train crew told them we had left for the hospital. After I had regained control, Uncle Boyd helped me to my feet and into the hospital. We waited until Dr. Caruthers came out to tell us Lee was alright. He had stopped the bleeding and stitched the cuts in the side of her head. However, he wanted to keep her in the hospital overnight.

We returned to Uncle Boyd's house. He then told me to take his car and go home. We needed to tell Mom about the accident before she heard about it from someone else. He told me to come back to town the next morning to take care of the car and he would go with me to talk to an attorney.

As expected, Mom was surprised and frightened when we told her of the accident and Lee's injuries. She lamented that it would not have happened if we would have just listened to her plea, "Don't go to town tonight, son; don't go to town tonight."

The next morning we drove back to town. My once beautiful but now battered car was still on the railroad right-of-way near the tracks. As we inspected the car we could see plainly what had caused the injuries to Lee's head. She had been sitting on Jack's lap on the right side of the car. When the train struck she was thrown forward and to her left. The right side of her head hit the rear view mirror, breaking it off the bracket. After hitting the mirror she was thrown further to her left and the injured side of her head had crashed against the top part of the steering wheel with sufficient force to break a spoke in the wheel and the bracket connecting the steering column to the dash. As she was being tossed about, she apparently also had hit her knee on the dash of the car.

With the advice of Uncle Boyd we talked to an attorney, A. Paul Johnson, who had been a long time friend of Dad's. In a few days, after Lee had been released from the care of Dr. Caruthers, we met with officials of the Burlington Railroad.

At first their attitude was arrogant and self righteous, and they insisted the railroad was free of blame. In fact, they informed me that the impact with my car had caused damage to the cow-catcher on the front of the engine and they expected full reimbursement. The attorney reminded them that according to law the train was required to sound its whistle as it approached the crossings in town. I had not heard a whistle. In addition the good Samaritan who had taken us to the hospital had told us he did not heard a whistle and would so testify if necessary.

After some haggling the Burlington Railroad, without admitting blame, agreed to pay Lee's hospital costs, reimburse me for the pre-accident market value of my car and take care of the attorney fee. In those days auto insurance was not required and we had none. In a few months Burlington installed flashing warning lights at the main railroad crossings in Broken Bow.

The damage to my car appeared to be limited primarily to the body. The left side was caved in; the rear bumper and left rear fender were out of shape. The frame was not bent so the car was still driveable. I had the left door pried open and the frame around it straightened enough that it could be opened, closed and secured. People stared as I passed by wondering how a car so badly damaged could still function. I was able to keep it running for a couple more months, but apparently it had suffered more damage than I originally thought. Reluctantly I sold it to the junk yard, ending a short but passionate love affair between me and my Terraplane.

ENLISTING IN THE COAST GUARD

I was approaching eighteen, but I had no intentions of being drafted. I thought the Army Air Corps sounded great, but assumed as a Gates High School graduate I did not have the academic credentials to fly. I also thought it might be exciting to drive an army tank. After all, I had experience operating many kinds of tractors, including track types. Operating a tank should be no trouble at all.

As my eighteenth birthday approached, it became essential for me to make a choice. My Aunt Mary Crable was my primary source of information regarding the various branches of the armed forces. She remembered WW I very well. She had a brother (my uncle), Bill Gates, who had served in Europe, was gassed by the Germans, and after his discharge from the army died from complications of the gas attack .

Aunt Mary advised against both the army and the Air Corps. She knew someone in the U.S. Coast Guard who thought it was a great outfit. She was sure if I joined the Coast Guard I would get good duty, fulfill my military obligations, and maybe never have to leave the States.

I took her advice, contacted the Coast Guard recruiting station, then made arrangements to go to Omaha to take the necessary aptitude tests and physical exam. If I met the qualifications of the Coast Guard, I would enlist.

About a week before my birthday I took the train to Omaha and reported to the Coast Guard recruiting station. I was given a battery of aptitude tests. While the tests were being evaluated, I was given a physical examination, the first one I had ever had. I was assigned to a group of other equally green and naive, potential Coasties.

We were herded into a cold barren room by an unsmiling young man in a freshly starched white uniform and ordered to strip to the skin. I was embarrassed. I had taken group showers after sporting events in high school and had gone skinny dipping in the river with friends, but never before had I bared myself in the presence of so many also naked strangers.

An officious young man in a white coat ordered us to stand in line. Another, whom from the gold on his uniform I assumed was a medical doctor, proceeded down the line in front of us. He removed a gadget that looked like a pointed flashlight from the pocket of his white coat and peeked quickly in each ear and my nostrils. He removed another gadget from the same pocket and waved it in front of my eyes. He told me to open up and say,"Ah." He pressed on my tongue with a flat stick, gave me what I took to be a reassuring pat on the shoulder, grunted something to a notetaker by his side and left me standing with my mouth open.

As he stepped on to the next recruit, my mouth snapped shut as I felt a cold hand on my shoulder accompanied by a crisp and even colder sounding order from behind, "Bend over and spread your cheeks."

I didn't know the vernacular of the military. I wasn't even a boot yet. I bent forward as ordered, grasping my cheeks and pulled outward to form a funny face. I wondered what kind of a military maneuver this procedure was to prepare me for.

I had little time to wonder. A sharp slap landed on my buttock as the medic retorted angrily, "Spread the cheeks of your ass stupid. Where do you think you are, at a masquerade party?"

I had heard a phrase before about someone so dumb that, " He didn't know his ass from a hole in the ground," but never before had I been confused identifying the opposite ends of my anatomy.

Feeling chagrined I quickly altered my position in a blind effort to do as instructed. Still unsure as to what came next, I grabbed my posterior with both hands and attempted to carry out the implicit order.

Before I had much time to analyze the situation, I had another totally new and startling experience. I felt another cold hand on my butt and simultaneously something cold and slick was thrust up my behind. The medic pressed hard, wiggled what I assumed was his finger, and muttered something unintelligible to his assistant. As the assistant hurriedly scratched something in his notebook, the medic stepped back from me and moved on to the next man in line. It was somewhat heartening to note that different medics and different equipment were assigned to opposite ends of my anatomy.

The surly medics with the cold hands must have determined that my body was warm, inside and out, and thus acceptable to the Coast Guard. I had satisfactorily passed the aptitude tests despite the problem I just had with my cheeks. In fact test results showed I was eligible to attend any training course offered by the Coast Guard.

I was sworn in along with the other recruits who survived the examinations. I was now a fledgling member of the U.S. Coast Guard, the oldest branch of the U.S. armed forces. I was told the Coast Guard was attempting to put together a company of recruits from Nebraska and Iowa and they would call me probably within a month.

I was now in a state of limbo. I could not make any but short-term commitments to a job. I helped Mom move and get established in the house she had purchased in Broken Bow. I took a job picking corn for Whispering George Dudley, a real estate promoter who also had a farm about fifteen miles southwest of Broken Bow. He picked me up early each morning, took me out to the farm, then came back out to the farm each evening and returned me to my home. That was great with me as I liked to be in Broken Bow at night so I could spend as much time as possible with Oma.

The flipside of Whispering George serving as my chauffeur was that he too had a great love. His was with a fiery hot mistress with whom he appeared to have a frequent liaison. But his hot and demanding mistress was the contents of the whiskey bottles he carried in his pocket or stashed under the seat of his car. On many occasions when he came to the farm to pick me up, it was obvious they had spent the afternoon together. During several trips back to town I clung tightly to the seat and braced my feet against the floor boards waiting for the accident I was sure was going to happen. On a few occasions I requested he let me drive. He was generally overly self-confident and kept his seat. However, a few times he surrendered the wheel to me. I don't know if on those occasions he realized he should not be driving or if he was so drunk he didn't know whether he was driving or not.

In about six weeks I had his corn out. I was out of a job and had heard nothing from the Coast Guard. I was puzzled as to why I was not called. There was a war on and I thought the military was drastically in need of men. But I waited for the call.

I spent some time with Mom and the kids, then took a job with another farmer, Dick Roberts. Following the death of his first wife, he had married Martha Christian, sister of my older sister Gee's husband. In this case I was expected to stay at the farm during the week. Roberts picked me up Sunday nights or Monday mornings and returned me to town Friday evenings so I could have the week-end in town.

I was assigned to clean up several straw-pile butts. I loaded the partially rotted straw mixed with cow manure into a manure spreader and scattered it over the farm land. It served as a fertilizer and helped to stabilize the sandy soil against wind erosion. Shoveling manure was neither glamorous nor exciting, but it was a job that needed to be done and kept me in pocket change. I suffered through the week on the business end of a pitch fork which had neither a self-starter nor a seat. The technology of the pitch fork has changed little in the last century.

TIME TO GO

When I came in from work one evening Martha told me Mom had called. I was to report to the Coast Guard Station in Omaha the following Monday. It was mid-week, and Dick indicated that since I did not have to report until Monday I might as well spend the rest of the week and finish cleaning up straw-pile butts. I finally convinced him that I had only a few more days until I had to leave for the service and I would like to spend them at home. He eyed the remaining manure piles which he would have to finish if I left, then reluctantly gave me my pay and drove me to Broken Bow.

Hay, Hell, Kids and Cattle

Mom and the family were not the only reasons I wanted to get back to Broken Bow. I wanted to spend as much time as possible with Oma. With her mother's permission, she had accepted an engagement ring from me several weeks earlier. Being engaged was important to me. I wanted to have something to come home to before leaving for the Coast Guard. Yes, I had a big family, but somehow I needed something more. Having Oma wearing my ring provided a psychological anchor and tie to that which I was leaving behind.

I spent the last few days at home saying my goodbyes and receiving wishes for good-luck from friends and relatives. The great thrill and spirit of adventure which prevailed when I enlisted had waned and been replaced by feelings of uncertainty and remorse. It was great to get pats on the back and admonitions to, "Give them hell." "Take care of yourself," or "Come back safely." But now that it was about time to go, I felt like I would rather stay home.

Sunday night I joined the other five Coast Guard recruits from the area: Jimmy Ecker, Kenny Bendowsky, Bill Porter, Clairse Fox and Bill Ingrahm and our friends and families at the Burlington railroad depot. Even, Anastasia, that little brown-haired gal with the big brown eyes, whom I had met at Gates High School, was lingering in the background to see me off. We clustered in small groups with those most dear to us and waited for the train from the west that would take us east to Omaha to the Coast Guard recruiting station and the rest of our lives. We knew when the train arrived, the stop would be brief so we needed to be prepared to leave.

As we waited we heard the whistle as the train approached from the west. At last, but now too soon, the train clanged into the station amidst clouds of steam and the squeaking of giant wheels against cold rails. The time had come.

The conductor called, "All aboard." I gave Mom a farewell hug and kiss. As I gave Oma a final embrace, we exchanged youthful vows.

"I'll come back." I whispered. *I did.*

"I'll wait for you." she promised. *She didn't.*

As the conductor gave the last call, "All aboard," I grabbed my duffle bag. Semi-dazed I stumbled through a cloud of steam and climbed the steps into the black behemoth waiting to carry me away. I entered the passenger car and rushed forward to claim an empty seat next to a window. I threw open the window hoping to get yet another glimpse of

Oma and Mom. I called from the open train window and reached out my hand. As the train chugged from the station Oma ran along side, reached up and for a fleeting, but indelible moment, touched my extended fingers. Then she was gone. My mother, my family, and my friends were gone. I guess in reality they were still there. I was gone. In the span of a few brief moments I moved from a familiar environment of security, love, and warmth to one which was unfamiliar, cold, and impersonal.

As the train picked up speed, moving me through long familiar farmlands toward a war which I did not fully understand, I hunkered down in my seat and stared through the darkened window. I was now on my own. I knew not what lay beyond the horizon. I didn't feel the charge of adrenalin that prepared the soldier for battle. I didn't even feel like a man. I felt like a country boy who had just been disjoined from all he held dear. Already I missed my mother. I missed my girl. I was frightened, and I was lonely.

THE END

Nona Ash (Pool, Goodrich) was born in Broken Bow, Nebraska, in August 1917. She grew up on dryland farms and attended rural schools. She attended Gates High School where she completed the 11th grade. In 1943 she moved to Portland, Oregon, where she worked as a welder making Liberty and Victory ships until the end of WW11. From 1945 through 1979 she was an industrial worker and the first woman welder for Freightliner Inc. Nona has been a member of the Oregon Society of Artists since 1950. She is the mother of two girls and now lives in Portland with her husband Hal Goodrich.